Praise for *JACK,*

"This is a fascinating and impressive̶ͣ ------------- a̶c̶c̶o̶u̶n̶t̶ ̶o̶f̶ ̶a̶ ̶m̶u̶l̶t̶i̶-
generational and truly American success story."

　　　—John McEvoy, author of *Great Horse Racing Mysteries: True Tales*
　　　　　　　from the Track and *Photo Finish: A Jack Doyle Mystery*

"One of the holes in racing's bookshelf has long been the spot where
a biography of legendary trainer Jack Van Berg belonged. Now it can
be filled. Chris Kotulak has written, with both affection and respect, a
detailed portrait of the man known for his uncompromising work ethic,
his vast and hard-earned knowledge of thoroughbreds at all levels of the
game, and an understanding of both horses and humans that enabled him
to get the best out of both species that passed through his barn."

　　　　　—Jane Schwartz, author of *Ruffian: Burning from the Start*

"A wonderfully detailed and descriptive biography of Jack Van Berg—
you truly understand why horse racing's Marlboro Man cried when he
won the Kentucky Derby. Fast-paced and often humorous, *Jack, from
Grit to Glory* also reveals the man whose name still is spoken in awe by
track old-timers: Jack's father, Marion."

　　　　　　—Jennie Rees, *The Louisville Courier-Journal*

"Chris Kotulak writes confidently—and with an abundance of heart and
feeling—about the hardscrabble Plains State conditions that would ultimately give rise to both the iron will and the sensitive horsemanship of
one of the greatest trainers the racing game has ever known."

　　　　　　　　　—Rich Perloff, TVG Broadcaster

"A fascinating and long-overdue glimpse into the life stories and racing
backgrounds of two legends of the sport: not only Jack Van Berg, but
Marion Van Berg as well."

　　　　　—Randy Moss, NBC television horse racing analyst

JACK
From Grit to Glory

JACK

JACK
From Grit to Glory

A Lifetime of Mentoring, Dedication, and Perseverance

The True Story of Jack Van Berg, an American Horse Racing Legend

By Chris Kotulak

Chris Kotulak began his career in horse racing as a teenager, when he worked with the thoroughbreds on the backstretch of Ak-Sar-Ben racetrack in his hometown of Omaha, Nebraska. A self-trained track announcer with an Applied Sciences Degree in Photography, Chris called races on the Nebraska horse racing circuit before leaving to work as an announcer in Louisiana and later to call races at Hollywood Park. Kotulak worked at the Los Angeles–based horse racing television network TVG for many years. As a host, analyst, and reporter, he is known for his folksy nature, horse sense, and vast insight and experience with all breeds of horse racing. He has covered horse racing in England, Australia, and Japan. Chris currently works full-time at Remington Park Racetrack & Casino in Oklahoma City, Oklahoma.

Bluestem Publications
Edmond, Oklahoma

Copyright © 2013 by Christopher C. Kotulak. Published by Bluestem Publications, Edmond, Oklahoma. Printed in the U.S.A. by Mercury Press, Inc.

Cover photos: Dustin Orona Photography (racing silks);
Tony Leonard (Jack in red jacket)

Visit the book Web site: JackFromGritToGlory.com

ISBN: 978-0-9891553-0-4

*To my mom, Caryl, who told me I could
be whatever I wanted to be.*

*To my dad, Joe, for his
quiet love and support.*

And to Jack.

CONTENTS

Preface   xi

Acknowledgments   xiii

In Memoriam   xv

Part I

1. The Van Berg Pedigree   3

2. Leaving the Farm   8

3. Columbus or Bust   11

4. Rising from the Dust   15

5. Along Came Jack   19

6. Jack'n Around   25

7. School Daze   29

8. A Winning Path Is Born   36

9. The Trainer in Training   44

10. Development of a Dynasty   48

11. The University of Hard Knocks   51

12. Jack of All Trades   54

13. The Decade of Dominance   58

14. The Columbus Connection   65

15. Rose's Gem   74

16. Marion's Way   83

17. A Heaving Heart   93

18. Memories of Marion   102

19. The Estate of M. H. Van Berg   108

CONTENTS

Part II

20.	Gold West Young Man	112
21.	Trainer for Hire	117
22.	Building and Rebuilding	122
23.	An Omaha Opus	126
24.	Merlin of the Midlands	132
25.	The Spirit of '76	137
26.	The Disciples	145
27.	A Road to a Renaissance	159
28.	The Inspiration of Laurie Bale	168
29.	A Cavalcade of Stakes	171
30.	On the Road with JVB	184

Part III

31.	Gate Dancer	193
32.	Montages in Print	211
33.	Alysheba: A Classic Name	219
34.	Alysheba: Glowing Pride and Growing Pains	222
35.	Alysheba: Evolution of a Champion	248
36.	Alysheba: Farewell to a Prince	263

CONTENTS

Part IV

37.	Family, Finances, and Failures	269
38.	That Damn California Ranch	272
39.	Now You Know Jack	281
40.	What Happened	294
41.	A Fight to the Finish	300

Appendix: Montage Essays, by Gary Simmons   303

Bibliography   333

Preface

Since I began writing this book so many wonderful stories have been shared with me, not only by Jack, but by the family, friends, and peers of Jack Van Berg. Maybe it's my pride in being a fellow Nebraskan, maybe it's my love of horse racing, or maybe it's my love of the iconic man "Jack" became, and still is. But regardless of *my* interest in it, the Van Berg story simply must be told.

It is a true story of hardship, heartache, and heartfelt joy. The life and remarkable accomplishments of Jack Van Berg are a testament to discipline, respect, and commitment. The characters are real, yet the accounts of humans and horses seem unbelievable, as if they are from a different time—because they are. Step back and feel the embrace and warmth of life and horse racing before the age of the Internet and the cell phone. Jack lived through a golden age of horse racing; he trained champions, broke records, and became a Hall of Fame trainer.

This biography reveals how a son, Jack, worshiped his father and how those he mentored would later worship him.

A trainer of horses; a leader of men; a hero to us all: JACK.

Jack would like to dedicate this book to his mother and father who provided him inspiration and wherewithal, and to his siblings who helped him achieve all that he did. He also dedicates the book to his children, now the most valued thing that he has.

Acknowledgments

I simply could not have written this book with any historical backbone had it not been for the meticulous record-keeping of Harold Scholz. Harold married Jack's sister Betty Van Berg and created an invaluable collection of historical information. By saving all of the year-end data provided by the *Daily Racing Form*, Harold compiled a handy reference to the accomplishments of Marion and Jack Van Berg. His diligence and accuracy, in what was essentially just a hobby, became priceless resources in the development of this book. In fact, Harold once identified an error in the win tally for Marion that had been published in the *Daily Racing Form*. He notified the Chicago office and received a thank you telegram with recognition for a correction of their official records. From 1937 to 1963, Harold Scholz wrote the book on M. H. Van Berg. He kept the numbers; I turned them into words. Harold was also the one who took most of the family pictures at home, around the barn, and at the racetrack. God bless you, Harold Scholz.

And similar thanks to Jack's sister Virginia and her husband, Dwayne Smith; they live in the big white house Jack grew up in on the property of the Columbus Sales Pavilion. Virginia and Dwayne dug out and scanned a number of precious photos for this book. The photos that did not make it into the book can be found on the book website, JackFromGritToGlory.com. Virginia and her older sister Helen kept Jack and his father's financial books for years.

Shortly after I agreed to write the book, Jack told me I needed to fly back to Louisiana to interview his eldest living sister, Helen. When Jack tells you to do something, you do it. I thought I'd make a good impression, so I did. It was awesome! Helen was a child with limitless devotion to her parents, and she worked for the family business well into her eighties. Now her two sons, Chuck and Dick, look after her. The farthest reaches of the Van Berg taproot are still alive in her mind. I hung on every word of her wispy, aging voice, although her hands, eyes, and heart expressed more than her words. Helen is pure gold.

Jack became known to be very handy with the microphone. For decades he has stepped up to the auction stand where his humorous and industrious delivery has earned him much praise. He credits his brother Bud as a major influence in that art.

For many years, many people have told me that I should write a book. Ed McNamara was the first author I contacted about writing a book. Ed is a sports copy editor at *Newsday* in Long Island, New York. He wrote the book *Cajun Racing: From the Bush Tracks to the Triple Crown* and he put some inspiring wind in my sails.

John McEvoy was a name I heard for years working in the Nebraska racetrack press boxes alongside the venerable *Daily Racing Form* trackman Dean Williams. The press box was Dean's den, and he had a roar and a bite like a lion. But when he received a phone call from his *DRF* boss, John McEvoy, Dean was a real kitten. I respected Williams for his wisdom and I was certain I could rely on McEvoy for his background in horse racing in the Midwest, his writing, and his journalistic wherewithal.

The 110-pound paragon of print (newsprint), Mark Gordon knows a thing about racing and writing about it. Years ago his byline appeared in the *Daily Racing Form* as well as the *Lincoln Journal Star.* Good Mark's exemplary work ethic and explosive expletives have always been an inspiration to me.

I appreciate the assistance of Breeders' Cup Limited, the National Museum of Racing Hall of Fame, and the Kentucky Derby Museum. Thanks to copy editor Emily Jerman, and to the many experts I polled in determining the styles in which numerals are presented in this book. I appreciate their advice, which we adapted for our purposes. Special thanks also to Abahazy Photography, Benoit Photo, Brien Bouyea, Ed Burgart, Allan Carter, Bob Curran, Eight Balls Racing, John Engelhardt, Kent Frates, Orlando Gutierrez, Sandy King, Preston Madden, John McEvoy, Ed McNamara, Frank Mirahmadi, Weaz Mitilier, Randy Moss, Jim Mulvihill, John Neal, Dustin Orona Photography, Mike Patterson, Mark Ratzky, Jennie Rees, Sally Sue Schultz, Jane Schwartz, Virginia and Dwayne Smith, Jeff Taylor, Kay Thurman DVM, Wendy Treinen, Scott Wells, Jon White, Mike Willman, Dave Zenner, Amy Zimmerman, C. M. Light, the incredible crew at Mercury Press, in OKC, and the entire Hoops and Van Berg family.

In Memoriam

I began writing this book in June of 2010; Jack had just turned seventy-four. Many of his family and friends have already passed away, and some important people have passed away since the process of this book-writing began. I want to recognize those dear family and friends who made a loving impact on Jack and me, and who are part of our horse racing fabric and souls.

John Tooley was a longtime friend of Jack and the Van Berg family and an assistant general manager at the Columbus Races; he was my direct boss when I called races there for three years. His son Chris ran a division of horses for Jack in the Midwest. John passed away in August of 2010.

John lived in Columbus, Nebraska, as did Bud Kuta and Frank "Zuke" Zuroski. I'll never forget the satisfaction and joy in the stories told by Bud and Zuke as we sat around Zuke's breakfast table. I have countless priceless memories of the immense research that went into the writing of this book—recollections of Zuke and Bud are some of my earliest. The two men spoke of "Mr. Van" (M. H. Van Berg) as if they had been infantrymen fighting for a beloved four-star general. Their devotion was electric that October morning as we all laughed and reminisced. Zuke was growing feeble by then, but he puffed with pride that morning; he passed away in February of 2011. Jack's sister Alyce Van Berg Cumming, the fifth child of Marion and Viola Van Berg, passed away in April of 2012.

In November of 2012, my dear friend Con Furay passed away. *Conal Furay* loved God, his family and horse racing—in that order. He was a devoted Catholic, husband, father, friend, and employee. A past president of the history department at Webster University in St. Louis, Con spent thirty summers working (and making $2 bets) at Ak-Sar-Ben. He worked some for the *Daily Racing Form*, but he was most noted for his graded handicap Ak-Sar-Ben horse racing selections that appeared in the *Omaha-World Herald* newspaper. In the Aks press box, Con and I worked alongside Don Lee, the late, great turf writer for the *Omaha-World Herald*. Both Con and Don were *my* mentors. An author of three books, Con was assisting me with this book when he passed away.

Eighty-seven-year-old Betty Van Berg Scholz was a ray of sunshine.

She and her loving husband Harold Scholz lived actively in Omaha and were always part of my trips back home there once I began the process of writing this book. I simply fell in love with that couple; they were like my grandparents reincarnate. Betty called me the night of November 29, 2012, to tell me how much she enjoyed reading the fresh book chapters I had just provided her. She told me she was overjoyed with the reading—remembering things she had forgotten; being informed of things she never knew. She told me to take some vitamin C to fight the cold I had and then she cheerfully wished me a good night. I spoke with Jack the next morning and he told me Betty had passed away that night.

Jack has his own dedication, which he requested be included in this book:

> I want this book to be written for my mom and dad and my family and children. I want to thank them, and thank all of the many friends and many employees who helped me achieve what I did. I love them all. And I especially want in there that this book is in memory of Betty Scholz. That woman was a gem. A real gem!

After that request, there was a long pause between Jack and me . . . and two pairs of teary eyes. Naturally, Jack followed that pause with one of his trademark barks: "I want that in the book, damn it! Do you hear me?" Yes, Jack, I heard you. No one evades *that voice*.

PART I

1

The Van Berg Pedigree

The blaze red sumac leaves had fallen. The rustling golden cotton-woods were now silent. Vital trees were transformed into simple silhouettes—reminders of a winter that was steadily advancing across the prairie.

The corn was picked; the harvest was weak. An exhausted Nebraska farmer stared blankly at a barren field and a profoundly pale prospect. His hope was gone. *Now what?* That was the question young Marion Van Berg asked himself as he assessed his empty land. It was a bitter horizon and a scene as gray as his future.

Generations of hardships had led to this moment, and the toil that Marion, and all those who carried the Van Berg name, had endured. In 1844, Marion's grandfather, Charles Van Berg, at age nine, had arrived in the United States as part of the precious cargo his parents brought with them on their ocean passage from Sweden. As a young man, Charles's interest in horses led him into the 5th Michigan Cavalry. He served in the Union Army during the Civil War and endured several months as a prisoner of the Confederates in their infamous Andersonville, Georgia, prison camp. He was fortunate to be released from the living hell of the stockade, under the agreement that he would no longer serve in the army. Charles obliged himself to the terms, but only long enough to get safely north of the Mason-Dixon Line and significantly west of it. He rejoined the Union Army at Fort Leavenworth, Kansas, and during his duty there, he met and married Sarah Jane Kealiher of Sparta, Michigan. The couple produced eleven children, including a son, Elwin Van Berg, born July 22, 1875. Farming became a way of life for the Van Bergs, and Elwin extended his forebears' inherent, emigrant ambitions as he trekked west of the Missouri River to become a hopeful homesteader.

As a young man, Elwin married Emma Titman of Aurora, Nebraska. The couple battled the elements on their small piece of land near Bradshaw, Nebraska, roughly fifty miles west of the capital city, Lincoln. Then, as now, making a living on a farm was dubious. Profit teetered on the often wicked whim of Mother Nature. Grasshoppers, floods, and drought, coupled with the hungry mouths of his ever-growing family, forced Elwin out of farming, and he moved his family to the nearby railroad-junction town of Aurora. He would ultimately settle in as a barber and in his spare time drive trotting horses in races at the nearby county fairs. But while Elwin, aging, welcomed the relief of a real job, his firstborn, Marion, intrinsically felt the pangs of wanting to sow and harvest from the land.

Born January 15, 1896, Marion Harold Van Berg was a young man well before the Great Depression. Before his parents moved the family to Aurora, he had grown up on the farm with a mixed bag of livestock to care for, crops of corn to look after, and seven siblings who both helped and hindered the process. The hard work aside, farming held appeal. There was a general alliance and bond among the farmers of the day. The farm provided food for those who lived on it and long-awaited income after the harvest. When one farm or family was stricken with a tragedy or bad luck, a neighboring family was there to lend a hand. With a little luck, a lot of sweat, and plenty of fellowship, farming could be a viable trade.

As a child, Marion learned these lessons of hard work and respect for others years before he would strictly instill those same values in his children. He also learned about respect for animals. The Van Berg farm, like most farms, raised livestock for sale and subsequent slaughter. These animals offered potential profit, but they also put food on the table along the way. A popular commodity raised on the Van Berg farm was Poland China swine. These pigs needed to be kept happy and healthy in order for them to reproduce on the farm and produce at the sale barn. They also provided an early means for Marion to observe, nurture, and come to understand animals.

On the farm, Marion's father, Elwin, always kept horses and mules, which he used as beasts of burden and for breeding purposes. He built quite a reputation that he could breed and raise a worthy work animal that could fetch a pretty price. The way to get the best price was at auction, but the way to get to the auction wasn't the best. The nearest sale barn of any significance to the Van Bergs' farm was in Grand Island, Nebraska, roughly twenty miles west of Aurora. Owning a stock truck to haul livestock was not a luxury of the day, or at that time. So Elwin took his animals to market by either riding or walking them himself. Or better yet, having one of his children do this. And thus a remarkable activity was born from a routine task on the farm that would come to summarize what it meant to be a Van Berg: horsemanship coupled with hard work. Learning these two dominant traits came at a very young age.

When Marion was just ten years old, he was part of what nowadays, aside from being a glaring infraction of child labor laws, would be simply unthinkable. On more than one occasion, a convoy of mules and/or horses was created by tying the tail of the leading animal to the halter rope of the one following directly behind. This perilous procession of livestock would trail down the roads, across pastures, over the Platte River bridge, and along fence lines bound for the Grand Island sale barn—led by Marion. It would have been an extraordinary feat in a controlled environment with adult supervision, but with a child solely at the helm, such an endeavor is simply mind-boggling. Yet this is the sort of responsibility that came second nature to those bearing the Van Berg name. If you were a Van Berg, you grew up quickly.

Despite all the work on the farm, young Marion did have enough time to attend school and, more importantly, meet his sweetheart. He fell in love with Viola Swartzendruber, whose family had moved to Aurora from Kalona, Iowa.

In the midst of all the sufferings Marion would endure, courting Viola was pure pleasure. Fortunately and conveniently, the Swartzendrubers moved into the farm across the road from the Van Bergs. The young couple would marry in 1917. Viola would become a pillar early in Marion's and her marriage and remain just as strong and supportive for decades to follow. She carried her weight on the farm and she also carried nine children to successful births. Her first six children were born at home without the services of a doctor.

Farming a section of land required more work than what a husband and wife could accomplish alone. Children were raised with the unquestioned intention of having them help with the chores on the farm. The children born in Marion and Viola's Aurora farmhouse were Eleanor, Helen, Jean, Betty, Alyce, and Wilma. Tough luck for the girls, there was hard work to be done. Helen tells the story of how one day she was with her father digging postholes for fence. The two gradually worked their way about a hundred yards from the truck Marion had driven to the worksite. Helen wasn't even a teenager, yet, and Marion told her to go back to the truck and to drive it up to where they were working. "But Dad, I don't know how to work the gear shift," said Helen. Marion replied, "You'll never learn any younger." There wasn't a child of Marion Van Berg's who didn't hear that phrase repeated a hundred times throughout his or her childhood. What Marion learned early in life is what he expected his children to learn early in their lives—if not sooner. That "no time like the present" attitude and his do-or-die philosophy were no doubt gained from years of self-preservation on the prairie. So the pint-sized girl dutifully dropped her head and trudged off to a ten-gallon task. Filled with fear, but with the desire to please the father she truly loved, Helen climbed up into the cab and settled in behind the steering wheel. There were a number of gear grinds and an equal amount of clunks and lurches, but Helen drove that old farm truck up to her father.

Praise and reward seldom flowed freely from Marion Van Berg's lips. When the able young girl slipped down from the truck, she simply went back to work alongside her father without any mention of her courageous accomplishment. Not a word was whispered between the two, but when Marion peered at his devoted daughter from the corner of his eye, his heart was filled with Van Berg pride.

2

Leaving the Farm

Marion, Viola, and the children were surviving on the farm, but it wasn't a frivolous existence. In the 1920s, townsfolk were starting to enjoy the luxuries of electricity and indoor plumbing, while, just down the road, farm life for many was still very raw. Marion had chosen to be a farmer, and he stayed committed to that decision. He did everything he possibly could to keep food on the table and to keep the farm. Corn, oats, wheat, rye, barley—he planted a variety of crops, but each growing season was a gamble. One year he might harvest a profit; the following year might set him back. He wasn't getting rich, but he was gradually developing his farm and providing for his family. Then came 1930, and with it the Great Depression. What resources Marion was able to muster and generate on the farm rapidly began to slip through his callused fingers.

The heavy haze of the Depression that crept over the world in the early 1930s spared no one and no thing. The weight of the dark economic times was a burden that emerged from the banks of New York City, loomed across the plains of Nebraska, and settled onto the shoulders of Marion Van Berg. If only the metaphoric cloud of the Depression would have brought rain. In reality, the gloom of the dark recession was coupled with a record drought in Nebraska. An international market collapse and statewide crop failure were the very last, sunbaked straws that broke a parched farmer's back. Marion's dreams dried up, too.

Marion knew he needed to get his family off the farm and he hoped to achieve some relative economic safety by moving into town. His parents were living in Aurora, but the savings offered by staying in their house in town provided no salvation for what was an increasingly hopeless situation nationwide.

A seed of hope was planted in the mind of Marion by a man from nearby Grand Island: John Charles Torpey. He was the owner of a successful sale barn there, specializing in mules and horses. Torpey had developed respect for and friendship with Marion over the years of doing business with him. John realized Marion was a hardworking family man and that he could be trusted. He had seen the way Marion interacted with the other men at the sale barn on sale days, and he saw something special in Marion. Grand Island was the third-largest city in Nebraska and at the time was the largest Nebraskan city west of Lincoln. Despite knowing that another auction barn in the region would cut into his own profits, Torpey sensed that Columbus, Nebraska, needed—and had potential for—a well-run sale barn. He knew Marion could be just the man to operate it.

Located roughly sixty miles northeast of Aurora, Columbus was not unfamiliar to Marion. He knew that it was the county seat of Platte County, and a small city of 7,000 with banks, schools, churches, a hospital, parks, restaurants, and bars. The age of the automobile had caused Columbus to grow rapidly. By 1925 all of the city's major thoroughfares had been paved and lighted. Most importantly, Columbus was a significant railroad town and a regional hub for commerce between Omaha and Grand Island.

Viola Van Berg's quiet strength was never far from Marion, and she helped him cultivate a new dream in Columbus. She supported him in every way and was influential in building his confidence in order to make the move. Viola believed in her husband, but as a mother of six, and with another child on the way, she also believed in shelter and electricity. She encouraged Marion to further discuss the venture of a sale barn with John Torpey. With a trusting wife in support, he did.

While Marion had two key supporters—his wife and Torpey— prompting him to transition to Columbus, his parents were strongly against the move. His mother, Emma, was known to have said more than once, "If the liquor doesn't get him, the Catholics will." Marion was not a drinker himself, but he was aware of the relative perils of moving into a much larger city. His children were all young girls at the time, and even though they performed chores as if they were stout young men, he was as protective of his children as his mother was of him. When it became clear that they were going to move, Marion called the girls up into one room and in his uncompromising manner and voice said, "We're going to move to Columbus, but there will be no drinking and no dancing."

And so what followed was a painfully common occurrence of the time, a farm dispersal sale. In order for Marion to take the first step on the path to Columbus, he needed to raise money for the risky road he was about to travel. This required selling off his farming implements. Only the essentials would be kept, the most important of which was the stock truck. Far from a shiny beauty off the sale lot, the truck was a treasured commodity, not only for the transport of the family's belongings to a new home, but for the transit of livestock to help pay for that new home. The plow and the thresher were no longer needed, nor was the scythe or the baler. Axes, shovels, and saws would be kept, and, of course, the anvil and Marion's two horses. But the Van Berg farming equipment, which for years had been pulled by heaving horses or operated by a sweat-soaked man, would no longer be needed possessions. That is, if the gamble paid off.

In an odd coincidence, March 5, 1933, was the date the dispersal sale was scheduled, but that very day President Franklin Roosevelt famously declared a national bank holiday and closed all financial institutions to stall a massive run on the banks. For better or worse, the sale would be conducted two weeks later. The raven roosted on the fence post.

3

Columbus or Bust

The move to Columbus got the Van Bergs closer to Columbus, but it didn't actually land the family *in* Columbus. Furthermore, Viola's quest for electricity didn't come as easily as the flip of a switch. Marion's budget, and the process of uprooting from the farm to the city, required a preliminary transitional stage when the family would live in a rental house outside of town. He simply couldn't afford to buy a house in town. The children would initially attend country school rather than be enrolled in the Columbus school district.

The Van Bergs' new home wasn't new. It was an old farmhouse north of town. The rental property also included a few acres so the residents could keep some horses and a milk cow. There was a barn for the livestock and a small granary that was transformed into a chicken house. Marion knew he would continue to rely on the animals as part of his master plan to help feed and support his family. The house had a coal-burning furnace system, which was a comfort their farmhouse south of Aurora didn't have. But the desire for electricity would remain on Viola's wish list. They would have to make do with kerosene wick lamps and lanterns until the amenity of electricity could be afforded.

John Torpey aligned Marion with a local Columbus banker by the name of Mort Taylor. The referral would prove to be a key introduction. Mort and Marion overtook the lease of a building in downtown Columbus on Twenty-Seventh Avenue between Tenth and Eleventh Streets. This was the site of a sale barn that had been poorly operated by its previous owners. The location was an awkward one for Marion personally because he was vehemently opposed to drinking—the structure had a door that connected to the adjacent Palm Garden tavern. Marion applied his individual touch to the sale barn by way of a hammer, a handful of nails, and a few boards. The result: the boarding up of a certain door to debauchery. At last, he was ready for business. Now all he needed was something to run through the sale ring.

Hogs were popular animals to raise in the region. They were practical to have around the farm and cheaper than cattle. With high hopes and the excitement of Marion soon being able to conduct his first sale, Marion and Viola trusted their daughters to care for themselves and then pointed their reliable stock truck north on Highway 81, bound for Winner, South Dakota, a 220-mile drive. They returned with a truck filled with sixty-pound feeder pigs ready for auction. Unfortunately, Marion also should have hauled in buyers for the sale. Despite his promotion of the sale, very few buyers came and he ended up losing money on the pigs. With a wounded but far from dead spirit, he tried again. However, on his second attempt he suffered the same result. Marion's calculations for success had a very narrow margin for error and another failed effort would mean certain devastation. In his third sale he was encouraged because there were more buyers from the area who came for the auction, but the end result was the same: zero profit.

In the span of a year, Marion had watched his crops dry up and blow away. He saw his farm equipment sold and hauled away. And he watched his farm disappear as he drove away from it himself. Seeing the misfortune that had befallen him and his family was simply overwhelming. Marion's eyes had witnessed far too much personal despair; they welled up and streamed tears that dotted the dusty sale office floor. He had gambled. He had lost.

Marion was defeated, hopeless, and nearly penniless, but his older sister Mary encouraged him to go see Mr. Torpey in Grand Island. So he grimly made the sixty-mile drive west on Highway 30 to see John Torpey to inform him of the wretched news. He drove by hearty fields of crops along the Platte, and he saw pastures filled with cattle that grazed on thick green bluestem grass. He wondered why none of that was meant for him. He wondered why he couldn't enjoy just a small slice of what others were able to taste. Wistfully, he drove on. Marion approached Torpey's sale barn and cleared his eyes as his car tires slowly crackled across the gravel lot. Hardly any dust was raised. He stopped the car, methodically set the brake, and then took a deep breath before stepping out. On his walk toward the office he glanced around the prosperous sale yard and asked himself again: why not me? Marion sat across the desk from Mr. Torpey and described what he had done, how he had failed, and how he surely couldn't continue.

When Marion completed his woeful story, John Torpey leaned back in his chair, reached into his suit coat, took out his checkbook, and said, "You're not broke." He tossed the checkbook across his desk and said, "Go back to Columbus and try it again, Marion. And use my checkbook to buy anything you need to get that sale barn up and running." When Marion shifted his car into drive, this time, the dust billowed around him. Limestone rocks spat out from behind his bumper as he rushed east onto the highway for his resurgent return home to Columbus. It was a far less melancholy drive; he mused that the cattle he passed might one day pass through *his* sale ring.

Armed with the confidence, and checkbook, that John Torpey had given him, Marion set out to conduct yet another sale. This time he had even more support from his Columbus banker friend. Mort Taylor encouraged his influential clients, farmers, and ranchers to give Marion's sale a try. The concept of conducting a sale in Columbus was genuinely a good idea and beneficial to both livestock sellers and buyers. Animals that were transported to the stockyards in Omaha suffered from injury, sickness, and significant weight loss. Livestock sold at auction at Marion's sale in Columbus were not exposed to such negative forces. They could be trucked in on the day of the sale, fresh off the farm or ranch, and experience virtually no weight loss. Without ever using John Torpey's checkbook, and with a deeper grassroots effort, Marion was soon ready to give it another go. For the first time, he even lured some cattle buyers to make the ninety-mile drive west from the Omaha Livestock Exchange building at the Union Stockyards.

It worked! After the sale, the receipts were tallied and a profit had been made. What's more, Marion's sale had made a positive impression on the sale-goers. Buyers promised that they would return, and ranchers and farmers promised they would bring more livestock. At the very next sale, big-time buyers came from the four major Omaha meat packers: Armour, Wilson, Cudahy, and Swift. Sellers drove off with empty stock trucks, and with thicker wallets. For the first time in years, Marion was able to walk with a spring in his step and to lay his head down at night with real hope for the next day. He could also foresee that his dear Viola's dreams of living with electricity would one day shine true.

4

Rising from the Dust

In 1935, times were still hard, but the grip of the Great Depression was beginning to loosen. The national unemployment rate was starting to ease, as jobless rates began to fall from as high as 25 percent. Closer to home, the move to Columbus was really feeling like a good decision for Marion. Business at the sale barn maintained steady growth, as did his family. Marion and Viola had their first boy, whom they named Elwin Swartz, after Marion's father and Viola's mother—Elwin would later be called "Bud." Marion and Viola then promptly added to the six girls, with baby Virginia. While Virginia was the couple's eighth child, she was the first Van Berg child to be born in a hospital. The luxury of giving birth in a sterilized room with doctors and nurses at the bedside was not only a sign of the changing times, but also an indication that the bucolic, unpredictable lifestyle of Marion and his family was becoming stabilized—and civilized. Recognizing all his newfound fortune, Marion thought to himself, "There is a God!" He knew it and was grateful. He also wanted to be sure his children felt the same and was emphatic that his family attend church regularly. The Van Bergs joined the Federated Church in Columbus, a church and congregation that still exist today.

Each day Marion would think of how he could further improve his sale barn. Sale days were becoming more and more hectic and were beginning to take place more than once a week. As always, he relied on his family for help. Marion's oldest sister, Mary, and her husband, Sterling Laurie, oversaw a grain elevator in the south-central Nebraska town of Hildreth. The Lauries were called upon to help out with office accounting matters and they taught Marion's young daughter Helen how to manage the books when she was just thirteen. Helen later would recall, "I went from slopping hogs and feeding cattle to being a bookkeeper." Some people thought she was too young for such a job, but, according to Marion, "You'll never learn any younger."

Business was becoming so good that both the downtown sale barn and Marion's business were beginning to experience growing pains. He had stomached his share of hardships, but this is one of the few hardships that he welcomed. With all the traffic at the sale barn, the facility needed routine upkeep and repairs. Marion always kept the checkbook John Torpey had given him in his chest pocket, but he had yet to use it. Thus far, the profits of his sales were also providing for capital improvements. However, it was becoming evident that with the popularity of the sale barn and the clientele of high-end buyers, he needed to start looking for a more accommodating facility. He needed a bigger barn. Marion wanted to maintain his balance of happy customers, but he also wanted to increase the volume of his sales. He needed more than just a bigger barn—he needed all aspects of the operation to grow, and soon.

Marion wasn't a big man, but the burgeoning success of his livestock sale business made his heart big. With the confidence he had gained in himself and with Mr. Torpey's checkbook close to his heart, he was starting to think big, too. He found the perfect spot for a larger barn in the southwest corner of town, on ten acres that backed right up to the Union Pacific main-line railroad tracks. Marion wasn't trying to outdo the mammoth Union Stockyards in Omaha, but he was trying to build an efficient, popular, and large sale yard. What he ended up with was the Taj Mahal of the Platte. Marion designed a facility that could handle a significant amount of livestock, offer transportation convenience, and provide comfort for his customers. Of equal importance was safety for the animals. Construction on the sales complex began in the fall of 1935.

Marion was building a new barn, but he had built a cache of respect that began paying dividends before the first nail was driven. The inroads into the community that he had made led to a tremendous financial benefit from a local lumberman. Lyman Mead owned and operated Mead Lumber, the lumberyard that served much of Platte County. He and Marion became friends, and Lyman trusted and believed in Marion so much that he allowed Marion to buy lumber and building supplies from him on a payment plan with no cash paid up front. Ted Kaufman owned Kaufman Hardware in Columbus, and he was also a believer in Marion. He welcomed a pay-as-you-go plan anticipating the future business that the Van Berg Sales Barn would bring to the community.

Marion was also building friendships across Platte County. He hired men to build his sales facility who would become both long-term employees and lifelong friends. Sweede Johnson, also playfully nicknamed "Pee Wee" Johnson, because he was such a large man, was hired along with Hardy Christensen. Both men were from nearby Stromsburg, Nebraska, roughly thirty miles southwest of Columbus. "Mr. Van," as Marion's employees and the locals would call him, was strong on hiring from within. Hardy's wife, Mars, would work in the sales office for years, and Sweede's son Max would become a close friend of the Van Berg children. Clarence Fusby, also from Stromsburg, became a key employee as the scale man in the sale barn once it was built.

Marion designed and helped build the sales barn, but he wasn't the architect of the house that would become the home of his ever-growing family. In a herculean effort, he orchestrated the moving of a two-story house from the opposite side of town to the sale construction site. Viola would get her much-deserved palace and her long-overdue electricity. The large white house would become a beacon of the family's accomplishment and a haven for the children's friends and Van Berg employees.

On March 6, 1936, the Van Berg Sales Pavilion was christened, without alcohol, and it was a thing of beauty. Stockmen from around the Midwest and beyond were awed by the newest sales hub in the industry. They appreciated and anticipated all the commerce and camaraderie that was customary at a Van Berg sale. A grand opening party was held for the facility, and more than a thousand people showed up to be treated to a barbecue featuring roast buffalo and soda pop. For decades to follow, those who stepped into the Van Berg sales office received a stern glare from the glassy eyes of a wooly, horned beast mounted on the wall—a reminder of just who provided the meat for that feast. Nearly three years to the day Marion had left behind his overalls as a starving farmer, he stood dressed in a tie posing for photos as a successful sale barn owner. With his wife, Viola, at his side, an unused checkbook for assurance in his pocket, and a workforce of eight Van Berg children surrounding him, the gamble had seemingly paid off.

5

Along Came Jack

The corps of laborers who lived in the Van Berg house got one member stronger on June 7, 1936, when John Charles Van Berg was born at Saint Mary's Hospital in Columbus. Marion and Viola respectfully named him in honor of John Torpey, the man who threw Marion and his family a lifeline. The newborn Van Berg boy, who would be nicknamed "Jack," made quite an entrance, and it wouldn't take long for folks to learn that big entrances would simply be his nature. Seven of Viola's first eight babies were born at home, but on this occasion, Viola was in a hospital bed during her labor and actually needed medical assistance. There was quite a panic, because ironically there were no doctors to be found in the hospital at the time. Jack was not born overdue, but he was a very large baby, which made for a difficult delivery. Luckily for mother and child, there were skilled nurses and nuns at the hospital to provide support. Of course the slap into reality tiny Jack received on his butt wasn't for bad behavior. However, disciplinary reminders would be readily applied as needed to the newest rogue in the Van Berg world in the years to come.

Baby Jack would be the last of the nine children that Marion and Viola would raise. By the time he was born, his oldest sisters, Eleanor and Helen, had already graduated from high school. Most of Jack's siblings grew up during the passage of the farm and hardscrabble early days. Jack was the first Van Berg child to be raised in a house that had both electricity and a father with steady income to pay the electric bill. But that didn't mean he was born with a silver spoon in his mouth. All of the Van Berg children worked, and they worked all of the time. An often heard expression from

Marion was "idle minds and idle hands make worthless children." Fortunately, Jack would have a few years' reprieve to play as a toddler and as a young boy before he had to prove his worthiness as a Van Berg.

While the sale barn was simply salvation for Marion, for young children it was more than magical. It was a forest of stock pens for tireless rounds of hide and seek, a cave with endless crawl spaces and trap doors, and a gymnasium with lofts, rafters, ropes, and billowy hay landing pads. Epic clashes of cops and robbers were battled there. The barn was everything a child's mind would allow. It was wholesome good times, albeit with the peril of a savage hog, the danger of a rusty nail, or the risk of a probable bump on the head. Shrieks of fun and yelps of pain were commonplace when it was playtime in the barn.

Jack's sister, Betty, was eleven years older than he, and she was often asked to babysit her younger siblings. She recalls Jack frequently making her nervous because he was prone to sneak out of her range of supervision. "Whenever he'd get out of my sight, the first place I would start looking would be the barns," said Betty. It wasn't uncommon to find young Jack in a stall, cozied up next to the family's matched set of draft horses, the gentle giants sharing their space with the inquisitive tot. Jack's innate horse sense shone early and likely saved him from being squashed by their mighty bodies.

Two other horses Jack spent plenty of time with as a young boy were Tiny and Pat. This twosome was not a matched set, just two good ponies that Jack often hitched to a wagon and drove around the barns. One of the first chores Jack ever had was to deliver lunch to some of Marion's hired men, Bob and Cecil Irwin. The Irwin brothers, along with John Pensick, enjoyed spending time with the youngest, precocious Van Berg. They saw how good he was with the animals and appreciated his evolving horsemanship. The men also enjoyed having some good fun at young Jack's expense. One afternoon, after Jack climbed out of the wagon as part of a lunch run, Bob Irwin hopped into the back of the wagon, grabbed the lines to the ponies, and pulled a tarp over himself to conceal himself from Jack. Hidden under the tarp he started to drive the ponies away from Jack. When an alarmed Jack saw this, he started out after them. Each time he'd get close to the wagon, Bob would urge the horses on. This stop-and-start chase went on for a while before Jack figured out what was going on. He whimpered a bit about being teased but soon saw the fun in it and was able to laugh along with the men. This small incident was key in Jack's development. He saw that hardworking men could make time to be playful and still get their job done. The understanding of this sort of workplace hijinks was a seed planted in Jack, which would sprout decades of practical jokes that he devised and cultivated himself. Bob Irwin would later become an essential element in Marion's racing operations. Cecil Irwin was a tremendous help to Marion at the sale barn.

Another Van Berg employee, and one of the children's favorites, was Bill Behrens, who was ruined as a farmer when the banks crashed and he couldn't get to his money before others did. Somehow, Bill was given the nickname "Boobly Bill," or simply, "Boobly." A German immigrant, he was a strange, raggedy character who could wiggle his ears. He always wore bib overalls—three pairs at once in summer and five pairs at once in the winter, the top layer just as threadbare as the layer down below. He lived in a little room in the big red Van Berg barn located near the base of the UP railroad viaduct. And he collected old newspapers and cardboard, which he used for insulation in his room. Boobly existed as frugally as imaginable. The only money he was known to spend was when he would go to Billie's Café on Highway 30 and routinely order pancakes, bacon, and eggs. Regardless of weather, he would walk downtown each New Year's Eve and order a Tom and Jerry. The hot eggnog and brandy was just what he needed to survive his round-trip celebration. Boobly had no faith in banks, so he asked Helen to keep all of his paychecks in the sale office safe—which is where they stayed until he died. He was the night watchman at the sale barn and could be trusted with anything and anyone, frequently giving the kids pony rides or keeping a close eye on young, wandering Jack. Boobly looked like he had crawled out from under a bridge and he smelled like he slept with the hogs, but he was as sweet as a rose, with a heart made of gold.

As a youngster, Jack liked to spend time frolicking in and along the banks of the nearby Loup River, which flowed into the Platte River. The French explorers got it right when they named the Platte. The French word *platte* translates to "flat." Early pioneers quipped, "The Platte was too thick to drink and too thin to plow." More sandbar than water, the languid river in the summertime might only be ankle-deep off the banks and sometimes just chest-high at the main channel. For a child it was less perilous than most rivers, but it overflowed as a natural playground. The Loup River was less than a half mile south of the Van Berg home. In the river's refuge, Jack could leap after slippery bullfrogs and catch whiskery catfish. He could trap aimless turtles and shoot hapless muskrats. He could swing like a chimp in the cottonwoods and swordfight like a buccaneer with the cattails. Tom Sawyer, Huck Finn, . . . Jack Van Berg!

But as Jack grew older, expectations of him grew, as well. All of his siblings played a role in the function of the sales barn, and young Jack was not passed over in that regard. His entry-level position was assisting his sisters Wilma and Virginia in the sale of soda pop and candy bars in the sale ring and throughout the facility. Fifty-pound blocks of ice were dumped into large stock tanks, into which cases of pop were then unloaded and chilled. The youngest children would carry pails of pop and ice and sell the bottles for a nickel each. All the money would be accounted for; this was not a paid gig for the kids, nor was there any commission to be earned. It was simply the duty of a Van Berg child. As Jack and his siblings aged, their responsibilities escalated. Helen worked like an ox and could milk a cow better than any man, but she and her sisters Eleanor and Jean were clerking in the sales office, while sisters Betty and Alyce had advanced to running sales tickets and receipts to and from the office for the buyers in the ring. Jack's role increased, as well. He learned from his brother Bud how to yard the hogs and cattle and did so in extreme conditions. He'd freeze numb working in the dour dank of December and swelter in the heat and humidity of August, lugging a heavy water hose to his mother Viola as she mercifully showered livestock in the transport trailers. A few years later, at age twelve, Jack was capable of parking big rigs and backing them into staging positions on the sales pavilion lot.

Jack wasn't born with a silver spoon, but he sure had a silver tongue. He knew it and his siblings knew it. He was an equally savvy salesman, and if the kids ever wanted something from their dad, they would send *Jackie* to soften him up. Jack would crawl up onto Marion's lap in the living room, snuggle up to him, and whisper into his ear. Next thing you knew, the kids were jumping for joy because Dad had sweetened and succumbed.

Don't be mistaken, while Marion was the taskmaster and had the almighty voice, occasionally Viola had veto power over him. She was known to scold her husband, saying, "Marion, your voice could take the skin off a snake." Now and then Viola would step in when Marion wasn't in the mood for compromise or leniency. One such occasion stems from the many notorious stories of Jack's covert smoking or, rather, his unsuccessful attempts to hide smoking from his father. The Stockmen's Café was part of the Van Berg Sales Pavilion, and, periodically, Viola or Jack's older sister Helen would give the kids the key to the café so they could get a pop. When Jack was involved, he'd take the opportunity to snitch some cigarettes from behind the counter and then later smoke them in the furnace room of the sales barn. This coal shack doubled as a sort of underground hideout for Jack and his chosen friends.

One afternoon Jack delayed some work at the sale to sneak a smoke. The plank door to the shack had a knothole in it to slip your fingers through in order to open or close it. When Billy, an unwelcome kid in the area, knew Jack was in the room, he'd attempt to join Jack by putting his fingers through the hole. Jack willingly stood guard to ping Billy's fingers with a hammer when this happened. With one hand on his cigarette and another on the hammer, Jack was privately puffing away when sure enough, two fingers poked into the hole. Just as Jack was ready to hammer them he realized the fingers were large and freckled—they weren't Billy's fingers.

The grace that God spared on Jack for preventing him from nailing his dad's fingers was not a similar grace Marion spared on his son. Marion jerked Jack out of the room and dragged him back into the sale, letting him feel the sting of a buggy whip in between strides. There Jack sat in the sale ring room, under the supervision of the infuriated eyes of his father. To further fuel the fire, each time the hog buyers would see that Marion might be cooling down, they'd offer Jack another cigarette. This did nothing to lighten the additional punishment Jack would face. Marion was not a smoker, but he kept a cache of cigars that he would occasionally receive as gifts from stockmen. Later that night, after chores and supper, Marion produced a cigar and made Jack smoke it in front of him at the kitchen table. "Take a bigger puff. Take a bigger puff," commanded Marion, as Jack sat there turning green as a gourd. Jack remembers standing up from the table in a nauseous daze and walking smack into the kitchen wall.

Viola saw that, and shouted, "Marion!" When Viola hollered *Marion*, she then had the voice. "That's enough!" she demanded. Even though Viola stepped in to save her son that night, it did not save him from decades of smoking. Jack's forbidden habit would later spark a legendary story, many variations of which have smoldered for years.

6

Jack'n Around

All work and no play make Jack a dull boy. No truer words were ever spoken, and to be sure, at least while he was young, Jack found time to play. One early spring morning, Jack and his buddies Tom Griffiths and Jim Nikolite decided to grab their guns and head out to go hunting. Never mind that pheasants weren't in season, cabin fever can take its toll during a Nebraska winter, and the boys were determined to blow off some steam. But instead, they nearly blew off their heads! Jack borrowed (without permission) his sister Helen's light green, well-kept 1950 Plymouth, and the three boys trundled out of town. It didn't take long before they flushed and shot their share of birds. After they had their fill of stomping around in the cold, they stowed their pheasants in a snowbank in order to pick them up on their return home. With some extra time to kill, they decided they would drive to nearby Schuyler and see what sort of mischief they could stir up.

Schuyler was less than twenty miles east of Columbus on Highway 30. The town offered a vital supply of similarly aged boys and girls, who often served as hormone-driven adversaries or admirers. Wars, but usually just in words, were waged for years and sometimes generations between the young bucks of the territory who frequently locked horns in battles of bravado. Jack and Jim emptied the ammo from their guns before they got into the car for the drive to Schuyler. As they were rumbling down the road in the Plymouth, Jack, at the wheel, looked over to Tom across the front seat and said, "Hey, did you unload your damn gun?" Tom mumbled rather unconvincingly that he thought he had, so Jack croaked, "Well, check the son-of-a-buck."

Now, Jack may not have gained his father's gruff voice yet at age sixteen, but he surely had his gruff attitude, and he barked out commands just the same as Marion would have. Tom Griffiths was packing both a pistol and a 16-gauge bold-action shotgun. He grabbed the shotgun first, and with the barrel pointed down, braced it on the floorboard and pulled the bold-action back. With an "I'll show you" attitude, Tom thrust forward the bold-action to demonstrate the gun was empty, and . . . whaboom!

Turns out the shotgun wasn't empty. The gun erupted. The boys almost jumped through the roof. And the car nearly swerved into an oncoming grain truck. The blast had blown through the floorboard, exposing the open road below. About the time the stunned passengers regained their hearing and realized they had just had a brush with death, they noticed the car was losing power. The gunpowder smoke and smell cleared from the blast, but then a new scent surfaced in the sedan. Jack pulled the crippled car to the side of the road to check the damage. Tom's not-so-empty gun had shot through the floorboard, ricocheted off the chassis, and made Swiss cheese out of the radiator.

The engine had taken a significant hit, but the boys' pride soon faced a more direct shot, as the first vehicle to stop to help was a pickup truck filled with some of their Schuyler rivals. As expected, the ridicule and name-calling flared up, but Jack knew when to use his brains and when to use his brawn. This was clearly a time for mind over muscle. With his golden tongue, he was able to coerce a tow into town by the same kids he might be scrapping with next weekend. Back in town, Tom Griffiths's dad was called to the rescue. Now the boys didn't go out of their way to tell Mr. Griffiths what had happened, they only said that they might have a leak in their radiator because they had lost all their water. Mr. Griffiths went up to the Conoco gas station and brought back two cans of Stop Leak.

But when he poured the contents of the cans into the top of the radiator, the fluid streamed out of the bottom just as fast as it went in. The boys may have shot their pheasant earlier, but their goose was now promptly cooked. The radiator additive didn't do the trick, but a tow to the Soulliere & Bray auto repair shop, plus a bill of $83.50, sure fixed the leak. Jack still remembers the cost of repairs because Tom didn't have any money, so he and Jim had to pay the bill. Another thing Jack recalls is a blast that occurred decades after the actual mishap. Jack was married, with a family of his own, when once more he set out to go hunting, this time with his good friend Sonny Pensick. He stopped by his folks' house to pick up a few guns, and when he was headed out of the house, Mrs. Van Berg calmly said, "Don't shoot any radiators, Jack." Roughly twenty years after he and his friends had shot out the floorboard and radiator of his sister Helen's Plymouth, that is all Jack's mom ever said to him about the incident. Jack's life lessons of the power of using a few choice words were evidently learned not only from his father, but also from an astute and even defter mother.

If Marion had a keen eye for appraising a horse, then Viola had an equally sharp eye for judging character. The Van Berg residence was large. Very often the two-story house and the surrounding sale barn and facility proved to be a playground and dining hall for many of the Columbus children. "Mrs. Van," as she was called by those children, would tell the children's parents not to worry when their children were visiting; she knew where they were, and they wouldn't be out on the street corner. One day Jack brought two boys (each named Billy) into the house after school; when they left to go home for supper, Jack's mom told him that they were not to be allowed back into the house. Jack griped and said, "Mother, you can't be that way." His mother replied, "Jack, those boys are no good and they are up to no good." Both ended up in prison.

Truth be told, Jack was no saint either. While it wasn't his gun or his finger on the trigger that resulted in the shocking shotgun story, Jack was prone to occasionally disobey orders himself. Long before the days of Big Wheel tricycles or Nintendo video games, good, clean fun didn't always mean clean behavior. When his parents were gone racing in Detroit for the summer, Jack would take a few liberties against the rules that had been laid down by Marion before he left town. One rule was not to use his father's good riding horse as a bucking horse—which is exactly what Jack would do. For thrills and of course kicks, it wasn't uncommon for Jack to buck some small bulls or heifers out of the chutes in the rodeo arena that was built on the property. One day Marion's good horse Silver was too tantalizing to leave alone. Jack and his buddies grabbed the bareback bucking rig and cinched him up for a spin. On a good day Silver would give them their money's worth. With a nod of his head and firm grip on the bucking rig, Jack gave a bellow to "turn him loose." The two left the chute with Silver's hind shoes flashing high. At the end of the arena Silver turned and broke into a dead run. Jack was still cowboying as best he could until, at full sprint, Silver suddenly turned sharply again and fell hard with Jack getting caught underneath. The horse popped back up, shook his head and trotted off. Jack laid there with a broken ankle—and a broken promise. Each spring, Jack would promise his sister Helen that he wouldn't do anything that would make her call Dad home. A call was made to inform Jack's folks that he had broken his ankle. That it happened astride Silver was not part of the phone call. And so a cover up, and not the first one on Jack's behalf, was permitted by dear sister Helen. But seldom is an artificial alibi air-tight. Helen never said how much flak she caught from her father when the facts surfaced, but she did say that when Marion learned the truth about Jack's broken ankle, all he said to Jack was "You're lucky it was your ankle and not the horse's."

Tough love, ever the Van Berg way.

7

School Daze

School and Jack Van Berg were like oil and water. Too frequently Jack's attention was far from the classroom chalkboard—that is, if his attention was ever in the classroom. His mind was frequently going a mile a minute, and school just slowed him down. Jack had more important things to consider, like the wonder of what the next sale might bring on the weekend. As Jack slogged his way through grade school, it became evident that his exposure to the buying and selling activity of the sales barn had enabled him to do math in his head. Unfortunately, arithmetic wasn't the only subject he had in school.

Years ago, students declared a major in high school and attempted to learn a trade even before they reached college. The path of least resistance for Jack was woodworking shop. But he still faced a challenge—in this case, the resistance turned out to be his reputation and a pugnacious past that initially blocked his future.

As a freshman at Columbus High School, Jack observed a few kids in his shop class who, as he put it, "really had their noses up the teacher's ass." Once, as these kids went up to get some sandpaper and to schmooze with the teacher, Coach Alpers, Jack seized the opportunity to glue their woodworking projects to the workbench. The humor in this was short-lived. Jack recalls the eruption that followed: "Mr. Alpers was a good son-of-a-buck boy, a good guy. But he grabbed me and whipped me and beat me and knocked every tool off that tool rack with my damn head. He beat the living shit out of me!" Subsequently, Mr. Alpers told Jack to never return to the shop class. Well, Jack needed woodworking to graduate, so the next year, as a sophomore, he approached Mr. Alpers about being readmitted. Impressed that Jack was man enough to address him face to face, Mr. Alpers saw to it that Jack would be permitted to carry on. Jack was back in the woodworking curriculum, but this time with a different teacher, Mr. Costello, who was also the football coach. But his sophomore year didn't get much better, because of a standoff in football practice. Jack's friends Jim Nikolite and Hart Keating were facing undue verbal and physical abuse from Coach Costello. When Jack had seen enough, he said, "Hey *Nik* and *Hart*, we don't need to take this shit, you know that? Let's leave. We ain't playing football anymore!" The boys didn't play football again until their senior year after Costello had been fired. But the damage was done, and the price Jack paid was a 4, then equivalent to the grade of D, in woodshop his sophomore year. Jack would later joke that a 4 average is great in college, but it's not the average you want to keep in high school. Jack knew that he had been wronged, so he took his case to the principal, Mr. Paul Miller. Jack told Mr. Miller that he had given his word to Mr. Alpers that if he was permitted to join woodworking again he'd work very hard. Jack had lived up to his word, and he showed Principal Miller photos of all that he had built: end tables, card tables, bed frames, and headboards. Jack really had done an exceptional job. Mr. Miller approved Jack's work in class for his sophomore year, and because of Jack's exemplary craftsmanship, Mr. Alpers made him the shop foreman for both his junior and senior years in high school.

Jack's activities during his school years involved much more than the classroom routine. He participated in school team sports and rodeo when time allowed. Throughout grade school and high school he also had chores to do around the barn and he routinely worked weekends. Jack had an enterprising mind, and he'd invite his buddies to ride his horses—but only after they had cleaned stalls for him or milked the cow. Milking was both Jack's primary chore at home and his number one aggravation. He hated that duty and did all he could to sidestep it. Jack was notorious for enticing almost anyone to take the bucket from him and to sit on the stool and squeeze, squeeze, squeeze. His siblings were lobbied; longtime Van Berg employee Bud Kuta was often goaded; even his milk-to-ride program with his classmates had decent success. Once Jack even attempted to bypass the milk cow and go straight for the milk bottle. Mrs. Roberts ran the Stockmen's Café and Jack bought some milk from her to fill his bucket with bottled milk. She warned him, "Jackie, your dad is going to know the difference, and that cow's utters by morning are going to be so full." But Jack ended up filling the bucket with bottled milk against Mrs. Roberts's advice. He figured the money he would spend would save him time. He thought he was so clever by squeezing just enough fresh milk into the bucket to create some milk foam on the top. But the next morning he had some explaining to do when the homogenized milk brought no cream to the top. There was no butter that day, and Jack's failed investment in a shortcut only churned up more chores as punishment. Jack's sister Virginia recalls many milk pail tales, but she avoided having to do the chore herself. "My sisters told me never to learn how to milk a cow. They said, 'If Jack tries to teach you, don't learn,'" said Virginia. Not all of Jack's tactics were a success, but he considered anything a triumph so long as he wasn't sitting under an udder.

If Jack wasn't making a fist to tug a teat, he was making a fist to knock a nose. Jack said it himself: "I was an ornery little bastard." When kids would come to town with their folks for business at the sale, Jack would lure them back behind the barns and attempt to coax them into a fight. Bob Kutilek was one of his buddies in school, but it was a fickle relationship. Jack recalls, "One day we might be peacefully walking home from school side by side and the next thing you know we'd be rolling on the ground tangled in a fight. Then just like that we'd be back walking again and I'd have my arm on his shoulder." Kutilek remembers it similarly: "When

Jack would put his arm around you he would always be fiddling around with your ear. Damn, I hated that! He'd constantly be twisting or playing with my ear." Jack's pal Jim Nikolite has a bump on his ear that to this day he claims was caused by Jack squeezing it.

Sometimes Jack would ask Bob for a ride home from school on his bike. "I'd let him ride on the back of my bike," Bob remembered, "but then he'd have to let me ride his horse when we got to his house. Oh, he'd grumble about that, because he had to do chores when he got home and didn't have time to play like I did." Jack had to bum bike rides because Marion wouldn't let him have a bike. "Either ride a horse or walk," Marion would say.

One day after school Jack was riding on the handlebars with his pal Curly Hengler seated behind him at the controls. As they were cruising down the sidewalk, a woman carrying two bags of groceries suddenly stepped out of the Hinky Dinky grocery story. She walked into their path so quickly that they ran right up behind her. Instead of plowing her over, Jack reached out and just grabbed her by the waist and picked her up. A circus act couldn't have choreographed the stunt any better. But when Jack clutched her from behind he may as well have goosed her. She flung open her arms in a reflexive release that scattered soup cans, spaghetti noodles, coffee, and eggs. The shriek the woman let out drew as much attention as the mess they had to clean up.

"Jack was an explorer," his oldest sister, Helen, explained. "A lot of times he'd go by the river and mess around or sneak off to the Waggoner sandpit lake before he would come home from school. He knew he'd be put to work when he got home, so I guess you'd say he took the long way home sometimes."

During the summer vacations of his school years, Jack was often on the road. His summer months were far from a vacation time. Marion's interest and success in thoroughbred racing had grown so much that it caused him and Viola to be away from Columbus for several months of the year. During the summer racing season, Jack would periodically spend several weeks in Detroit with his parents, oftentimes arriving or departing via horse van. Summers meant vacation from school, not vacation from work. Jack spent summers working at the barn, grooming and walking horses, or performing whatever task his father might have for him. Jack was worked anywhere and everywhere and he was given no amnesty. One summer he was in Detroit and he helped van some horses back to Omaha. But his help didn't come from riding in the cab of the truck; he was in the back with the horses. Young Jack was assigned to a beast named French Admiral. The son of War Admiral had class in his blood, but not in his behavior. "He was a nasty, mean son-of-a-buck," Jack recalled. "I had to ride in the back of the van with him, and he tried to savage me the whole way back to Omaha."

Nevertheless, Jack formed a close relationship with the horse, and he got the colt to soften up and become gentle. French Admiral set a track record that June at 1 mile 70 yards and then came back two weeks later to set a track record at 1 mile and 1/16. "I loved that horse. I got him eating apples and oranges out of my hand, and you didn't even need to tie him up in the stall to be around him," Jack remembered. "But you could never hit him or whip him in a race."

Tommy Osment rode French Admiral in all of his Ak-Sar-Ben races. However, when Marion shipped in another horse to run in a big race, he wanted Tommy to ride the ship-in. "We got Hank Manifold to ride French Admiral and he was specifically told not to whip him. At the top of the stretch, just as he was starting to move to the front, Hank reached back and popped him. French Admiral stopped like he ran into a brick wall. Oh, that made me so mad," steamed Jack. "I never forgave Hank for that."

When Jack wasn't in Detroit with his folks or riding in a horse van over the summers, he might be making a daily round-trip trek from Columbus to Omaha. Sometimes he'd stay overnight in Omaha with the horses stabled at Ak-Sar-Ben. Most boys went to day camp, spent time at the swimming pool, or played baseball during summer vacation—Jack was busy becoming a man.

When school was back in session, it didn't interrupt work, nor did work yield to weekends. Oftentimes, the forces of work and weekends would collide. In one such confrontation, Jack came home at 2 A.M. and was tip-toeing up the stairs to his bedroom with his shoes in his hands. After the wrong board creaked, he heard a voice call out, "What time is it, boy?" Jack mumbled back, "I don't know." To which the voice responded, "Well I do!" The next morning the snow was blowing—it was a nasty Nebraska winter's day. Marion told Jack that he wanted him and Jinks (Jack's buddy, Boyd "Jinks" Hopkins) to drive out to the farm in Genoa and haul back several loads of hay. Jack asked his dad why, since he knew it was already arranged that Bud and Cecil Irwin would handle the work detail. Marion responded, "I decided I want you to do it since you have so much energy." Oh, that pissed Jack off to no end, but through his seething he was also thinking. Jack and Jinks hitched the hayrack to the back of the grain truck and successfully, albeit very dangerously, cut the job time in half.

Genoa is roughly thirty miles west of Columbus, and what with the blowing snow and road conditions, it took the boys until 7 P.M. to complete the job. As he walked into the kitchen to warm up, Jack stomped the snow off his boots and tried to shake off the chill. Marion was at the table and asked Jack how much hay he had hauled. He didn't believe it when Jack told him they had hauled it all. When Jack convinced his dad that he had made two loads for every haul, Marion was impressed by his ingenuity but sarcastically replied, "That's very good; I'll bet you go to bed early tonight." Jack defiantly responded, "No, I'm not; my friends are going out ice skating tonight, and I'm going out, too." Jack made it to the ice rink in the park, but a half-hour later he was back home, zonked out, face-down and motionless, fast asleep on his bed. Jack showed Marion how hard he could work, but it was the father who taught his son the hard lesson.

At the sale barn, at the racetrack, or en route to either, Jack was trusted to accept a great deal of responsibility, but with it came equal parts of opportunity. His brain was always ticking, and if he had an interest in something, he could soak it up like a sponge. The commotion in the sales ring was captivating to him, as was the clamor and cadence of the auctioneer. He was so intrigued by the sounds and actions that after the sale or on a midweek night, he'd often climb into the auctioneer stand, turn on the microphone, and mimic the auctioneers. Armed with some auctioneering tips from his brother, Bud, Jack would coerce his sister Virginia into being a pretend buyer and would solicit make-believe bids from her. In the car or truck cab, he'd drive crazy whoever was riding along with him as he practiced his auctioneering: "Two-and-a-half, five; five, now seven-and-a-half; ten!" Or he'd chant, "Wanna bid fifty; would ya give me sixty? Sixty, sixty, sixty! Now seventy? . . ." And so Jack rambled down the highway as he rumbled down the highway. This, like so much of what he learned, was on-the-job and over-the-road training. Very little of Jack's education came while he was seated behind a school desk.

8

A Winning Path Is Born

In 1937 Marion's curiosity in racing got the best of him; he bought a thoroughbred racehorse filly named Julia R. But there was a catch to his whimsical buy. The filly had thrown a nasty fit in a horse van and gashed and skinned herself badly. She was an unsightly mess, but something about her caught Marion's eye. He had a vision beyond her unpleasant appearance. Julia R became quite a project for Marion, and she nearly took some lives along the way. The filly had a bad tendency to flip over when a saddle was placed on her back. One day, while she was in the stall, Marion and a few bold helpers began tinkering with a tempest. They tightened the girth on Julia R and, sure enough, up she went up like a rocket with her front legs striking and her hind legs kicking. The men scattered, all of them seeking shelter from the bomb they had just detonated. Marion dove toward the manger in her stall, but John Pensick was quicker in the scramble and beat Marion to the cover. John said, "To hell with you, Marion! I got here first." In the meantime, Pee Wee Johnson was on the business end of the lead rope, trying to wrestle Julia R with his herculean strength. This left Marion pinned in the corner, hoping the filly was only filled with vinegar and not vengeance. Fortunately it wasn't angst—only energy—and everyone survived the explosion. Through the working experiment, the men brusquely learned that if they saddled the filly at a walk, that slight diversion would allow them to get the job done with far less chance of a detonation.

That was just the first lesson in the remarkable Van Berg expedition into the world of racing. A journey that joined generations, inspired hundreds of lessons, and led to thousands of wins and millions of Breeders' Cup Classic earnings—and priceless Kentucky Derby glory.

Julia R first ran for Marion at the Madison County Fair in Madison, Nebraska. After her encouraging effort at Madison Downs, known as the "Saratoga of the Midwest," Marion decided to send her to Omaha, where she would be placed in the care of trainer C. A. "Charlie" Tanner. A retired cattle buyer for Armour and a friend of Marion, Tanner was a notable horse trainer at the Ak-Sar-Ben races in Omaha. Charlie guessed that Marion's excellent horse sense and business practices would be a big help for both men to win some races. So Marion dipped his toe in the water and it didn't take long for him to become immersed. Never one to sit back and relax, he was soon managing an evolving stable of racehorses and a prospering sale barn, and he still had John Torpey's yet unused checkbook right at his side.

With initial guidance from Charlie, Marion purchased and claimed horses from around the immediate region in the Midwest. He had started to build a modest stable of horses when, on June 6, 1937, there was a horrible barn blaze at Ak-Sar-Ben Field in Omaha. The fire killed Julia R and a half-dozen Van Berg horses stabled in the large livestock barn near the racetrack. Despite the significant setback, Marion mustered and rebuilt. He began by claiming a filly for $700 named Customized. She won her subsequent start, thereby providing M. H. Van Berg with his first win as an owner. When he ran Customized again two weeks later, she was claimed away for $800. The nature of buying and selling horses via the claiming game cuts both ways. But Marion's appetite to win was whet, and he honed his winning ways via the claim box. Another Van Berg winner in the early days was the filly Flaghorn. Her win in an $800 claiming race at Fairmount Park resulted in a $390 windfall. The win, or more likely the winnings, was an inspiration and invitation to seek more, even if more meant a venture from home. More ventures and more wins would follow in what would become two Racing Hall of Fame careers.

Back when racing was conducted at Riverside Park, a bush track near Kansas City, Missouri, Marion claimed a nine-year-old gelding named Bud Smith. Van Berg didn't have a halter with him for the $800 claim that day in June of 1937, so the horse was led back to the truck with baling wire. He later ran third in three straight races for Van Berg. The competition was tough at the dusty, rustic track. Hall of Fame trainer Ben Jones was running Woolford Farm just across the Missouri River in Prairie Village, Kansas. In 1938 the farm produced Lawrin, the first and only Kansas-bred Kentucky Derby winner. 1938 was also a better year for Bud Smith; he won 3 of 13 races and earned $1,633. "Bud" was solid as hickory that summer. Marion ran him on July 1st, 3rd, and 5th, and at the end of that demanding sequence, the gelding was claimed away for $800. The valiant stable star had become such a family favorite that in collective family outrage, Viola and the kids demanded that Marion claim him back. He did, and at age thirteen, Bud Smith made his final start in Omaha, adding one more apple to the bushel when he earned $30 for his third-place finale.

Marion was off to the races after that first sweet bite of the apple. The livestock sale facility he so passionately created was prospering, and his horse racing interest rang extra cash into the till. But more than anything, training and trading racehorses offered him a rush he had never felt before. Marion was not just smitten; he was bitten.

In his first two years of racing, Marion ran exclusively in the Midwest, at Sportsman's Park and Fairmount Park in Illinois and in Omaha at Ak-Sar-Ben. He won 2 of 20 races in 1937 and 8 of 53 the following year. In 1939, Marion caught the fever of shipping his horses cross-country. Typically, he transported horses by horse van, but the Union Pacific Railroad line dissected Columbus, Nebraska, making it easy to load horses directly from his back yard. And so, in the same year that legendary Hollywood movie director Cecil B. DeMille released his film *Union Pacific*, starring

Barbara Stanwyck and Joel McCrea, a star Van Berg runner, Tetrashera, was loaded onto a Union Pacific Railroad livestock car. Along the Platte River Route, the Portland Rose 484 locomotive chugged west over the Green River to Salt Lake City, over the Columbia River and on north toward Seattle—destination: Longacres Racecourse, located just a few stops south of Seattle in Renton, Washington. Marion bought his trainer a ticket, too, and C. A. Tanner boarded the train wearing his big western hat, with a cigar in his mouth and, most importantly, the purple and gold Van Berg racing silks tucked safely under his arm. Tetrashera finished fourth in the prestigious Longacres Mile, earning $400 for the effort. For more than four decades, the $10,000 Added Longacres Mile was the richest race in the country that was run at the mile distance. Marion was delighted and proud to have earned a slender piece of the pie.

But Van Berg did register more than a fourth-place finish with his venture to the Great Northwest. Pandisco, a mare, made the trip in the same stock car as Tetrashera for the purpose of providing companionship to the gelding during the round-trip journey. But she was more than a pal. Two weeks after the return to Columbus, a large envelope with a Renton postmark arrived. Inside the manila envelope was a win photo of Pandisco. She wasn't just along for the ride—she proved to be worthwhile cargo along with Tetrashera. Marion closed out the year with a record of 67-10-13-6 and earnings of $6,780. He did it with just six horses, with an earnings average of $10 per start.

In 1940, Marion returned to Renton with a pair of gray moneymakers. This time, in addition to Tetrashera, he sent a speedy gelding named C Note. Marion's sprinter won the $2,000 Speed Handicap and this time Tetrashera won an important mile race. Though it was not the Longacres Mile, the race earned Marion $500—important enough. Before the end of the year, the range of the Van Berg runners would stretch west of the Cascades in the Pacific Northwest and extend east as far as the banks of the Ohio River, to River Downs in Cincinnati. It was the first year Marion had more than one hundred starts. With just twelve runners, his record was 104-20-12-8, for $11,685.

Marion was just getting his legs underneath him as an owner and was having good results with his trainer Charlie Tanner. His foundation runners of C Note and Tetrashera were an excellent base in the very early '40s, and his gelding Bert W won 7 of 21 races in 1942. But Marion wanted to win more, and in order to do that he needed more horses—and more trainers. Marion began to hire trainers to help run his racing operations while he was tending to business elsewhere. In 1942 Max Johnson trained seventeen head at Fairmount Park in Collinsville, Illinois, for Marion, while Charlie Tanner maintained the bulk of the operation in Omaha, Chicago, and Detroit. In 1943, R. L. "Bob" Irwin took the reins at Fairmount while Tanner maintained the remainder of the Van Berg runners. He struck gold at the Detroit Fairgrounds and won 10 of 48, with four wins earned by the stout filly Rodia. The $11,850 accumulated at Detroit pushed the Van Berg horses to a best-ever-year annual earnings mark of $19,025, which was accomplished with twenty runners making a combined 129 starts.

In 1944, Earl Fouts flashed on the scene and trained all eighty-four of the Van Berg starters that year. Horses at Detroit, Sportsman's, and Thistledown earned $33,405 with their twenty-two wins. The star runner that year was one of the nine Kentucky-bred fillies Marion had bought from Charles Nuckols two years prior. Marion named seven of the fillies after each of his daughters, one after his wife Viola, and another "Missy Van." All of the fillies had the suffix Van as part of their name. Without question, the best of the bunch was Wilma Van. The precocious debutante won all five of her starts at age two. But Fouts was forgettable. In 1945 he was gone from the Van Berg scene just as quickly as he had arrived. It would, however, be a memorable year in the racing operation as yet another name emerged on the program as a trainer of the Van Berg horses. This time it was a very familiar name. The program read: M. H. Van Berg.

Ak-Sar-Ben did not conduct racing during World War II, but Detroit sure did, and Marion made a meal of races there. In 1946 he started 290 horses with 41 wins and 40 seconds. Two hundred and eighteen of those races were in Detroit. A bay gelding named Take Courage was responsible for seven of the year's wins. The following year Marion started 237 of 366 races in Detroit alone, and for the first time, the Van Berg horses earned more than $100,000 in a season. Henny Penny was Marion's stable star then, winning 7 of 19, while Wilma Van regained her good form to win four. Goats didn't earn a dime on the racetrack, but they often were kept in barns and stalls as companions for horses. Henny Penny needed no such friends; she hated goats and would frequently strike out at them, killing them anytime they were within her reach. Good sport for Henny Penny; bad news for the goats. The resulting barbecued *cabrito* always pleased the grooms.

In '48 Marion didn't tarnish his billowing reputation; he took Detroit by storm with a 20 percent win rate, winning 43 of 215. For the year, he trained 73 winners of 349 overall starters. Henny Penny had to share the limelight with another mare named Rose Bed, who was just beginning to find her best stride. Marion's year-end earnings were $160,625. At the conclusion of 1949, Rose Bed doubled the single-season earnings mark of any Van Berg runner thus far by winning $31,945. She was a multiple stakes winner in Detroit and led the charge of the Van Berg light brigade, a brigade that had direction and dominance. With sixty horses, Marion amassed a record of 542-118-90-73 and $266,882 for the year. He was the leading owner at the Detroit Fairgrounds and Hazel Park meets, and second in the nation for wins as an owner.

The post–WWII days gleamed the dawn of a legendary horseman and the evolution of an annual racing calendar that ticked along with clocklike precision. In the wintertime, Marion would be home with his family, but by the time the groundhog would appear, or not, Marion was readying his stable of horses for their upcoming year of racing. After a dozen-hour trek, snaking through Iowa on narrow Highway 30, the Van Berg band of runners would first appear in the spring for the Sportsman's Park meet in the Chicago suburb of Cicero. After that meet ended, the troupe would take to the trail again, this time for a loop below Lake Michigan and an eastward push on Highway 12, ending in Motor City. There, at the Detroit Fairgrounds, the Slovaks and Polacks from Hamtramck would come to cheer for the purple and gold silks of M. H. Van Berg. They'd watch from the rail with their mouths full of savory kielbasa, fresh kolache, and cold Stroh's beer. They happily spent the hard-earned money they made from riveting, wrenching, and sweating on the auto assembly lines. Many came from the confines of the Gratiot Avenue corridor. The Irish came from Corktown and near Briggs Stadium, the blacks from Lafayette Park, and the Italians from the lower east side. The Canadians took the tunnel from Windsor, and the Armenians rode the street cars north from Dearborn. A robust mix of blue-collared fans went to the Detroit horse races and they often bet on seeing a smart-suited man arrive in the winner's circle, with his sweet, smiling wife at his side. Marion and Viola Van Berg were a comely couple, and for their many and popular winners, the fans hailed the lovely pair as if they were royalty.

The purple and gold was just as regal in Chicago. In November 1949, in eight race days at Sportsman's Park within a span of ten days, Marion won seventeen of twenty-three races, including a pair of wins by Olo's Star and Agrarian Son.

When the easy breezes off the Great Lakes turned to a brisk chill, this signaled the end of the Detroit racing season, and it was time to migrate west, back toward Chicago and home to Columbus for the fall and winter. Marion and Viola's seasonal routine meant that youngster Jack was frequently with his parents in Detroit during the summer. But as Jack became a teenager, Marion delegated him to helping oversee things in Omaha at Ak-Sar-Ben. Marion never ran any horses in Omaha while listed as a trainer, only as an owner. This was the result of his getting crossways with the track manager, Dick Lee. Marion told it to you like he felt it. Dick Lee didn't like what Marion felt, and the two maintained a bristly relationship. Because of Marion's suspicions of Dick Lee, Van Berg chose only to be licensed as an owner at the track, speculating that this would ease any negative forces Lee might attempt to leverage on him. That is where, when, and why Jack came into play.

9

The Trainer in Training

Jack became much more valuable to the Van Berg racing operation once he got his driver's license and his trainer's license. At the ripe age of sixteen he made his first solo drive from Detroit to Omaha—and he did it hauling a full load of horses. While he was still in high school, Jack frequently left Columbus after school on Friday afternoon with a load of horses bound for Chicago. He'd arrive early Saturday morning, attend the races at Sportsman's Park that afternoon, and then drive back to Columbus on Sunday. Jack was a trucker before he was a trainer.

By the '50s, Charlie Tanner had aged into his eighties. He was still training the Van Berg horses in Omaha, but his memory was beginning to fail him. As a result, Jack acquired the additional duty of tenderly monitoring how Charlie trained the horses. Charlie had been known to work a horse a half-mile one day and then to want to work the same horse a half-mile again the next day. He would forget the paces he had put the horse through just the day before. Young Jack was guarding the old man—and the horses. This meant long days and nights for Jack. He often roughed it overnight in the stable if he didn't catch a ride back home to Columbus later that day. A covered stall in the horse barn soon became Jack's first home away from home.

Marion had men working for him year-round in Columbus. Some tended to the racehorses at the breeding and training operation just east of the house. Others worked at the sale barn through all four seasons, and some, like Columbus native Bud Kuta, did it all. Bud and Jack often drove into Omaha together from Columbus, sometimes beginning the 180-mile round trip at 3 A.M. and arriving back in Columbus in time for a late lunch. Once Jack turned sixteen he began to split the unpopular driving duties with Bud. The two were constantly trying to goad the other into driving. Bud would drive to the halfway point, Fremont; then Jack would take over and complete the remainder of the commute. More than once naps were taken by the driver while he was still behind the wheel. After Jack nearly put the pair into a ditch west of Omaha at 4 A.M., Bud decided he should do all the driving in darkness. Jack provided no resistance and relished the extra time to sleep.

Jack and Bud were watching over the horses in Omaha, plus keeping an eye on Charlie. With Charlie's diminishing memory, and the increasing uncertainties that caused, it made sense for Jack to have his trainer's license to help manage affairs. Back then, a trainer needed to be sixteen years old to get licensed, so at age fifteen, Jack falsified his application and was granted a trainer's license. But out of respect for Charlie, Marion allowed the majority of the Van Berg horses to continue to race with "C. A. Tanner" listed as the official trainer. The horse trainer's license Jack held was just a flattering piece of paper.

Jack might have been just a teenaged, peach-fuzzed kid, but during his summer vacation from school the man-child recorded his first win as a trainer. It came at Ak-Sar-Ben with a horse named Compensator. The striped-face chestnut colt was one of the runners Marion sent to Jack from Detroit with designs on finding a spot to win in Omaha. Two days before the race, Jack wrote out the name Compensator on an entry blank and entered him to run in a $2,500 claiming race. Jack liked his chances with the colt and rubbed in the Bigeloil muscle liniment with extra vigor in the immediate days leading up to the race. The colt's feet were good, his coat shined, and he had been taking ahold of the bit in the mornings. On race day, Jack and Bud were hopeful they'd get their first win of the summer with Compensator. Young Jack gave top jockey Bobby Mundorf a leg up in the saddle and ran his hand off the horse's hip as the pair moved out toward the racetrack. The crew from Columbus then gathered up their halter, lead rope, and pail of soaked leg wraps and left the paddock bound for the winner's circle. Jack thought about running to the concession stand to grab a Coke, but he was afraid he might miss the race. Instead, he found a spot on some steps that led up into the grandstand and waited. The gates opened and the field launched away. A few seconds later, Jack saw what he was looking for: a chestnut horse and purple and gold colors at the front of the pack. At the top of the stretch there was daylight between Compensator and the rest of the field. At the 1/16 pole Jack began to jump and whoop and holler as he rushed down to meet the boys as his first career winner raced across the finish line. Compensator; owned by M. H. Van Berg; trained by Jack Van Berg. Jack beamed with pride as the announcer's remarks reverberated in his head when Compensator stepped into the Ak-Sar-Ben winner's circle. After the race Jack thirsted for that ice-cold Coke again but knew he had to go back to the barn with Bud. After the test barn and after the stall mucking and after the leg work, Jack plopped down on a bucket. With an exhausted gaze, he stared blankly down the shedrow, his mind filled with personal satisfaction, his body racked with fatigue.

The sun rose and fell over the tops of the maple trees on the Ak-Sar-Ben backstretch. In the routine of the day, something memorable had occurred. Jack never did get to enjoy the Coke he so truly deserved; there was work to be done and simply no time to celebrate. That didn't matter much to young Jack, though; the rush of training his first winner was far more satisfying than any recipe of Coca-Cola. Jack entered Compensator to run back two weeks later. Bobby Mundorf advised Jack against it, warning that the horse wouldn't be ready to win again so soon. But the fledgling trainer shrugged off the warning, Jack felt he was a trainer now and he didn't think he needed to take advice from a jockey. The horse ran poorly and didn't earn a check.

Jack overcame that humbling early setback. He continued on to win more than six thousand races, and he joined his father, Marion, in being inducted into the National Thoroughbred Racing Hall of Fame. In horse racing, few reach fame, but everyone gets humbled. Fresh slices of humble pie are served daily on the racetrack.

10

Development of a Dynasty

While Jack spent his high school vacations as a deputy trainer in Omaha, Mr. Van was still the head honcho in Nebraska and beyond. M. H. Van Berg began his remarkable run as the all-time leading owner and trainer at Detroit Race Course and Hazel Park and was on the verge of reaching a national milestone. One of his most lucrative claims came in May of 1952, when he spent $6,500 on a three-year-old gelding, Vantage. Marion went on to win seven races with Vantage that year and just short of $30,000. That money was key. It was an important percentage of the $311,560 in total earnings from Van Berg's 140 wins, enough for the M. H. Van Berg stable to be designated the leading stable in the nation in wins—for the first time. And both Marion and Vantage were just getting warmed up. At age four, Vantage won 6 of 20 and earned $32,150. He would go on to win the '54 Chicago Handicap on turf at Hawthorne and the $50,000 Charles W. Bidwill Memorial Handicap, and to go 13-6-0-2 $77,412 for the year. Nice claim! And it wouldn't be the last time Marion took a runner from claim box to stakes cup.

Now Van Berg began to push the envelope even further—if not to keep horses in training year-round, to keep his operation up and running year-round. Traditionally, there was a cooling down time for Marion in the winter, when he, Viola, the horses, and the road crew would return to Columbus for Thanksgiving through Easter. Instead, Marion chose to mush on. He funneled some horses south for the winter, where they could race at the Fair Grounds in New Orleans during the holidays and then push back north to Oaklawn Park in Hot Springs, Arkansas, for the early spring. In

1955 Van Berg horses made 60 starts at the Fair Grounds, winning 14 and finishing second in the owners standings. Marion was in Columbus; his trainer, K. D. Kepler, was in New Orleans. And what Mr. Van won early in the year helped at the end of the year. In 1955 he was the leading owner in the nation again in races won.

Van Berg rocked and rolled through the remainder of the '50s, continuing to win titles and trophies in Chicago and Detroit along the way. And he produced some very popular chart toppers that were hits across the land.

Marion had developed a vein of success with claiming horses, which involved purchasing a horse for the designated claiming price without a pre-race, hands-on inspection prior to the purchase, or "claim." But in 1957, he chose to purchase a horse privately and risk a significant sum. Technically, the acquisition was less of a risk than claiming a horse because Marion had an opportunity to inspect the horse and actually lay his hands on his investment before the sale. Nevertheless, the purchase price would be the most Marion would ever spend on a horse. In the early winter of 1957 he bought an accomplished Argentine-bred filly named Estacion. Marion had never raced in Florida, yet the Nebraska farm boy travelled to Miami and ventured more there than he ever had before. He bought Estacion for $50,000. The major purchase wasn't the same risk as the all-in act of desperation that took place when he and Viola spent their last dime on a load of pigs in South Dakota, but it was a major gamble nonetheless. Estacion won the $25,000 Suwannee River at Hialeah, but it was her only win of 1957. Initially, her results may not have been overwhelming, but favorable results did come, and they came for years and generations to follow, not only on the racetrack but as a blue hen broodmare for the Van Bergs.

Estacion would later produce a number of winners, including a pair of multiple stakes winners. British Ross, by the Great Britain–bred stallion

Nivrag, won three Ak-Sar-Ben stakes and ultimately 17 of 73 races. And British Fleet, by the Van Berg–campaigned Sonny Fleet, broke his maiden in the Ak-Sar-Ben Futurity and then went on to win five more stakes races, earning more than $135,000.

Of equal significance in 1957 was the emergence of Van Berg's home-bred gelding Rose's Gem. After being winless in two starts at age two, Rose's Gem won 5 of 15 races at age three, early days of what would become a stunning and lengthy racing career.

Things improved in 1958 for Estacion, as she won the $50,000 Arlington Matron, a race that Marion declared his all-time favorite win. With three additional wins that year, she earned more than $44,000. Also in 1958, Marion claimed Cal's Choice, who went on to win four stakes races that year. Rose's Gem, now age four, won 7 of 21 races and ran second 8 times.

In 1959 Redbird Wish reeled off an amazing average of a race every other weekend. With his 26 starts, he won 6 races, including the Omaha Handicap and a pair of derby wins. He won the Michigan Derby off 10 Mile Road at Hazel Park and then caught the "Wheeling Feeling" on a bend of the Ohio River and won the West Virginia Derby. Meanwhile, Rose's Gem continued to take on all-comers and he also sought them out. He won 8 of 16, closing out the year with $53,523 in earnings. The luster of Rose's Gem would shine well into the next decade, too.

11

The University of Hard Knocks

After graduating from high school, Jack gave college a go, enrolling at the University of Nebraska in 1954. His daily curriculum would be the same as it was in grade school and high school: attend class during school hours; work the remaining hours—both day and night. Marion knew what time Jack's final Friday class let out at the university in Lincoln. At the end of the school week, Jack was expected to be in Columbus at the sale barn ready to work exactly an hour and a half later. That didn't leave much time for horsin' around on campus—at least on the weekends.

Jack did compete on the university rodeo team. As a Cornhusker athlete he missed being all-around cowboy by just two points. But he knew he had more horse and cow sense than a number of young veterinarians who had crossed his path, so he thought that vet school might be an interesting, though extremely demanding, option. Nevertheless, Marion's friend, Merle Mitchell, a cattleman from Brush, Colorado, helped Jack get transferred into the veterinarian program at Colorado A&M (now Colorado State). During his ill-fated quarter there, Jack rented a room from a kind, elderly couple. "I remember I'd be upstairs sleeping after dinner and they thought I was up there studying," said Jack. Despite hiring tutors to help him make the grade, academia was not for him. Although he knew he had failing grades when he was back home in Columbus with his family for Christmas break, he didn't let on. When he returned to Colorado for school there was a letter for him from the university sitting on his bed. Jack opened the letter, which contained the phrase "academic dismissal."

Jack purposefully waited until the next day to call home to break the news. He knew his dad would be at the sale barn and that he would only have to speak with his mom. After informing his mother, Jack headed out to have some beers with his buddies—an act of sorrow and celebration. Later that night Marion phoned the elderly couple's house and the land-lady told Mr. Van Berg how awful it was that Jack had been dismissed because, as she said, "He was upstairs studying so hard all the time." During Jack and his father's call, Marion empathetically encouraged Jack and told him that he had some connections in Colorado who might get him readmitted. This made Jack feel even worse. He had siblings who had graduated from college with good grades, but in his own words, Jack said, "I was just a flunky." Not wanting his father to pull any strings for him, Jack told Marion that he would go back to the office of the veterinarian school and speak to the department head himself. When he did, Stella Morris, the woman in charge, told Jack, "Let me tell you something young man—it takes a superior person to become a veterinarian, and you'll never make it."

Broken and frustrated, Jack fired back, "Well, let me tell you something; I know more than most of those who have already graduated out of here. And there's one of your dumb graduates back at our sale barn in Columbus, Nebraska, who is a disgrace to the veterinarian society. He's so damn dumb he tried to treat a steer that felt better than I did. He doesn't know a sick steer from a healthy one." Needless to say, the only door this opened for Jack at Colorado A&M was the door he used to exit the office and campus. Jack called his dad, told him they wouldn't let him back in school, and said he'd gather up all of his belongings and find a job some-where in Colorado. Surprisingly sympathetic and considerably content that Jack would be returning home to the sale business, Marion said, "No, no, don't do that; go on over to Sterling and buy a couple loads of cattle and bring them back." And with that, Jack had been released from college. He drove to Sterling, Colorado, cutting through the southeast corner of

Wyoming on the way. With his natural instinct and some remaining college cash, Jack bought six Shetland ponies along the way. Shetlands were starting to get popular at the time, but the fella Jack bought them from hadn't been to a sale recently and was obviously unaware of the horse's market value. Jack didn't need a degree to know how to turn the ponies into profit. He would do all right with the ponies he sold at the sale. He would do all right with the loads of cattle he bought at the sale. And he would do all right by shedding the stress of school. At last, his thoughts of homework disappeared in his rearview mirror.

Driving home from Sterling, Jack knew what he had left behind at college, but he was unclear of what was ahead down the road. As the sun eased into a dusk splendor across the endless rows of weathered crops, a magenta-orange glow washed over the muted land. Jack pressed east, quietly. It was just him and the steady hum of the engine. Cutting through the dark blue of night, he whisked by the twinkle of lights at Ogallala, then North Platte, and then Grand Island. His eyes were fixed on the road, but his mind wandered in wonder of what Columbus might bring for him once he returned home.

The very next morning he got his answer, when he heard . . . "Hey, if you're too damn dumb for school, then you better get up and work." That loud voice bellowing up the stairwell came from Marion, and *that* is what Columbus brought him home to. Home sweet home? Jack may not have had any specific plans for himself, but his father sure did.

12

Jack of All Trades

As soon as Jack returned from his ill-fated attempt at higher education, his father had him working on the floor of the Van Berg Sales
Pavilion, moving hogs and cattle at the feet of the buyers. Then, nearing
the end of a long day, at roughly ten o'clock at night, Jack was forced to
step up for some on-the-job training. Marion called him up to the auctioneer's stand where he would have to get on the microphone and conclude
the sale by selling some cattle. That meant Jack would actually have to
auction, something he had never done before. For years his father had listened to him and his brother mimic auctioneers as they worked or played
around the barn. Now, it was time for Jack to do it for real. One of Marion
Van Berg's favorite expressions, "you'll never learn any younger," once
more rang loud and true.

Jack's heart was pounding right through his chest when he climbed
up into the stand. The old dusty steps creaked with each footfall. With his
head held down and eyes low, Jack saw only the tips of his boots when
he trudged up the worn stairs, each step bringing him closer to what he
thought would be certain doom. The pressure was on like never before.
When he reached the top step, the lights of the sale ring washed away
his dark ascent. He lifted his head and eyes to see his dad's eyes fixed
right on his own. Jack sat down alongside his father and when he raised
his head once more, he saw the countless pairs of eyes that looked across
the sale ring, focused entirely on him. The cattle buyers were impatiently
waiting for the kid to get started. It had been a long day and they were
ready to go home. The cattlemen were in no mood for a greenhorn. Jack

began his auctioning chant just as Bud had schooled him. He was trying to find a rhythm through the terrible tremble in his voice and body. Fear coursed through his veins; he could hardly breathe. It wasn't seamless, but Jack got his chant under way. He was surviving this live auction audition! He steadily moved the bids up—twelve dollars, then twelve-fifty, then thirteen; he was finding his stride. Then, he unknowingly jumped from thirteen dollars to fifteen dollars and got a sudden, sharp nudge on his leg. "Boy, boy, boy! You forgot fourteen," Marion hissed. And with that, the next thing out of Jack's mouth was, "Oh, shit!" Well, Jack had sure said worse, but not into an open microphone. Everyone in the sale ring heard his expletive. Jack froze in embarrassment. But his blushed face was quickly cured by a collective, hardy, tension-breaking laugh from the amused cattle buyers. He also got a wry smile from his proud father. And with his first successful attempt at auctioneering, Jack showed yet another dimension in how he could play a significant role in the prosperity of the family business.

At the same time Jack was gaining new experience at the sale barn, Marion was on the trail of achieving remarkable feats in thoroughbred racing. In the '50s he was twice crowned the leading owner in the nation for races won, and he was clearly gathering his horses to gain further national domination. But Marion just as clearly did not want Jack to become a full-time trainer. Bud had settled in as a very important cog in the Van Berg sale operation, along with his sisters, and Marion wanted the same for Jack. In the immediate months and years to follow, Jack's keen sense of assessing animals on the hoof kept him busy at the sales. He was either working at the Columbus Sales Pavilion or on the road, buying and hauling livestock. Business at the sale barn would typically decrease in the summertime; it was then that Jack was called on for temporary training duties at Ak-Sar-Ben or wherever else Marion may have needed an extra hand. Despite whatever his father's vision may have been for him away from the racetrack, the reality was that Jack was never far from the race-track.

And with that, what might have sounded like an abnormal life and lifestyle began to become normal—the everyday life of Jack Van Berg.

In November of 1956 Jack married a cute and sweet-tempered girl named Mary Jane Sokol. She was from the small town of Duncan, Nebraska, located just eight miles west of Columbus on Highway 30. Jack had known Mary Jane since high school, but the two didn't begin dating until he returned from college. Mary Jane's father, Leo Sokol, had a reputation for his bright ingenuity. He and his friend, Frank Zybach, are known for having created the prototype of the center-pivot irrigation system that globally revolutionized the process of watering crops. Thus, Mary Jane's father is partly responsible for the hundreds of thousands of giant green circles seen from the air when flying over farmland. As newlyweds, Jack and Mary Jane moved into a house in Columbus that had formerly been owned by Mort Taylor, the dear friend and banker for the Van Berg family, who had been key in Marion's early success.

Van Bergs grow up quickly, and Jack was no exception. At age twenty-one he had experienced as much as someone twice his age and had been on the road more than most people are in a lifetime. He had far-reaching responsibilities with the family businesses and had to be ready to leave town on a moment's notice. In just a few short years, Jack achieved the important responsibilities of husband, homeowner, and father. He was expected to do it all, and for the most part, he did.

Timothy Ray Van Berg was born to Mary Jane and Jack in 1957. But Jack couldn't, or didn't, let fatherhood slow him down. He maintained his demanding work schedule at the sale barn, at the racetrack, and on the road. In fact, sitting in the cab of a stock truck hauling down the Nebraska and Kansas highways and gravel roads represented a good percentage of the father-and-son time Jack had with young Tim. "I took Tim to the cattle

sales with me all the time. He was so easygoing and likeable," Jack recalled. "He grew on a lot of people very quickly when we were out on the
road together." The young Van Bergs' second child was a daughter, Tami
Jo. Jack remembered, "Tami was a feisty little devil. She used to tease my
dad all the time. She'd get to where she would be just about arm's length
away and then jump out of reach so she couldn't be caught. But she was
hardheaded; if you told her to do something you had to keep after her to
make sure she got it done." Tori Lynn, Jack and Mary Jane's third child,
was just the opposite. "She was her grandpa's buddy," said Jack. "She
loved the horses and she'd go everywhere with Dad and me, and when she
got old enough she groomed horses at the track."

By the time the couple's fourth child was born, Jack had become totally immersed in his work and travels. "Traci Dee was more of a home-
body and stayed closer to her mother, but I suppose that was because I
was gone racing so much," reflected Jack. "Traci didn't spend much time
with horses as a child, but now she loves them and she says to this day
how she wished she would have been with the horses more when she was
younger."

In 1959, Tomy Lee won the Kentucky Derby. He also was the name-
sake for Jack and Mary Jane's fifth child, Tommy, born the same year.
"We named him after the Derby winner and we all called him 'Tom the
Bomb.' But shoot, I was gone by then. I was never around," a glassy-eyed
Jack Van Berg said regretfully. "I was at the racetrack more than I was
home. I guess, just like my dad."

As the pages on the calendar turned, Jack became very much just like
his dad.

13

The Decade of Dominance

M. H. Van Berg's two national leading owner titles in the 1950s were just the hors d'oeuvres leading to the main course. In the 1960s, Marion devoured a decade of satisfying horse racing wins, leaving only crumbs for the remaining owners and trainers. Incredibly, he was the leading owner based on races won every year of the decade. He also led the nation in earnings four times within those fantastic feast years, lapping up the money in 1965, 1968, 1969, and 1970.

The start of 1960 ended the derby season of Redbird Wish, but Derby fever carried over into a new season with a new horse, Marion's Spring Broker. A chestnut son of Money Broker, Spring Broker won 7 of 19 as a two-year-old, and at age three won a division of the Arkansas Derby. Marion dreamed of running a horse in the Kentucky Derby, but he always said he would never run for the roses unless he thought he had a horse that could win. Well, even the resolute can waiver under pressure. Peer pressure set in and forced Marion into submission. Against his better judgment, and for the only time in the history of America's grandest horse race, the name M. H. Van Berg appeared in the charts of the Kentucky Derby. Spring Broker was part of a three-horse field entry that went off at 40-1. In the 1960 Derby, favorite Tompion attempted the lead, but second-choice Bally Ache set the tempo for more than a mile. When the field turned for home, 6-1 Venetian Way glided to the front to win by three and a half lengths under Bill Hartack. The M. H. Van Berg entrant ran mid-pack throughout and finished eighth. Winning owner Sunny Blue Farm got $114,850 and a $5,000 gold cup. Spring Broker got hot and dirty;

Marion got nothing.

After the sweats of Derby fever had come and gone, the year got better for Marion and Spring Broker.

"Broker" won 6 of 15, and the now six-year-old Rose's Gem continued to lay waste to his competition. Rose's Gem did not race in Nebraska in 1960, but if he had, his earnings of $52,267 would have qualified him to be the leading Nebraska-bred that year. Nevertheless, it still evolved into a landmark year for Marion Van Berg. In Detroit, his Hazel Park runners surpassed the $1,000,000 earnings plateau, money that had begun accruing when HP was founded in 1949. At the conclusion of 1960, Van Berg's 221 winners set a world record for national wins for an owner in one year.

It was a banner year and Marion had reason to beam with pride. It was a noteworthy year for Jack, too, but for shame-inducing reasons instead. Jack recalled a less-than-shining moment . . .

I got the biggest ass chewing I ever had in my life involving a horse named All Gone. He hadn't won a race in over a year so I turned him out with the cattle and some saddle horses in a sandhill pasture west of Columbus. I figured I was doing the right thing for the horse. Well, Dad and I went up to check on the stock one afternoon and they all looked good until along comes this gaunt-looking horse that was nearly skin and bones. He looked so bad you could have hung your hat on his hipbone; it was sticking out so bad. Sometimes a thoroughbred won't hold up too well on their own if they've been at the barn and pampered and routinely fed grain. If you turn a racehorse out on his own on grass they might fall apart. This one did, and oh, did he give me hell. Dad said, "You ought to be turned in to the humane society for letting that horse get like that." And he didn't let up on me the whole time we were up there and on the drive back home. When he finally got done chewing my butt, I told him that at least the horse will appreciate it when we get him back into training. Oh, hell! I should have just shut up, because oh, man, he started back in on me again. I deserved it.

In 1961, after having been winless in nearly two years, All Gone won 11 of 25. He appreciated the training, racing—and grain. Rose's Gem had a relatively quiet year winning just 4 of 14. At age five, Redbird Wish won two stakes at Hazel Park; the stakes he didn't win in Detroit were won by Space Commander, who won four HP stakes and earned more than $41,800, leading all Van Berg runners in earnings for 1961. Spring Broker won three races, including the Ak-Sar-Ben Governor's Handicap. Marion bought Space Commander—sired by Tom Fool, 1953 Horse of the Year—from Dixiana Farm in Lexington, Kentucky, after the horse broke a bone in his foot. Marion laid him up with hopes of racing him again and then standing him at stud, which is exactly what happened. But young Jack got a good scolding from Ak-Sar-Ben racing secretary Lou Elkin along the path of Space Commander's comeback. Jack asked Mr. Elkin to write a conditioned race for horses that had not won a race in a year's time. At the time the race was offered, Space Commander's registration papers were not in the racing office for Mr. Elkin to review. After the race filled and entries closed, the oddsmaker set the morning line, the expected odds for the horse, on Space Commander at 3/5. Lou Elkin was furious at Jack and screamed at him, saying, "I don't write races for 3/5 cinches!" To make matters worse, the racetrack came up muddy on the day of the race and Jack scratched Space Commander because he was shod in a protective bar shoe to help a defective hoof. After scratching him, Jack tiptoed around the Aks racing office for a few days; Space Commander stomped on his competition the remainder of the year.

In 1962 Space Commander won another five races, as did the stalwart stable icon Rose's Gem. And a new star emerged in the galaxy of Van Berg racing: Little Everett, bred by Claremore, Oklahoma, horseman

Everett Lowrance. The colt won 6 of 14 races his freshman year of racing and caught Marion's eye; Marion struck a deal and bought him from Lowrance. The twinkle at age two ignited at age three as Little Everett won 8 of 20 races for Marion during his sophomore campaign.

Little Everett and Estacion weren't Marion's only successes *outside* of the claim box. In 1962, he bought both Ramblin Road and Royal Course in a package deal from Gordon Huntley, a respected bloodstock man. What Marion spent on the two-pronged investment would be a personal unprecedented price. Van Berg knew Huntley knew his horses; so without the aid of any X-rays, and after simply feeling the animals' legs and watching them jog, Marion had gathered enough appropriate information and agreed to the deal. With an educated eye and a seasoned stroke of his hand, he purchased the pricey pair for $80,000. Within a few years, the one-two punch banged out more than $250,000.

In 1963 Marion gained another nice three-year-old in the barn, when the California-bred Sonny Fleet won 5 of 13 starts and was Van Berg's highest money-winner for the year with more than $60,000 in earnings. His win in the Michigan Derby made Van Berg the first two-time winner of the race, having previously won the Michigan Derby in 1959 with Redbird Wish. Sonny Fleet also won the Society of North American Racing Officials (SNARO) Handicap at Sportsman's Park in 1963. Marion's Kurri San only won 2 of 22, but his Hazel Park Handicap win and his 8 second-place finishes equaled a bankroll of $50,494; he was the second-highest earner for the stable that season. And, in what would be the final year of racing for Rose's Gem (who won the SNARO Handicap in 1960), the nine-year-old gelding won 6 of 18 races—including the final start of his career. Rose's Gem was then sent back home to a retirement in Columbus, where he gently grazed on grass and just narrowly nibbled into the $230,964 he had earned as a racehorse.

At the start of the decade, Marion Van Berg had become the first owner in the history of the sport to break the barrier of 200 wins in a year when he crushed the mark of 165 wins that had been set in 1958 by the W. H. Bishop Stable; M. H. Van Berg won 221. Early in 1964, Audley Farm of J. F. Edwards was on pace not only to supplant Marion as the nation's leading owner, but also to eclipse the Van Berg record of 221 wins. On May 1, 1964, Audley Farms was 53 wins clear of M. H. Van Berg. But the Van Berg horses kept winning. By the end of September, the gap had narrowed, but Marion was still 33 wins behind Audley Farm. Was it time to fly the white flag and surrender, or would the purple and gold silks fight on? During the autumn months of October and November, Van Berg outscored Audley Farm 65 wins to 22 wins; indeed the fall was on. At the start of December, Marion Van Berg led J. F. Edwards's Audley Farm by 10 wins. The stage was set for a battle that might go all the way to the stroke of the new year. But in the end, the Van Berg colors shone through, establishing a new record of 258 wins, eight clear of the 250 wins of Audley Farm. Assuredly, the 10 wins of Hymient helped the Van Berg cause in 1964, as did You Look Cute's 5 consecutive wins at four different tracks (Detroit, Raceway, Sportsman's, and Fair Grounds).

If the outcome of 1964 seemed unlikely, topping that performance the following year seemed just as unthinkable—but it happened. The recap of the 1965 year of racing from the 1966 *American Racing Manual* tells the story:

> Fielding a stable that won 270 races (new world record) and earned $895,246, Marion H. Van Berg swept both owner crowns in 1965. He became the first to annex both titles of winning the most races and earning the most money since the late Warren Wright's Calumet Farm completed the sweep seventeen years ago. Van Berg garnered his sixth consecutive winner's title with ease, his 270 winners swamping runner-up T. Allie Grissom, who had 154. However, the money race afforded a more dramatic cli-

max. In winning monetary honors, Van Berg was called on to repulse a desperate bid from Louis Wolfson, master of Harbor View Farm. In the end, the Nebraska-owned stable won out by only $5,325 as Harbor View Farm banked $889,921.

Van Berg raced as many as three divisions at the same time, handling one himself, another by his son Jack, and a third by Robert L. Irwin, and had 1,453 starters in 1965. In addition to the 270 wins, his horses were second 220 times and third on 183 occasions, for an almost 50 percent in-the-money performance.

There can be no doubt that Marion H. Van Berg is a master turfman, deserving homage in racing along with such men as John E. Madden, H. G. Bedwell, Sam C. Hildreth, Ben Jones, Hirsch Jacobs, and others. The latest of his feats came during the recently concluded season when he swept the boards clean in regards to owner honors. It was expected that he would again emerge as the owner with the most winners, but it did not seem likely that the Columbus, Nebraska, horseman would also out earn the power-packed stables boasting a Buckpasser, Tom Rolfe, Roman Brother, or a Kelso.

"Truthfully, I did not think we would win the most money even as late as October," Van Berg said. "With Flash Climber not himself, the only big horses we had were Ramblin Road and Royal Course—neither a serious threat in a $100,000 race. However, we just kept staying in front. About mid-December I was threatened with the possibility of being nailed in the final weeks if I didn't buy up some horses or drop a few of mine below their worth. In the end I decided to race my usual way and make no changes. In fact, the final day of the year, when the outcome was decided, I ran but two horses. Championships don't mean too much if the cost comes too high."

Championships don't mean too much if the cost comes too high—wise words from a wise horseman. Jack recalls a phone conversation he had with Marion on the final day of the year. "I said, 'Dad, I'm gonna scratch a few of those horses today. We have them in too cheap and I'm not gonna just give them away. If we don't win the title that's just the way it goes.'" Van Berg won the title.

The '60s were explosive: Vietnam, JFK, MLK, Beatlemania, the Apollo missions—all the while, the Van Berg cavalcade carried on. In 1965, the bay gelding Herb Scott won the first of three consecutive Black Gold Handicaps for Marion Van Berg at the Fair Grounds in New Orleans. Later in the year, Ramblin Road was feeling festive and won both the Thanksgiving Handicap and the Christmas Handicap in the New Orleans. Mike's Red won the 1966 Black Gold and then won it again in 1967 (when it was not restricted to three-year-olds); he also won the Pelleteri Handicap. And in 1968 Ramblin Road sprinted home first to win his Pelleteri Handicap in the Crescent City. In the meantime, in Chicago, Royal Course won the '67 SNARO Handicap and the National Jockey Club Handicap, as well as two other stakes that year in the Windy City. And the decade concluded with a remarkable national father-and-son feat. In 1968, 1969, and 1970 Marion was the national leading owner in both races won and earnings, while Jack was simultaneously the leading trainer in the nation with races won those same three years. Without question, it was a decade of dominance. The Van Berg colors flew high over the national racing scene as the purple and gold silks scored stakes and earned awards at race-tracks through the Midwest, the South, and beyond.

14

The Columbus Connection

The royal colors of the M. H. Van Berg racing stable were revered across the land. Marion's brilliance was deliberated with esteem, but the professor in purple had his pupils. While Marion was responsible for the syllabus and curriculum, in practicum, superior subordinates were a prerequisite to the Van Berg stable's success. Marion, just as his student and son Jack would do years later, recruited *men* and developed them into *horsemen*. There was no deviation from Marion's course and school of thought. The protocol involved mutual respect and trust between employer and employee. If a man or boy was willing to prove his devotion and mettle to Marion H. Van Berg, that person might one day have the honor of calling his leader *Mr. Van*. Many from Columbus, Nebraska, did.

Louis "Bud" Kuta began working for Marion on weekends at the Columbus Sales Pavilion. It was there in the stock pens and within his chores with the horses that his dedication to the Van Berg family was born. Bud and Jack spent plenty of time together in Columbus, Omaha, Chicago, and Detroit; or in the truck shuttling between those cities. They were pals, but Bud always seemed to be a guiding shepherd to Jack. The two young men happily agreed to share the overall training responsibilities. Typically, Bud stayed at the barn when Jack was handling affairs in the racing office. But an issue developed in Detroit once when Jack left the barn to go enter horses in the racing office. Entering horses wasn't the issue; the friction that followed stemmed from Jack not returning to the barn after he made the entries. This frustrated Bud to no end, because it left him to do all the stall mucking and legwork. One morning Bud finally had enough and he bleated, "Jack, where have you been?" "Oh, I was up entering horses," Jack replied sheepishly. "Well, did you enter any?" Bud asked accusingly. "No, those races didn't go," Jack guiltily replied. Bud had done and heard enough, and exploded, "From now on I want you back from the racing office by ten o'clock so you can help out back here." Bud was only two years older than Jack, but occasionally he had to pull rank over Jack. But despite the sporadic spats, he did gain admiration for Jack. "He would get distracted now and then, but boy could he work when he set his mind to it. He'd get down in that straw and work and work and work, without taking any breaks or shortcuts," said a respectful Bud Kuta. The days of Bud scolding Jack became an ironic thing of the past. However, Jack always respected his Columbus comrades, and Bud's firsthand involvement with the Van Berg icon Rose's Gem made Bud an indelible element in the fabric of the Van Berg family. To this day, Jack refers to Bud Kuta as the best *legman* in horse racing.

Of course Kuta's primary boss was Mr. Van Berg, and Bud would never think of raising his voice to Mr. Van. But now and then he would question some of Marion's actions. Bud remembers one summer morning in 1958 on the backstretch in Detroit, when from sitting astride his big, white pony, Mr. Van called out, "Hey Bud, bring a halter up to the paddock for the third race." Having read the *Daily Racing Form* from cover to cover the night before, Bud had already seen the field of horses in the third race, and he felt there was nothing in the field worth claiming to bring back to the barn. Nevertheless, Marion claimed Cal's Choice for $6,500. He was a chestnut colt by Polynesian. Bud recalled, "He was a big devil, but he was always finishing last or getting soundly beaten." Bud was overcome with curiosity, so he asked Marion why he claimed the horse. "Let me tell ya," Van Berg said. "I've been watching this horse, and every morning he runs off. The exercise rider can't hold him. We're gonna put Leonard on him and fix that." Leonard Iwan was from Osceola, Nebraska, a town less than thirty miles south of Columbus. He was a beer-drinking son-of-a-gun, but most of all, he was a gallop boy who was an important part of the travelling road show. The first time Bud tacked up Cal's Choice and gave Leonard a leg up into the saddle, Marion rode over on his pony and said, "Leonard, until you tell me you can gallop this horse, you're going alongside the pony. Let me know when you can hold him, but not until then." After a few weeks had passed, Leonard approached Mr. Van Berg and said, "Mr. Van, I think I can hold him without the pony." "Are you sure, boy?" Marion asked with a glare. "Yes, sir!" said the confident, or at least hopeful, gallop boy. There was only one way to find out. So the horse and rider headed off to the racetrack for a trial run. When Leonard slid off the back of Cal's Choice after his first unescorted gallop, he was wringing his hands in pain from throttling the horse. His palms were the color of ripe cherries. Leonard's shoulders and triceps were sore the following day from a tug of war he wasn't exactly sure whether he had won or lost. But steadily Cal's Choice became rounded, less headstrong, and began using his horsepower in a more productive manner. He started to train. Before the graduating gelding could race again Marion wanted to work him in the morning at top speed to see whether the horse had completely transformed or would revert to his unruly behavior. Jesse Dehoyos was part of the Columbus caravan, by way of Detroit, by way of Mexico; he was one of Marion's most trusted gallop boys. Jesse purposefully worked the horse a fast half-mile. After the gallop, Bud met the horse and rider in the stall and he asked Jesse how it had gone. With a glint in his eye, Jesse said, "Go to the windows—this is a running dude!" On race day, the horse obediently laid off the pace, waited for his cue from the jockey, then kicked clear to win going away. That Van Berg vision paid $28. Cal's Choice later went on to win the 1958 Ak-Sar-Ben Handicap and stakes races at Waterford Park (now Mountaineer) and Hazel Park.

Lee Larson was from nearby Columbus; he became involved with the

Van Bergs as a kid and matured into a fine man and an excellent exercise rider for Marion and, later, Jack. He taught many of the Van Bergs' riders how to gallop and work horses and was credited with teaching Leonard Iwan to gallop. Cal's Choice wasn't the only tough horse Iwan tamed. Leonard famously won a bet in New Orleans when he was challenged that he couldn't gallop and control a very difficult horse named River Cat. Days later, Leonard was securely galloping River Cat in front of the two men who had issued the challenge. As Leonard galloped by, he shifted his cross grip of the reins to his left hand and then reached back with his free right hand, pulled out the hankie from his back pocket, and blew his nose at the two stunned losers. It was a winning achievement that was nothing to sneeze at.

Frank Zuroski was another member of the band of merry men from Columbus. "Zuke," as he was more commonly known, gave his heart and soul to the Van Berg family. He primarily stayed in the Midwest, galloping horses either at the racetrack or at the Van Bergs' training operation in Columbus. Zuke started working for Marion at the sale barn in his high school years in the early '50s and recalls the joys and pains of working for *Mr. Van:*

> He sounded like a drill instructor. And boy, could he bark at you and work you, too. Mr. Van taught me how to gallop. In the winter when it was no good to be outside we'd gallop horses inside in the big barn. He'd tell me to go twenty rounds in the barn to make two miles. And he'd keep track of you. *"How many rounds have you gone, boy?"* I'd say, *"Fifteen, sir";* then he'd say, *"No, damn it, you've only gone eleven."* Then he'd tell me I had to put twenty BBs in my mouth and spit one out each round. Oh, he was a corker, but I loved the man. And when the weather was nice I'd have to harrow the track with a hitch of horses. We had tractors and pickups, but he wanted that track harrowed by horses

with someone walking behind it. That someone always seemed to be me. Jesus! I worked my butt off for Marion—and Jack, too. The apple didn't fall far from the tree with that pair. They wanted things done their way, and if you didn't do it the way they wanted, boy you'd hear about it. But if you took care of things, they'd take care of you. He worked you hard, but he treated me like aces. Oh, I loved the man.

In later years Zuke found life on the road to be less desirable and preferred staying at home with his wife and family in Columbus, but Marion wanted him to gallop horses at Sportsman's Park. Zuke told Marion that he'd have to ask his wife. Instead, Marion called Zuke's wife and asked her if she would allow Zuke to go to Chicago for two months. Zuke went to Chicago. Two weeks later after morning chores in the Windy City, Marion went up to Zuke and handed him the keys to his Cadillac and told him to go pick his wife up from the airport. Marion had paid for Zuke's wife's flight and all her expenses. And he did it again a month later.

Of course, Zuke had similar stories of tough love from and for Jack, too:

Jack wasn't afraid to work, I guarantee ya. He'd pony horses in the morning and sometimes we'd have a couple rogues that we'd have to snub to the pony. *Whew!* I don't know how Jack and I made it back some mornings. Those horses would lunge and buck. Boy they were tough, but we made it around. And Jack would be alongside hollerin' at me the whole time. *Geez!* But we'd always have a good laugh about it on the way back to the barn. Oh, those were some good times.

And Jack has stories about Zuke . . .

Zuke was a great guy and a dedicated worker and everybody liked him, but everyone seemed to like to mess around with him and tease him. One time after a race, the guys were hanging around the scale at the finish line; it was Leonard Iwan, Loren Rettle, Jesse Dehoyos, and Zuke. When Dad walked by them, one of the guys told my dad he thought Zuke looked like he was getting heavy. So they made him get on the scale. Well, hell, every one of those guys was heavier than Zuke, but Dad heard that and hollered at Zuke and told him he wouldn't let him work horses any more. Zuke got hopping mad because he loved working horses in the morning and thought he was pretty good at it.

And then another time when we were in Omaha, Zuke went out to gallop a horse named Iron Side who Dad claimed at Sportsman's in the spring. The horse pulled up lame in the race Dad claimed him, so Dad sent him back home to Columbus to give him some time off. A month or so had gone by and Dad had the horse back in training. One morning I was leading a set up to the racetrack to gallop; Mark Wallerstadt was on one horse, and Zuke was on Iron Side. Zuke, who was prone to stutter now and then, asked me, *"JaJaJa Jack,* is there anything wrong with this one?" I looked over and winked at Mark, then told Zuke that after Dad claimed him he was off behind. That's why Dad sent him home. So we're riding back to the barn after the horses galloped and Dad pulls up on his pony and asks Zuke, *"What did you think of him, boy?"* Zuke says, "He's pretty good but a little off behind, boss." *"Off behind!"* Dad screams, "You damn dummy, there's not a damn thing wrong with that horse." All the while Zuke is stammering, *"Bababa boss,"* trying to come up with some explanation for why he said he was off. Meantime, Mark and I are just laughing our asses off. Oh, God bless Zuke—he got more ass-chewings than anybody.

A few years later, Marion named one of his horses after Zuke. He bred Space Commander, a stallion he stood after the horse won several stakes races at Hazel Park, to his homebred mare Mrs. M. H. The resulting foal was a colt he named Zuke's Bad Boy. Zuke beamed with pride to have a namesake racehorse, and one to care for personally. When Zuke's Bad Boy became a multiple stakes winner and put up a lifetime record of 90-25-18-6 $103,508, it was a personal accomplishment for Frank "Zuke" Zuroski, too—one for which he radiated joy for the rest of his life.

Another Van Berg faithful, Max D. Johnson was the son of Swede Johnson, a longtime friend of the family, who helped Marion build the Columbus Sales Pavilion. Max learned how to train horses under Marion and got some good private training jobs as result, including a gig working for Dearborn Farm in Midway, Kentucky. But Max was inclined to get homesick and he would always return home to Columbus.

Foy Conyers didn't stray far enough from home to get homesick. Raised in Creston, Nebraska, roughly twenty-five miles north of Columbus, he worked for the Van Berg Sales Pavilion for more than forty years. Foy raised a son, Don Conyers, who was a horse trainer and auctioneer. And Don's son Billy Conyers also became a horse trainer on the Nebraska racing circuit. A similar path was taken by generations of the Engel family from Silver Creek, Nebraska, just twenty miles southwest of Columbus. Roger Engel is a prominent and leading trainer in the Oklahoma thoroughbred racing scene. His brother Rick also trained and provided for his family via Nebraska horse racing. The boys learned horsemanship from their father, D. A. "Andy" Engel, who learned under Marion and trained horses throughout the Midwest. Their uncle Fritz Engel was a farmer and auctioneered some at the Columbus Sales Pavilion. And their grandfather Fred Engel was a longtime friend of Marion. Fred helped in the preparation and presentation of the buffalo sandwiches that were served at the grand opening of the sales pavilion.

The Irwin brothers, from Columbus, were a hearty three-of-a-kind. Robert, Cecil, and Ray all contributed to the Van Berg success story. Robert "Bob" was a longtime, right-hand man to Marion and was one of the original travelling deputies who trained for Marion. Cecil stayed in Columbus and was a significant employee of Marion's at the sale barn. Years later he found his way to St. Louis, Missouri, and became a primary caregiver to, and hitch-driver of, the World-Famous Budweiser Clydesdales. He returned home to Columbus and in his retirement years worked as handyman at Agricultural Park, home of the Columbus Races. The Van Berg Derby has been run at Columbus for decades as a tribute to the Van Berg family's importance to horse racing and Columbus, Nebraska.

Direct relatives to the Van Berg family were also involved in Marion's operation. Dick and Chuck Karlin, nephews to Jack and sons of Marion's daughter Helen, essentially became surrogate Van Berg children when their father abandoned Helen after he returned from the war. He had flown "the Hump" (the name of the treacherous air route flown over the Eastern Himalayans by U.S. and allied forces in WWII) and when he returned home, he was a different man. "They gave those pilots drugs to wake up, drugs to sleep, and drugs to give them the nerve to fly over the Hump. When he came home, he was a complete stranger," said Helen. In essence without a father, the boys gained two fathers. Uncle Jack drove them to places they needed to be and Grandpa Marion doled out the discipline and structure.

The Van Berg crew wasn't completely Columbus-based; Platte Center, just up the road, was also a feeder into the VB operation. Ben Ciboron, the primary groom of the Argentine mare Estacion, grew up in Platte Center and worked many years for Marion, as did Joe Pedraza, a big farm boy from outside of Platte Center. And the silent yet volatile Jim McGuin also joined forces from Platte Center. McGuin was known as a strange bird. He was an avid reader and would often disappear into his books. He was also known to battle the bottle and would occasionally disappear into it, too. Jim could stay flat and sober for weeks at a time, but in time, something always triggered him inside and he'd go off stride—and AWOL.

Once while racing in Omaha, Jim was sent to the store to buy some falsies. Prior to the age of silicon, falsies were padded cotton inserts used in bras by women who wanted to accentuate or de-accentuate their frontal features. All Jim McGuin knew was that the barn had run out of the cotton pads they used to wrap around the horses' ankles. The shape of the pad was ideal to help prevent abrasions and irritations caused by the horses' heels running down into the base of the track. Poor Jim—when he told the women at the counter of Woolworth's that he wanted to buy some falsies they both began to giggle at him. Red-faced, but not wanting to leave empty-handed, Jim stood his ground with the ladies. When they asked him what size he wanted, Jim replied honestly, "I don't know; they're for my horses." It's hard to gauge who erupted more—the two women who broke out in riotous laughter, or the man who bolted from the store and was not seen back at the Van Berg barn for days.

15

Rose's Gem

Before Nebraska racing enshrined their immortal Who Doctor Who, or Maryland racing cherished their Little Bold John, or Louisiana exclusively experienced Dixie Poker Ace, horse racing had a star like no other; his name was Kelso. The unprecedented skein of Kelso's five consecutive Horse of the Year titles, from 1960 to 1964, quite likely will never be matched. Simultaneous to the zenith that Kelso enjoyed—and earned—Rose's Gem, a sort of Kelso of the Midwest, was racking up similar numbers to those of the illustrious national champion. Rose's Gem's annual win tallies were similar to Kelso's, and his annual earnings would have been equally comparable but for want of an important extra digit that measured Rose's Gem's earnings in tens of thousands rather than hundreds of thousands.

Rose's Gem was pure Van Berg, not just in accomplishment, but in origin. A homebred, his mother, Rose Bed, was campaigned by Marion, and she won 23 of 102 races and ran second 23 times, too. In the late winter of 1953, Marion walked Rose Bed out to the back, north gate of his Columbus Sales Pavilion, up a slatted wooden ramp, and into an airy boxcar. A Union Pacific locomotive then trundled her east, to Goshen, Kentucky. Upon arriving at the legendary Hermitage Farm, owned by Warner L. Jones, Jr., she was bred to Royal Gem II. He was a flashy stallion that had been imported from Australia after winning several primary stakes races in Victoria, including the Ascot Vale Stakes, the Goodwood, the Caulfield Guineas, and the Caulfield Cup. In the spring of 1954, a simple bay colt was foaled in Columbus, Nebraska, and he was given a simple name. Rose's Gem would also be given a lifetime of care from Columbus native Bud Kuta. Bud had put in his time with the Van Berg racing operation, and both Marion and Jack knew that Rose's Gem would be in the best of hands with Bud. Rose's Gem developed so quickly and favorably that he was raced in April of his two-year-old season—against winners! In his debut at Sportsman's Park in Cicero, Illinois, Rose's Gem went off at 50-1. He took the lead three times in the battle to the finish, and with four horses on the wire, he got beat by just a neck! When jockey Bobby Mundorf got off him after the race he was upset that his mount had run so courageously but still lost. Mundorf knew Rose's Gem could have trounced the competition if only he had run against fellow maidens. As he told Bud, "This is terrible! We could have cashed a big ticket on this horse." Bud knew Rose's Gem was a runner, too, but now so did everyone else who had seen the race or could read a racing form. The cat was out of the bag.

The process of developing a racehorse so quickly can often be double-edged, and Rose's Gem started to get sore shins, just as many athletes, equine and human, encounter in the early days of their training. In the follow-up race of Rose's Gem, Mr. Van Berg instructed Bud to put elastic leg wraps on the racehorse's forelegs to help provide strength and stability. But when Rose's Gem broke from the gate, he dug in so hard that the flexion of his leg muscles caused the elastic wraps to squeeze down tighter on his shins. This resulted in extreme discomfort—and in Rose's Gem pulling himself up and not running at all. He shin-bucked and was eased in the race. This unfortunate lesson made Marion give Rose's Gem several months of rest and recovery back home in Columbus. But in the span of just two losing races, Rose's Gem had won the love of both his groom and Viola, Mr. Van Berg's wife. Viola adopted Rose's Gem as her own. Bud summed him up: "He was a running little devil. He was ornery, but not mean. Just small and with a big heart. Oh, and Mrs. Van loved him so much."

Rose's Gem was gelded in the winter of his two-year-old season, while getting a chance to freshen and mature back in Columbus. In 1957 he rebounded from the aches and pains of his freshman year and was ready to roll as a sophomore. Jack was supposed to lead Rose's Gem to the starting gate but was keen to bet on him because he knew how well he had been training. Leon Hall, who became an iconic Ak-Sar-Ben outrider (along with Bob Young), took Rose's Gem to the gate while Jack went to bet $20 to win on him at 30-1. After the post parade, his odds hadn't changed, so Jack bet another $10 on him. Then a few minutes later he bet another $10. As the field reached the starting gate, Rose's Gem became as anxious and ornery as his trainer. In his eagerness to run, he bucked jockey Bobby Mundorf out of the saddle, took off down the backstretch, and was scratched. By the time he ran again, the word had gotten out that Rose's Gem could run and he went off as a favorite. He won that race and then started to win Nebraska-bred stakes races for fun. Rose's Gem had blossomed. He didn't win a derby, but at age three, he did win the Ak-Sar-Ben Breeders' Special Stakes and the Midwestern Stakes at Sportsman's Park. And his recognition as the Nebraska Horse of the Year in 1957 would be just the first award of what would become a gaudy collection of Nebraska-bred racing honors—and ultimate induction into the Nebraska Racing Hall of Fame.

But Rose's Gem didn't just rough up restricted Nebraska-bred competition, he also won stakes in open company in Omaha, Chicago, and Detroit. And he even pressed farther east than the Great Lakes. Van Berg shipped Rose's Gem as far away as New England, to Lincoln Downs in Rhode Island. Race fans from New York City and Boston took the Gansett Express trains to the Pawtucket track and many locals rode the UTC streetcars. On October 3, 1959, they saw a Nebraska-bred sweep by local legend Charlie Boy and win the Hartford Handicap. On October 17,

Rose's Gem ran third to Battle Neck in the Springfield Handicap. Then, on October 24, he won the seven-and-a-half furlong Rhode Island Handicap at 2-1. The Daily Racing Form comment for Rose's Gem read: "Won easily. In hand early, moved well when called upon, wrested command just before the final eighth and won with speed to spare." In doing so, the Columbus, Nebraska, interloper set a track record for the distance. Not a bad month's work. Cape Cod Country was off the beaten path for Rose's Gem, yet the newcomer humbled his opponents just the same.

"He could run anywhere and at any distance, from six furlongs to a mile and one-quarter," reflected Kuta. "He'd usually lay just off the pace, but if they sent him to the front, then he'd just go on with it from there. Oh, he tried so hard—always!" Rose's Gem could break the hearts of the horses he repelled and win the hearts of jockeys who rode against him. After repeatedly being outrun by Rose's Gem, jockey R. L. "Bobby" Baird, who won more than 3,700 races in his career and rode in the Kentucky Derby five times, was known to have asked Marion Van Berg if he could ride Rose's Gem—at no charge. "I'm tired of getting beat by that horse; I just want to know what it feels like to be on him and I won't ask for a penny of purse money," said a bewildered Baird.

Richard Rettele sure knew what it was like to be on Rose's Gem. He galloped him throughout much of his race career and made the winning trip with him to New England. "Rosey (Rose's Gem) was a tough little guy. He was the king and everybody liked him. It seemed like each weekend there was a stakes race for him to run in, so he ran what seems like every Saturday," said Rettele.

Of course there was plenty of animosity, too. Bud and Zuke were always under fire from the grooms of competing horses. Envy, jealousy, and hope filled and fueled horsemen, and Rose's Gem was frequently a target, too. After a particularly rough race at Hazel Park, in which he was almost put over the inside rail due to some rough and questionable riding,

Rose's Gem got shuffled back and was pulled up. He'd also lost his previous race, so the form of the then eight-year-old gelding at the time did not look good. Bud recalled what followed:

> When he showed up next in the entries at Chicago, a groom popped off to me, saying, "What's Rose's Gem doing in that handicap? He don't belong in that race." And then another groom who had a horse in the race with five-straight wins said, "You better scratch that damn horse!" I asked why. "We're gonna school him," said the groom. All I said was "you might," but I knew they weren't going to school Rose's Gem. So they ran the race and their horse was in front till about mid-stretch, then along comes Rose's Gem and he beat 'em by three lengths. And the best part of it was, before the race Zuke was sitting with Mr. Van, and the sun was shining hard on the tote board, creating a strong glare. Mr. Van asked Zuke, "What's he at, 2-5, 3-5?" Zuke says, "No, he's 25-1, Mr. Van!" So Marion reaches into his pants and gives Zuke $200 and says, "Go bet this to win on Rose's Gem, boy." After Zuke cashed the ticket he had well over $4,000 crammed into his pockets. Zuke saw there were some guys who followed him to the windows and they were still on his tail after he cashed the big winning ticket. Well Zuke was getting nervous holding all the money and he knew he was being followed. He also knew there was a $100 fine for cutting under the rail as a shortcut back to the barns. But Zuke figured that a fine was good enough insurance to protect Mr. Van's winnings, so he shot under the rail and sprinted back to the stable area. When he got to our barn he was hollerin' for me and Bob to come help him and stash the cash. Oh, that was quite a scene. But Mr. Van made sure Zuke didn't get fined for the shortcut and we made sure that Rose's Gem got plenty extra carrots for the win.

After his underdog win, Rose's Gem lost his sheen and stopped winning races. Marion knew he still had a sound horse and thought he needed to help his champ regain the winning feeling. At a huge risk, Marion entered Rose's Gem in a $10,000 claiming race and included Admiral Van as an entry mate. Shock waves rolled throughout the Van Berg domain. Bud was horrified; Zuke was suddenly speechless; the entire barn crew was confused. When Mrs. Van Berg heard what her husband had done, she shamed him and told him he shouldn't return home if her pet horse got claimed. Everyone sunk into a sickening spiral. Bud explained what happened:

> We were up racing at Sportsman's Park at the time and everyone was sweating it out that Rose's Gem might get claimed for $10,000. But in the days and hours leading up to the race I kept telling folks not to worry because surely Mr. Van would scratch Rose's Gem and he wouldn't get claimed. Well, Bob Irwin came out of the racing office and said, "Bud, you're not going to believe this, he scratched Admiral Van." I said, "What!" I couldn't believe it and I just knew Viola would have a fit if he got claimed. And Mr. Van knew the circumstances, too. All day long Mr. Van was very quiet and he looked sick. He looked white! I asked him if he was okay. "No, no, I'm fine, boy," he said. But he knew it and I knew it and we all knew what trouble he was in. And his mistake was starting to show and make him very nervous. Well, I knew I had to do something to try to save this horse and prevent him from getting claimed. So I put cold water bandages on his ankles and on one knee. And sure enough, there were some guys who followed us up to the paddock when I led him up for the race. I heard one guy say, "I wonder if he's got a bad knee." They followed me all the way up there. Up in the paddock all three guys were huddled together and planning. Finally, I walked by

and said, "Guys, don't take him." Oh, Mr. Van was just a mess; he was sweating and worrying, but as soon as we made it past claim-time and we knew he hadn't been claimed, Mr. Van looked like a changed man—he got his color back and was all cheerful again. There's no way he could have faced Viola again if he would have lost that horse.

Rose's Gem won that $10,000 claiming race, and for an encore, the old-timer set a track record for six-and-a-half furlongs in 1:16.3.

His overall numbers and achievement are remarkable; 125-41-34-12 rings loud in any racing genre. But Rose's Gem's lifetime earnings sum of $230,964 is especially astonishing. He won stakes races at six tracks in five different states. The richest stakes in which he finished in the money was the 1960 renewal of the then $25,000 National Jockey Club Handi-cap; Rose's Gem earned $5,000 for his second-place finish. To calculate what the modern-day earnings for Rose's Gem could have been, simply add a zero; in 2007, the purse of the National Jockey Club Handicap was $250,000.

Of course, all good things must come to an end. Rose's Gem conclud-ed his racing career with a fitting victory in his final race. After the end of the racing season in Chicago, Rose's Gem was vanned back home, west to Columbus, Nebraska, for his final trip down Highway 30. Perhaps the most captivating element of horses in racing is that these gentle giants can subtly or immediately become part of the hearts and souls of their keepers. Coping with their departure, whether it be immediate or planned, is often more difficult than expected. For Bud Kuta, not having Rose's Gem in his shedrow left him with a heavy heart. Each month that passed drove Bud into further self-reflection; he missed the nuzzles, warmth, and love he shared with Rose's Gem—he missed his family, too. Bud had given much of his life to Marion and Jack. He was an honest, hardworking, and de-voted employee, much like the iconic Van Berg father and son for whom he worked for decades, and much like the iconic horse for whom he cared for nearly a decade. It was time for Bud to go home to Columbus, too.

Back home, Bud continued to work for the Van Berg family, but his duties centered mostly on the horses that were kept in Columbus or raced at the tracks in Nebraska. He still spent time on the road, but the shuttles to-and-fro were much shorter. Bud was home with his family and he was back with Rose's Gem. One of the first things Bud did when he returned was to check in on his old pal, who had begun his retirement at the Van Berg sales complex. When he discovered that Rose's Gem had been given a rear stall in the horse barn, Bud wouldn't have it. He immediately moved him to the first stall and also noticed the reemergence of an old injury. Bud tells a most touching story:

When I heard Rose's Gem was back in the west barn, I said, "No sir, I want him up close so I can keep an eye on him." At times he could develop quite an ankle on him and sometimes he could barely walk. His ankle had gotten as big as the moon. So I threw down some fresh straw and started to work on that ankle. I did him up every day for about thirty days and got that ankle down to nothing. Then one day when Mr. Van Berg had come home, I turned him out in the paddock just south of the barn. I saw Mr. Van stand there and look at the horse and he just stood there looking over the fence at him. I told the guys, "Look, he's puzzled; he doesn't know it's Rose's Gem." And Mr. Van was renowned for being able to identify not only his own horses, but horses of other horsemen, too. I asked him if he knew who the horse was and he said, "No Bud, I'm sorry, I don't know that horse." When I told him it was Rose's Gem, he squawked, "Rose's Gem! I thought he couldn't walk?" "He can walk now," I said. Marion, he was tickled to death to see the horse doing so well. So he rushed to the intercom phone near the sale barn and called Viola. He told her to come outside in ten minutes because he was going to bring a horse by that he wanted her to see. When Viola stepped out on the back porch she immediately began to weep. Smiling through her tears she cried out, "I thought he couldn't walk?" "Well, he can now," said Marion. I led him into the front yard of the house and I've never seen Viola give a horse such a big hug. And she wouldn't let go.

The story gets even better. Marion was so proud of Rose's Gem and of Bud that he told Bud, "Next week they're running the Rose's Gem Stakes at Ak-Sar-Ben; I want you to get him ready and take him down to Omaha for the race. He'll lead the post parade, but I don't want you to leave his side, you got that?" Bud assured Marion that he would take good care of their champ. When Rose's Gem arrived to the paddock he got a deserving hero's welcome. The Ak-Sar-Ben race fans, many of whom came by bus from Des Moines, Kansas City, Topeka, Denver, and beyond, crammed the grandstand apron to have another look at a horse many considered their friend. There was plenty of picture-taking and hoopla, but when the field approached the starting gate at the mile-and-seventy-yard position, Bud knew he needed to return the horse to the paddock. There was already enough commotion; he wanted to avoid any more. When the starting gate doors began to be latched closed, Rose's Gem lifted his head, pricked his ears, and his eyes became fixed on the gate. "And boy, when the latches flung open and that gate bell rang, he went to digging and pawing at the ground; I could hardly hold him," Bud said, sentimentally.

It was a treat for Bud and the Van Bergs to get reunited with Rose's Gem. It was a treat for the fans to get reunited with Rose's Gem. And it was obviously a treat for Rose's Gem. But the glitter of Rose's Gem was far more than just a treat—it was a treasure. And he was a genuine gem.

16

Marion's Way

The national success of both Marion and Jack Van Berg was measured not only by how well their horses ran, but how well the horses were run—and by whom. It was physically impossible for Marion and Jack to be on hand to tend to the daily affairs of training when there were multiple barns being operated simultaneously throughout the nation.

For decades, the name "M. H. Van Berg" was omnipresent in the owner line of the official racing programs sold from the Great Lakes through the Midwest and deep into the Mississippi Delta. In the thirty-four years that Marion watched his horses run, if *his* name didn't appear as trainer, a list of more than two dozen names may have been printed as trainer instead. The honor roll of trainers who raced the Van Berg gold and purple includes: J. D. Burns, D. Denham, W. A. Fabry, E. W. Fouts, F. E. Fitzgerald, F. E. Heeb, L. Horton, R. L. Irwin, M. C. Johnson, Max D. Johnson, K. D. Kepler, H. Kirby, C. C. Kranz, F. M. Lee, E. H. Mahoney, J. McFarlan, H. Nutter, C. W. Pierce, M. Resseguet, W. Resseguet, M. Stubbs, C. A. Tanner, Bud Van Berg, Jack Van Berg, F. E. Waldron, L. N. Willey, and R. H. Wiley.

The original trainer—and thus travelling trainer—for M. H. Van Berg was C. A. Tanner. "Charlie" Tanner was Marion's exclusive trainer dating back to the 1937 origins of the Van Berg racing operation. In the early 1940s M. C. Johnson and R. L. Irwin also appeared as trainers. Marion established a much-travelled path from his home in Columbus, Nebraska, that stretched along the present-day Interstate 80 beltway from Omaha to Detroit. That primary route then branched out, reaching to racing below

Lake Erie in Ohio and on south to St. Louis. In 1945 and 1946 Marion raced only in Chicago and Detroit and "M. H. Van Berg" was exclusively listed as the trainer. He had a 20 percent win rate in 1945, saddling 31 winners from 149 starters.

The first leading owner title Marion earned was in 1948, the final year of racing at the Detroit Fairgrounds. He would finish the meet second in the trainer standings. Van Berg would conclude the year by winning his first leading trainer title at the fall Sportsman's Park meet. The end of the '40s marked a new beginning for Detroit horse racing. With the closing of the Detroit Fairgrounds, two new tracks opened in the city soon thereafter. Hazel Park opened on August 17, 1949, and Detroit Race Course opened on May 25, 1950. The floodgates also opened for M. H. Van Berg as he and his able assistants quickly conquered Detroit—and Chicago. From the late '40s and deep into the '60's, Van Berg was essentially the lone leading owner and trainer at DRC and Hazel Park. And what happened in the Motor City also happened three hundred miles away in the Windy City. It was all Van Berg—all the time!

The summary of Marion Van Berg's lifetime stats is simply stunning. He was the leading *owner* at either the spring or fall meet at Sportsman's Park twenty-four times and he was the second-leading owner another ten times. Marion deployed his deputies across the nation with a mission of winning wherever, whenever. Columbus, Nebraska, was central command, but Sportsman's Park in Cicero, Illinois, is where M. H. Van Berg held court as a *trainer*. He was the leading trainer at Sportsman's twenty times and he finished as the second-leading trainer eight times. At Detroit Race Course, in a twenty-two-year span, he was the leading owner twenty times and was second twice, while he was also the leading trainer there six times and the second-leading trainer on four occasions. At Hazel Park he led the owner standings sixteen times and led the trainer standings seven times. He was the leading Ak-Sar-Ben owner fourteen times but he never was listed as a trainer in Omaha. Although he oversaw plenty, he left the Ak-Sar-Ben training honors for his son Jack.

At Oaklawn Park, Marion was the leading owner seven times and the second-leading trainer three times. His (assistant) trainer Bob Irwin got credit as a leading Oaklawn trainer four times. The breadth of tracks where Marion was the leading owner is a mindboggling list . . . six times at the Fair Grounds in New Orleans, twice at both Latonia and Laurel, four times at Pimlico, once at Hawthorne and Wheeling Downs. Marion was the second-leading owner at Maumee Downs, south of Toledo, Ohio, in 1958, until Raceway Park opened in Toledo, where he promptly swept the owner standings six times. He crushed at "The Rock" when in 1969 he sent Jack to Rockingham Park in Salem, New Hampshire, and pummeled the competition with a 23 percent strike rate; winning 39 of 167 races. Curiously, he left the members of the competition to themselves in his own backyard. At the Columbus Races at Agricultural Park in Columbus, Nebraska, Marion's numbers from 1947 to 1968 were just 59-9-8-8 $8,650. Similarly, his lifetime stats at Fonner Park in Grand Island, Nebraska, were just 7 wins in 50. This said, Marion did win 17 of 89 in Lincoln, Nebraska, and he took a title there, too.

In his racing career, M. H. Van Berg started nearly 24,300 horses and he owned more than 99 percent of those runners. He won a total of 4,775 races, but he was the *trainer of record* for roughly only 1,500 of those 4,775 wins. Approximately 3,300 of Marion's winners carried another name in the program as the *official* trainer. His son Jack trained more than 2,000 winners for his father. In the early days, Charlie Tanner trained 119 winners and K. D. Kepler was responsible for 351 wins. R. L. Irwin trained more than 500 winners for Mr. Van and was ever the stalwart servant.

In 1970, M. H. Van Berg received one of his highest career honors when he was inducted into the National Museum of Racing Hall of Fame.

The tribute plaque that hangs in the Hall of Fame in Saratoga Springs, New York, gives specific mention and credit to Van Berg's "longtime assistant" R. L. (Bob) Irwin.

Marion Van Berg owned racehorses for thirty-four years, and Bob Irwin worked for Marion for thirty-two of those years. Irwin came from a Depression-era family of ten children that was barely surviving in Columbus. At age twelve, Bob, and his brothers Cecil and Ray, began working for Marion at the Columbus Sale Pavilion. Their earnings were pooled to help keep the Irwin family fed. Even before Marion had run his first racehorse, Bob showed an interest in working with horses. As Marion got more involved with racing, he hired Charlie Tanner to train for him. He then purposefully positioned Bob under Charlie's wing. The young pupil soaked up all he could from Marion and Charlie and quickly stood out as a budding horseman. Bob began to evolve as the horse racing entity of Marion's business interests also began to grow. In true apprentice fashion, young Bob Irwin was spending time with the horses day and night. He was actually given a bed in a makeshift bedroom in the attic of the big, white Van Berg family home located on the sales grounds. Bob ate his meals with the Van Berg family and was for all intents and purposes part of the family. By the early '40s Bob had been out on the road, making the loop from Chicago to Detroit or wherever Marion needed a trusted hand to care for his horses.

So much of Bob's time (as it was for anyone who worked for Marion) was spent on the road. The A.M. radio became a true friend when sitting behind the wheel of a Van Berg horse van. At nighttime, Bob's companion was the strong signal of Omaha's KFAB radio, which escorted him along the Platte River bends of Highway 30 and then east through Iowa. Over the years, Glen Miller, Benny Goodman, and the Dorsey Brothers frequently played for Bob in the truck cab. He laughed out loud at "Fibber McGee and Molly" on WMAQ in Chicago. And he learned about

D-Day and Tigers baseball on WJR in Detroit. Convenience stores did not dot the interstates in those days—there were no interstates. Food was available for the haul, but only if sandwiches were made or cookies were purchased before departure. The trusty coffee thermos was always within arm's reach. Telephone communication along the way *might* only have occurred in the event of an emergency. It wasn't an easy trip, but it became routine. The entire Van Berg racing season had become a routine. Racing and running the roads from Easter until Thanksgiving was the norm; then it was home for the holidays. Winter in Columbus meant weaning foals, breaking yearlings, castrating colts, blistering legs, and allowing horses genuine downtime before cranking back up again in the spring.

"I don't ever recall a time that Dad wasn't with the horses for Mr. Van," recalled Ralph Irwin, Bob's son. "Dad also did all the trimming and shoeing of the horses for Marion during the wintertime. Jack Reynolds, a highly regarded farrier, always told me that Dad was an excellent shoer." Reynolds shod Spectacular Bid and was often flown all over the country to work on high-profile stakes horses. Bob often worked closely with the famous Kentucky veterinarian Dr. Alex Harthill, providing shoeing advice to Harthill and his clients. Following in his father's footsteps, and continuing the already-established Van Berg/Irwin relationship, Ralph Irwin became a longtime assistant to Jack Van Berg. He currently trains at Oaklawn Park and Louisiana Downs.

In the early '50s Marion added a few more tracks to his yearly roster. Aside from the Chicago and Detroit tracks, Wheeling Downs and Churchill Downs stretched the Van Berg racing season and span. Before Bob Irwin became Marion's main man in Detroit, he won 3 of 10 races at Keeneland in 1955.

Then, as an experiment with an earlier start to his annual racing campaign, Marion got a few selected horses on the muscle several weeks before the others. It began with sending nine runners to Oaklawn Park with K. D. Kepler. Initially, the Hot Springs, Arkansas, maneuver did not prove to be a winning way to start the year, but by the end of the decade, Marion would find that the Fair Grounds in New Orleans was a nice way to finish the year. In the fall of 1959, Kepler would win 13 of 54 races in the Crescent City. Of course those New Orleans–based horses continued to run well for Marion beyond New Year's Eve. A Southern stronghold was shaping. The introduction of year-round racing did not sit well with Marion's wife, Viola. But she didn't have much of a case against this new tactic when both meets produced leading trainer titles. It was a Fat Tuesday—and then some—at the Fair Grounds. As a result, things at Oaklawn Park went from famine to feast. While the Bay of Pigs invasion was still a year away, M. H. Van Berg was already enjoying the fat hog he had cut from his very own strategic southern placement.

JFK took heat for his failed invasion; MHVB took heat for a successful invasion. Viola Van Berg simply did not like being away from her husband, and truth be told, Marion was famous for missing Viola and wanting to be with her. The success of keeping a string of horses going in the South from November through April interrupted what for years had been key family time in Columbus. Both Viola and Marion were known to have an open-door policy at their home in Columbus during the holidays. Having three and four turkeys in the ovens for Thanksgiving and Christmas was the ritual, as was inviting employees who were away from their families at this special time. "We'd sometimes have thirty or forty people over," said Dr. Dick Karlin, DVM, grandson of Marion and Viola and nephew to Jack. "Grandpa would hitch up a team of horses and give everyone buggy rides around the place, and the kids would have footraces while they were waiting for the meal. When there was snow during the holidays he'd have Jack get two long logs for a sled and tack in some two-by-fours to create bench seats, then hitch it to the draft horses. That was Grandpa's way of showing his love."

The year-round racing caused a need for a supply of reliable, able-bodied assistants. A corps of assistants was put into position at the various divisions across the land, and there was a proper protocol with the racehorses. Things needed to be done Marion's way . . . exactly! There was no wiggle room. It was this rigid attention to detail that Marion (and later Jack) demanded, so that he could accurately monitor the training of his horses while he was hundreds of miles away. The certitude of Marion's methods allowed for extremely effective remote training.

"You had to call him every night and tell him what was going on with the horses. Then when he came to town you'd have to get them all out and jog each one down the road in the stable area. And them sons-of-bucks better jog perfect," said Jack. "He didn't go for any of that 'oh, they just got that way' crap if they were off or sore." There was routine in the morning at the barn and routine in the evening, too. A specific routine was put into place whereby the assistant called the trainer each night after the races. Aside from being tireless, devoted men, Van Berg assistants had to be part veterinarian, part chart caller, and part race caller. Back then there was no full-card simulcasting of every track from every state. There was no simulcasting at all.

Oddly, Marion didn't see the majority of races his horses ran. He relied on the description of each race from all of his assistants. Marion was told how the horse acted in the post parade, how the horse behaved in the race, how he finished, what the jockey said after the race, and how the horse cooled out. Keep in mind, if an urgent issue developed, the assistant might not speak to Marion until hours later. There were no cell phones and few pay phones. Occasionally, an assistant might have to make a significant decision on his own. "Just use your best judgment," Marion would say. That was the refrain his assistants were told to follow. Of course that was fine, as long as the assistant's best judgment was the same action Marion would have taken. In the event it wasn't, the assistant (or son) heard a few choice words from the trainer on the day or days that followed.

The impressions and accounts of journalistic observers also played into Marion's comprehension of races or performances he might not have seen. Teddy Cox covered horse racing at the Fair Grounds for the New Orleans newspaper *The Times-Picayune*. In 1965, the Van Bergs had a nice filly named You Look Cute, who was evolving into a stakes horse. Following her fifth consecutive win and her second straight at the Fair Grounds, Jack recalled telling Cox, "Dad doesn't know how good this filly is." The next morning at the barn, when he was digesting his coffee, a doughnut, and the newspaper story on You Look Cute, Jack read, "Jack said his dad doesn't know what he's doing with the filly." Jack snorted out his coffee and nearly choked on his doughnut. He went storming out of the tack room and was bent on straightening out Teddy; he just as eagerly could have bent Teddy's nose. Fortunately there was no physical discussion. But this time, the spoken word from trainer to reporter was completely understood. Jack also saw to it that the printed word in the newspaper never found its way into the hands of his father. He simply described the filly's fifth win to Marion over the phone and that concluded the cautious chronicle of You Look Cute.

Beyond the telephoned race reviews, the assistant also gave a report to Marion on each horse's legs. Were their legs cool? Was there any swelling? Had a suggested treatment worked? How were their hooves? Those were the important questions Marion asked. *No hoof, no horse!* Marion got a frequent and comprehensive summary of every horse he had in training, at every track, several times a week. But Van Berg assistants didn't easily become assistants. Marion observed his men's demeanor, ability, and potential as soon as they began working for him. He assessed them much like he would observe his horses in the barn or on the racetrack. When he saw key characteristics in a prospective assistant, he gradually put that candidate through a battery of tests, often times unbeknownst to the employee. Marion knew he couldn't possibly be with all his horses all the time, so he essentially developed an elite legion of assistants who could and would do things the M. H. Van Berg way.

What's good for the goose is good for the gander. That expression held true in Marion's way of thinking and expectations. It applied not only to how he wanted his help to treat his horses, but how he wanted his help to treat themselves. What Marion believed, he wanted you to believe—and Marion believed in God. Marion attended church and he insisted that the younger men who worked for him also attend weekly services. Marion's daughter Helen recalls a remark she heard her father say countless times: "Dad said, 'You can go to church every Sunday, but if you don't live it during the week there's no use going. Go to church, but live it!'" Most of all, Marion was rigid when it came to honor. "In Dad's world, if you said something, that's the way it was," Helen said. "You lived up to your word and there was no way around it. It was just that simple."

Marion also had zero tolerance for smoking, at least within his immediate family. He didn't smoke, so his children wouldn't smoke, and none did—except for one. Unfortunately, the cigar-smoking sentence Marion had handed down to Jack as a child didn't linger long. Shortly after Jack cleared his lungs, head, and stomach from that near death penalty he faced in the kitchen, he was back smoking again. Jack was not a heavy smoker by any stretch; nonetheless, he attempted to conceal his smoking from his father for years. A legendary story has been told and twisted for years about this. Once and for all, Jack clears the air . . .

Back in Columbus at the sale barn, after a sale we'd all go to the café attached to the barn and have some soup and a sandwich. After we ate, Dad left and went to the house to be with mother. A few of us went back to the sale office to have a smoke before we went back to check the cattle to make sure they were in their proper pens. We're in there bullshitting, and in walks Dad. I had a lit cigarette in my hand, so I just cupped it and squeezed it tight to put it out in my hand. I was a grown man with a few kids at the time, but I'd rather feel the burn of that damn cigarette than catch hell from my dad.

A final flashpoint occurred years later in Chicago at Sportsman's Park . . .

We were racing at Sportsman's and I was in the racing office with Dad. We had finished entering horses and Dad left to go up to the grandstand to the races. I bummed a cig from a guy and had just taken my first puff off that thing when Dad walked back into the racing office. He looked at me and I looked at him and all I said was "*oops!*" He said, "I guess *oops!*" That time, I just threw it down and stepped on it to put it out. But I would have put that one out in my hand, too, if I had a chance. The next morning I was cleaning a stall and he came up to me and told me that as old as I was I didn't need to start smoking now. I could hear that he had a crackle in his voice, so I peeked up and saw that he had big tears in his eyes. I was ashamed, so I just kept my head down and kept mucking and said, "Yeah, you're right."

Jack felt awful, mostly because he knew he had really disappointed his father. Marion did not always show his love in a conventional manner, but he was a father who loved all his children, and he hated to see his son harming himself with smoking. Ultimately, Jack did quit smoking entirely, but not without memories of cigarettes first being singed into his hand, head, and heart.

17

A Heaving Heart

In tenacity, Marion's heart was undeniable; in generosity, his heart was charitable; but in basic physicality, Marion's heart was vulnerable. The metaphorical giant heart that he presented was perpetually vexed by the biological weak heart he actually possessed. Marion had an overworked heart, which kept him going, or rather, which *he* kept going.

Whether his woes were inherited, or created, matters not. The life and chosen lifestyle of Marion H. Van Berg took a mighty toll on his health. As a young man he battled through many uncertainties, took major risks, and faced serious setbacks. The breath he did catch when his Columbus Sales Pavilion started achieving success was quickly sucked away by the effort it took to maintain that success. And the rigors of racing were no picnic either. Here was a man who was as rags to riches as they came. Reverting back to the threadbare days of living hand to mouth was a haunting concept for Marion. The kingdom he lived in was self-constructed, and his immense pride restricted him from any form of easing up. Marion's early days motivated him all the way to his final days.

As Marion battled his own health problems, he was known to help others with their own personal misfortunes. Gallop boy Leonard Iwan had badly bruised his foot and it gave him problems for several weeks. He was really hurting. Before he left town to go to New Orleans he went to the hospital in Columbus to have it checked out. The day he showed up at the Fair Grounds the hospital called him and told him that he had cancer in his foot and that they would have to amputate his lower leg. Marion shuddered at the thought and wanted him to get a first-rate opinion. He saw to it that Leonard got admitted to the Mayo Clinic in Rochester. Leonard had been misdiagnosed and he kept his leg thanks to Marion. Bob Irwin was also a recipient of Marion's love and generosity, and he too received treatment at Mayo, undergoing surgery for a longtime issue with his throat. Marion's kindness was present in acts of sympathy, too. The shoeshine man at Detroit Race Course was working and living away from his family and was understandably despondent when he received news of the death of his young daughter. When Marion learned that the man couldn't afford to buy a plane ticket to attend the funeral, he reached into his wallet and gave the man cash to purchase the ticket. In turn, it would be Marion who needed medical assistance, but he rebuked all acts of sympathy shown to him.

Marion felt his first warning shot in 1954. Otter Brook was a hard-knocking nine-year-old who won 30 of 100 races; but he was equally hardheaded. It was in the early spring of the year and Marion was home in Columbus. Otter Brook needed to be shod, but the stout gelding was known to be unruly, and it often took extreme measures to accomplish the simplest things with him. Marion was on hand to supervise the shoeing process. Sure enough, Otter Brook became obstinate, and sure enough, Marion became involved. The two got into a wrestling match and neither would back down. There was quite an exchange of bumps and tugs and lunges and stomps. Both battlers were gnashing their teeth and showing the whites of their eyes. Then, Marion suddenly shuddered, stepped away, and yielded to his rival. Otter Brook merely glared back. Van Berg had suffered myocardial infarction; he had a heart attack.

At age fifty-eight, after such a threatening episode, most heart attack victims would have altered their routine, but Marion recovered and kept on pushing. In addition to his evolving heart issues, Marion dealt with sleep apnea throughout much of his adult life. He was a man who typically got little sleep anyway, and the apnea symptoms only compounded his physical challenges. Van Berg developed the habit of taking several aspi-rins throughout the course of the day. He'd drop a handful into his trouser pockets each morning before heading to the barn. The seemingly innocu-ous pills helped him battle the headaches he got from a pattern of ragged sleep. In turn, the aspirin doubled as a blood thinner, which helped keep his blood pressure from running wild. Of course, a significant amount of aspirin is never kind to the stomach. But that was how the engine was maintained in the human machine that was M. H. Van Berg.

Nearly a decade went by before Marion suffered another heart at-tack attributed to his appetite for winning. In the summer of 1962, he had already won the leading owner title at Sportsman's Park and Ak-Sar-Ben and was weeks away from doing the same at Hazel Park. On July 2, a piercing lightning bolt ripped through his heart. Marion was rushed to Henry Ford Hospital and was treated for another heart attack. Jack was in Columbus, and his wife Mary Jane was only hours away from having the couple's third child. Tori Lynn Van Berg was born later that day after Jack had left to be at his father's side. Indeed, hearts were attacked.

Jack's juggling continued. He left his wife and newborn daughter with the infrastructure of his family in Columbus and began caring for his fa-ther and a barn of horses in Detroit. Much of Jack's recollection of oc-currences is traced and connected to incidents associated with his horses. The accomplishments of Indian Nation in the summer of 1964 serve as a bittersweet beacon for Jack.

Dad had just come home from Ford Hospital, and we were stay-ing at the Shirberg Motel while we were racing at Hazel Park. He and I were in the hotel room—Dad was on one bed and I was on the other. I got a phone call from Jim Hall, a steward from the Ne-braska racing circuit. Jim told me they were desperate for a horse to help with entries to fill a small handicap race at the Columbus Races. I told him we had no horses in training back there to help him out. The only horse I had was Indian Nation, but he had been up in a pasture near Columbus turned out for a few weeks and he was just a cheap claimer. Well, when Dad heard this, he said, "Hell, run that son-of-a-buck—it can't hurt him." We ran him and he won and set a track record. And that's the way we trained that horse from then on.

Marion's health improved well enough for him to resume his routine of training. Unfortunately, he didn't follow the same approach of rest and light work that he directed for Indian Nation. As the racing season evolved in Detroit, the races moved across town to Detroit Race Course.

One morning, Jack had just arrived to the stable area after driving all night with a van full of precious cargo from Columbus. His children, Tim and Tami, had ridden along with Jack in the cab; in the back, one of the horses in the big Van Berg horse van was Indian Nation. That morning, Marion was leading horses up to and back from the racetrack from astride his buckskin pony, Buck. On one of his trips he began to waver in the saddle. Marion was arching backwards and beginning to fall, but his pony sensed this and kept stepping back to try to help his rider retain his balance. It wasn't long before some other horseman saw this and ran over and helped Marion out of the saddle. Marion was taken directly to Ford Hospital for treatment of his third known heart attack.

After roughly a week of hospital care he was released from the hospital. He was free to go home. Home at this time of the year in Detroit was the Compton Village Motel located directly across the street from the racetrack. Marion was still too weak to return to the races so he, impatiently, was confined to the motel room while the races were being run only a few furlongs away. Tim and Tami were outside playing in the pool but were advised by their grandfather to stop their frolicking each time the horses left the gate. The motel was so close to the racetrack that track announcer Alan Drake's race call could be heard from across the street.

Indian Nation was one of the Van Berg runners in that day and Marion was intent on knowing how he ran. Immediately after the race, he called Tim in for a report, "How did it go, boy?" said Van Berg. An excited young Tim Van Berg exclaimed, "I don't know for sure, but all I heard was the track announcer say 'Indian Nation owns the racetrack!' I think he won big, Grandpa?" He won by eight lengths. After going 0 for 15 the year before at age six, Indian Nation won 7 of 25 at age seven. At age sixty-six, M. H. Van Berg would not experience a similar regeneration. But despite multiple sieges on his health, Marion mustered, recovered, and resumed his routine as best he could.

One fall day at Hazel Park in 1965 Marion was carried to the racetrack first-aid room after suffering a mild heart attack. The nurse and doctor ordered the television monitor turned off so they could focus their attention on the patient. Their patient had no patience and requested that the monitor be turned back on so he could watch his horse run in the next race. After Marion saw his horse leave the winner's circle, he was taken to the hospital by ambulance. But Van Berg refused to be carried to the hospital on the gurney in back; he rode up front with the ambulance driver.

Marion's routine was to maintain the vise grip he had as the national leading owner of thoroughbred racehorses. But in the mid-'60s he began to alter the number of days he was on the road and away from Columbus and Viola. In 1965 he was the trainer of record for just 86 starters; the previous year he had already cut back to 295 starters. Marion Van Berg wasn't downsizing, he was just leaving the training and travelling to his son Jack or to Bob Irwin. In 1966 he trained only 49 horses, and in 1967 M. H. Van Berg started zero horses as a trainer, yet he carried on as the nation's leading owner. 1968 was the first year Jack led the nation in races won for a trainer: 1,152 starters, 256 winners. It began a title-holding father-and-son one-two punch that continued for three years. While Jack was primary in the day-to-day training of the horses in the late 1960s,

Marion still remained active in ownership. He purchased the Argentine-bred Zorba II who had been prominent in the principal stakes at Monter-rico Racecourse in Lima, Peru. For two summers, Zorba II routinely made headlines in the handicap races at Ak-Sar-Ben and led the M. H. Van Berg stable in earnings in consecutive years beginning in 1969.

However, it was in 1969 that Marion's world took a direct shot to the bow, and it had nothing to do with his own health. His loving wife, Viola, had a stroke. The quiet, nurturing, often unsung hero of the Van Berg family was now in a battle to save herself. But she was not left help-less. Viola became confined to a wheelchair, and so the family roles were reversed. Her children and husband now doted on her. Viola's daughter Betty Scholz lovingly remembers her mother: "Mom was always so calm and compassionate and kind. Even after her stroke, she never grumbled or complained. I guess you could say she was close to a saint." On September 24, 1970, Viola Van Berg joined the heavenly saints.

Viola was Marion's rock, and when she was gone, he was crushed. So many of his life's trials and an equal amount of his travels he had shared with his beloved Viola. Marion endured financial ruin and bounced back from heart attacks, but his heart had never felt this sort of pain and loss. Things would not get better.

In December of 1970, at age seventy-four, Marion underwent surgery for the overdue repair of a hernia injury. Jack flew into Omaha to be with his father for the operation. After the surgery at Bergan Mercy Hospi-tal, located just up the hill from Ak-Sar-Ben, Dr. Pantano informed Jack that the surgery had gone as expected, so Jack caught the Braniff airlines direct flight back to New Orleans later that day. But a few hours later, complications developed with Marion's recovery. The years of working with an overtaxed heart took a catastrophic toll. Marion had a stroke. The following morning, after Jack had just returned to Mary Jane and the kids in New Orleans, he received a call from Dr. Pantano informing him of the bad news.

"I was in the process of looking at a horse for Roger Wilson and he heard the news about Dad, so Roger told me to go the airport with Mary Jane and he'd have his plane waiting for me to fly us back to Omaha to be with Dad. That Roger was a good man," said Jack.

This time the impact of the trauma was significant. The stroke caused Marion to lose his ability to speak, and he was left a considerably weaker man. When he was able to travel after the incident, Marion was flown down to New Orleans to live with Jack and his family at their lakefront home. While his strength was sapped, his spirit was not. Marion still wanted to be at the barn to oversee what he could. Often, he would make his observations from the car as horses were jogged by for his examination.

One morning, Marion had enough strength to work his way into the barn. While seated inside he noticed a horse take an odd step as it was being walked around the corner under the shedrow of the barn. Marion pointed and kept pointing to that horse with his cane. His speech was so bad that he couldn't vocalize what he wanted to express. Finally the horse was brought up to him and he pointed to one of its hooves. "The hoof looked fine, but he made us poke around on the underside of the hoof, which we did," said Jack. "Sure enough, the horse had a hidden abscess that popped open at the coronet band above the hoof. My dad was amazing with what he could see inside a horse."

At the conclusion of the Fair Grounds meet in April, the Van Berg family made its northern migration back home to headquarters in Columbus for the start of the Ak-Sar-Ben meet. But even the comforts of home would not prevent what would ultimately be the final days for Marion. Still, his wisdom, passion, and discipline would prevail. Driving home to Columbus after looking at the horses in Omaha, Jack pulled over to get a hamburger and french fries from McDonald's. He and his dad were eating their lunch while heading down the road and Marion offered Jack his fries.

Jack reached over and took a bigger handful than Marion had expected. Marion snatched the fries back and actually spoke out, "I didn't say you could have all of them." Jack was never too old to be scolded. Those would be the last words Jack heard from his father. The final weekend of April, Jack was back home in Columbus after another week of traveling. He had promised to take his wife Mary Jane out to dinner that night, but before dinner she told Jack that "Dad" wanted to see him. When Jack got to the house Marion pointed to the sale barn. He knew that his dad wanted to hear him go auction some at the sale. So Jack went out to the barn and auctioned cattle for two hours straight. Dinner with Mary Jane would have to wait.

The following day Jack was up early to drive to Omaha for Sunday morning training at Ak-Sar-Ben; Marion stayed home. On Monday morning, May 3, 1971, Jack was back in Columbus tending to horses at the racehorse barn and readying for another sale. He got a call to come over to the house. Marion was not doing well, so he was driven straight to Bergan Mercy in Omaha. Shortly after Marion was admitted Jack was told that he'd better get to Omaha. Once again, Jack was headed east on Highway 30. He knew the reality at his destination would not be good. Jack remembers, "When I was headed to Dad's room in the hospital I could see Dr. Pantano walking down the hallway towards me, and he was crying. He told me what I already knew. He told me my dad was gone."

The funeral in Columbus was a major event. It was as if the town had shut down. A genuine local, regional, and national hero had died. Horsemen and cattlemen from around the country arrived to show their respect to the family of Marion H. Van Berg. An announcer for the local radio station, KJSK, reported from nearby the Columbus Cemetery: "Throngs of people and cars are still passing by the cemetery and it is long after dark. I've been here for forty-four years and I've never seen anything like this happen before." Jack has his own bitter memory: "The day of the funeral

I went out back and sat on a cattle pen fence for hours. I didn't want to be around anyone. Dad and I were close."

Three days after the death of a legend, Omaha recognized that legend with a Marion H. Van Berg Memorial Day at Ak-Sar-Ben. In the gray misty rain, a caparisoned, riderless horse was led in front of the grandstand; empty boots facing backwards—honoring a deceased comrade— were fixed in the stirrups. The Van Berg box, where Mr. and Mrs. Van had sat for decades, was empty and shrouded in black draping. It was an eerie sight that was made even more mesmerizing when ten thousand patrons stood silent and motionless and listened to the bugler play taps. All was calm. Everyone was moved.

18

Memories of Marion

With Marion's passing in 1971, he left behind innumerable memories in the hearts and minds of those who knew him. "I found out that the older I got, the smarter my dad was," said Jack Van Berg, "and not just with the horses, with many of his approaches to life." That said, Jack did have some favorite lessons from his father regarding horses. He recalls, "If I told him a horse was sore in his shoulder, he'd say, 'If you fix what's underneath he'll be okay up above.' Or if I said I had one that was off behind, he'd say, 'If you fix the front the rear will follow.' Things like that you learn, and it sticks with you."

The 1971 *American Racing Manual* spells out Marion Van Berg's training philosophy, in his own words: "Winning is the name of the game. However if you can't win the race, be second. And if you can't get second money, try to be third." That's a pretty simple approach. That's purely no-frills Nebraskan.

It was a rare event for a Van Berg to take a vacation, but the oddity occurred once when Jack and his wife Mary Jane went to California in 1966. From the command post in Columbus, Jack's sister Helen delegated their sister Ginny (Virginia) to go down to the Fair Grounds in New Orleans to keep an eye on Marion while Jack was away. Virginia had a wonderful ten days in New Orleans with her dad—she recalls that it involved both enjoying and *enduring* some of her father's quirky ways . . .

Dad was a horrible creature of habit. And he was equally horribly impatient. He loved going to the same places for service or to eat. He liked to establish himself so that when he would show up, the staff would get to it. I remember setting my alarm clock extra early so that I wouldn't keep Dad waiting. I'd get dressed, fix my hair, and then lie back down in bed and wait for him. At six o'clock he'd knock on my door, I'd hop into my shoes, and away we'd go. We ate at the same place for breakfast, lunch, and dinner the whole time I was at the Fair Grounds. Only once did I get him to take me to the Roosevelt Hotel, just off Canal Street, and he was so uncomfortable the whole time. He liked simple food, too. I remember when he raced in Detroit, we always ate dinner at Wigwam—and it was a buffet. I loved caring for Dad when I was in New Orleans, and the kicker was, he told a friend that he thought I was down visiting because I was having troubles in my marriage. It never dawned on him I was there for him. And Dad hated to drive, but he loved to give driving instructions—if he stayed awake. He was famous for falling asleep in the car almost immediately. But if he was awake, you knew it. Once on a drive into Eppley Airfield in Omaha, he told me every car to pass and every lane to change, and when to speed up and when to slow down. My sister Eleanor was in the car with us, too, and when we dropped him off at the airport, I looked at my sister and told her if she said one word about my driving she'd have to *walk* back home to Columbus. Dad was so much better in the car when he was sleeping.

Family members aren't the only ones who remember Marion's quirky ways and wisdom—not to mention his delivery.

Larry Snyder was the leading jockey in North America in 1969 after he booted home 352 winners. He was a leading jockey at Arlington Park twice, but it was in the mid-South where Snyder sparkled. He was a six-time leading jockey at Louisiana Downs from 1981 to 1986 and topped the Oaklawn Park rider standings eight times. Voted the George Woolf

Memorial Jockey Award recipient in 1989, at the time of his retirement
he was one of only six jockeys in U.S. racing history to ride more than
six thousand winners. Throughout his career, Larry rode more than one
thousand races for Marion and Jack and did so with an amazing 20 percent
win rate. Of course the down side is that he lost 80 percent of the time he
rode for the Van Bergs. Larry recalls that the otherwise like-minded father
and son differed in the manner they would give you a piece of their mind
after the race.

> Mr. Van would wait until the next day to tell you what he thought
> you did wrong in a race; Jack would let you have it right then and
> there. The morning after a race, Mr. Van would say, *"Boy!"*—
> he'd always call ya "boy." "Boy! I told you I wanted you to be
> off the pace—why were you up on the lead?" And then I'd have
> to explain myself in what I knew would be a losing battle. But if
> he told you he wanted you to lay third and you laid third and you
> still lost, well then he wouldn't blame you. He was fair like that,
> but he sure hated to lose. Jack, on the other hand, was different.
> He'd undress you before you got a chance to get back to the jock's
> room to change silks. Jack would start in on you before you could
> drop your feet out of the stirrup irons and he'd walk with you
> scolding you all the way back to the room. That's a long walk
> back when you've got Jack in your ear and on your ass.

Phil Georgeff is in the Guinness Book of World Records for having
called more than ninety-six thousand races in his career. He is known for
his distinct voice and his famous race call expression *"Here they come,*
spinning out of the turn!" Phil started galloping horses as a young man.
He worked at the thoroughbred tracks by day and called races at the trot-
ters by night. The bulk of his work in racing was at the Chicago-area racetracks where he has fond memories of Marion. "M. H. Van Berg didn't
make much noise at the national stakes level; he was primarily a regional

claiming trainer. But he was respected by so many for what he did without having a barn full of stakes horses," said Georgeff. "I think he was the sweetest man in racing."

Although his career in the saddle was relatively short for a rider who was the 1960 leading rider at Oaklawn Park and at Ak-Sar-Ben, Larry Spraker forged a career and lifetime in horse racing. After his riding career ended, "Sprake," as he is commonly called on the racetrack, was an assistant trainer to Johnny Hart and later trained some on his own. He then became a jockey agent and had immediate success with David Whited and later kept book for George Woolf Award–winning jockey John Lively. Larry Spraker gushes with pride and awe when he recalls M. H. Van Berg. "I worshiped the man," said Spraker. "He'd do anything for you to help you, as long as he could see that you were trying to help yourself. He would help you if you were a jockey, another trainer, whatever you were." Larry still speaks in amazement of Marion's training prowess and his willingness to share his knowledge. "I remember we claimed a horse in Detroit and the horse had bled badly. This was years before Lasix was used to treat bleeders. I was coming off the racetrack and Mr. Van could see that I was pretty overwhelmed by it. He said, 'If you want some advice on how to stop that bleeding, boy, I can help you out.' He told me to tie some copper wire around the base of the horse's tail and I'll be damned if it didn't work." Spraker concluded, "He was an amazing man and he was everybody's friend."

Richard Rettele is from a family of jockeys, exercise riders, and trainers who came out of Baileyville, Kansas. He spent most of his career with thoroughbreds but gained national attention as a senior citizen, riding and winning quarter horses well into his early seventies. Richard galloped many of the stars trained by Marion and Jack, such as Bouncer, Little Everett, Redbird Wish, Royal Course, and Ramblin Road. "Marion was as good a horseman and as good a man as there ever was on the racetrack," Rettele said. "He could look at a horse that wasn't right training or doing something wrong and he would claim him or buy him and turn that horse into something good. He knew horses as good on the inside as he did on the outside." Richard was equally impressed with how Marion observed and looked after his help: "He took those boys from Columbus under his wing and really made something out of them. He was a father figure to them and he'd watch after them and doctor them and do whatever he could to care for them. For me, working for Mr. Van was a great and important experience in my life."

David Whited was a popular jockey throughout the 1970s. He was a leading rider at Fair Grounds, Ak-Sar-Ben, Keeneland, Churchill Downs, Detroit Race Course, and Hazel Park. Whited currently operates a thoroughbred training facility east of Hot Springs, Arkansas. He is equally skilled as a trainer as he was as a rider. Much of what David learned about training he learned from Marion Van Berg. "I don't feel there was any greater horseman. Mr. Van saw everything," said Whited. "Once in Omaha Jack claimed a horse and it ran third. A few days later Mr. Van was observing all the horses in the barn. After seeing, for the first time, the horse Jack had just claimed, Mr. Van said, 'Don't run that one back until Detroit.' Well, they waited and it won in Detroit." And then, understatedly, yet tremendously poignantly, the Arkansan stated something eloquent: "Jack and Marion were exactly alike; the difference is that the world caught up with Jack, it didn't catch up with Marion." Think about that.

Chuck Karlin—grandson of Marion, son of Marion's daughter Helen—recalled Marion's words and actions in moments of adversity. He shared the remarkable story of what occurred after a barn fire at Hazel Park.

During and after the fire, many horses were released from their stalls to be freed from the barn fire and kept away from potential danger. The loose horses were routed off the backstretch and into the infield of the racetrack for safe keeping. When it was time for the horses to be returned, there was confusion as to which horses belonged to whom. The infield had become a remuda of refugees. Marion was renowned for his uncanny ability to identify horses, so his memory was called upon to help the sorting process. They positioned him at the track gap and when a horse was led by, he identified the horse and to what trainer it belonged. Marion did this until the infield was cleared for all but one horse. Marion struggled to identify it and finally gave up, concluding that the horse must not have ever galloped over the racetrack. When the animal was finally identified, it was determined that it had come in on a trailer just hours before the fire. In fact, the horse had never stepped onto the Hazel Park racetrack.

Chuck further recalls Marion's tough love and pragmatic side when he was a child and spent the summer with his grandparents in Detroit. "I was sniffling and whimpering and feeling homesick and Grandpa heard me and asked me, 'What's the matter, boy?' I told him that I missed Mom and wanted to go back home. He said, 'Let me tell ya, boy, life is tough! It gets tougher all the time. Just get prepared for it.' That's about as good a lesson as I ever had," smiled Karlin.

Chuck's mother, Helen, was a tireless worker for Marion and the family business. She worked at the Columbus Sales Pavilion well beyond retirement age. When asked what she valued most from what she learned from her father, with a purposeful pause and in a calmly, contemplative manner, Helen succinctly said, "No self-pity! Whatever comes your way, you work through it."

It is a motivating mantra. Long live the memories of M. H. Van Berg.

19

The Estate of M. H. Van Berg

Technically, the torch had been passed to Jack months, if not years, prior to Marion's passing. A path had been paved, an infrastructure was in place, and the result was many racehorses in several barns across the nation. But for Jack the emotional result coursed much deeper. A son had lost his father; however, the flame of his father's message and his father's mission still lit his path. The *message* was unwavering horsemanship; the *mission* was to win races. The difference was that now the owner line in the official racing program read "The Estate of M. H. Van Berg."

When Bob Irwin and Jack had some time together after Marion's death, Jack assured Bob that they'd keep running the stable the same way they had. Jack said, "We'll just keep going and you can stay if you want to." But Irwin said he'd rather go out on his own. Jack told him that he understood and invited him to not only take whatever tack he wanted, but also whatever horses he wanted. "Bob took five or six horses and I didn't charge him a thing. He spent his whole life with Dad. He was responsible for a lot of our success," Van Berg said gratefully.

The show must go on, and it did, but in the immediate months that followed when Jack was alone, his emotions and memories of his father would often spill out. And in the solitude of driving a load of horses down the lonely road, Jack would remember his father and begin to cry. "I had gotten into the habit of calling him every night to tell him my thoughts about training the horses. I did this for years with him," Jack said. "It was quite a loss to not have him to talk to. He was my father; he had become my best friend and he was my mentor."

Jack dealt not only with the personal sorrow and stresses he that felt in-side, but he also faced negative exterior forces. There were more than a few people on the racetrack who predicted a collapse of the Van Berg creation with Marion's passing, and many preyed off of Jack, too. Trainer Hal Bishop readily claimed horses away from the vulnerable Van Berg. Jack remembers how he lost his confidence and how he gave the naysay-ers good reason to think what they did:

> I felt a lot of pressure because many people were expecting me to fall on my face, and it began to take its toll on me. It seemed like until about November of the year Dad died I was afraid to run horses in the spots where they belonged. I was training like someone who had never been in the claiming business. I was not putting horses in the right races. Someone would claim a horse from me and do good with it and then make me look bad. People were talking behind my back and saying, "You won't see Jack anymore." Or they said, "He's done." That kinda talk was all over the racetrack, and it really got into my head for a while.

Fortunately, Jack had support from his family, his close friends, and his key employees, and he and his sister Helen managed the estate as their father had prescribed. But it was a rough half a year of racing and living for Jack. The summer and months that followed became a blur as Jack just went through the motions in the Midwest. With the change in the season, it was time for him to migrate to the South, to his second home in New Orleans.

Racing in New Orleans was nothing new for Jack; he had previous-ly been the leading Fair Grounds trainer for five consecutive years. But Jack approached the change in atmosphere with an optimistic outlook. He was hopeful that his return would be a welcome and refreshing relief from what he had battled since May. It worked. The shift to his south-ern surroundings was just the boost and change that he needed. With a cleared mind and new possibilities on the horizon, Jack plotted a course that would have him pointed to the West. Instead of entering the racetrack via a familiar stable gate off of Gentilly Boulevard in New Orleans, Jack would be a newcomer accessing a backstretch off of Baldwin Avenue in Arcadia, California. It didn't signify just a new chapter in his life—it was part II.

PART II

20

Gold West Young Man

The divisions of the Van Berg dominance flowed from the Missouri and Ohio River Valleys deep into the Mississippi Delta, and touched as far east as the shores of the Atlantic Ocean. In 1849 a path to the Pacific proved both fruitful and fateful for tens of thousands who wallowed in Northern California millstreams and wandered in redwood forests in pursuit of their golden fortune. In Southern California, more than a hundred years after a great gold rush, a driven man drove his horses west, seeking fortune under some swaying palms at the foothills of the San Gabriel Mountains. It wasn't Sutter's Mill; it was Santa Anita Park, but the luster and lure were just as captivating for thirty-six-year-old Jack Van Berg.

In the winter of 1971, while Jack was racing at the Fair Grounds in New Orleans, Catfish Smith arranged for Jack to meet Nelson Bunker Hunt, the oil company executive and former billionaire who would become infamous for his catastrophic investment mistake in the world silver market. Catfish (Clarence L. Smith) was much more than an introducer; he was a former Georgia Tech and Chicago Bears football player who raced the incredibly talented thoroughbred Hillsdale. The Indiana-bred colt won nine stakes races in 1959 and collided with the likes of Bald Eagle, Round Table, Tim Tam, and Sword Dancer. Jack recalls a day that pushed his paper-thin patience to the limit:

> I didn't know Bunker Hunt from a load of hay, but he flew me to Dallas to meet with him at his farm. They were having a Charolais cattle sale that day and Bunker sat down in the front row and watched that damn cattle all day long. I sat around in the back

all day waiting to meet him and it was starting to get dark. I told Catfish that my time was just as important as his time and that I was going back to the airport to fly back to New Orleans. So Catfish quickly got Mr. Hunt out of the cattle barn and we finally got to visit out back in the hog shed. Bunker told me that he wanted me to train for him, but I told him, "Mr. Hunt, you don't know me and I don't know you. You might not like me and I might not like you." I said, "I'll train by the day for you and we'll see how we get along." He said he wanted me to take thirty horses to California to train at Santa Anita. I told him I wanted $25 a day; I was getting $20 a day in the Midwest. When he told me that he was paying $17 a day, I told him then he must have been getting cheated along the way. I said there was no way I could do it for less than $25. So he agreed. Bunker told me he'd assemble them up in Kentucky so I could go up and look them over. Well, there really wasn't much to choose from, but I took seven of them and they all did okay.

Another golden reason to go west was Golden Eagle II. The colt was a son of Right Royal, the French-bred winner of the French Derby and the French Two Thousand Guineas. Marion purchased the horse after Wayne Murty told him, "This colt is the best-looking horse you'll ever see." Wayne and his brother Duane, from Guymon, Oklahoma, were jockeys in their younger days, and in 1953 the pair finished in a dead-heat win at the Columbus Races. The two Okies went on to make quite a name for themselves in the European bloodstock industry. When the import from France finally arrived in Chicago, the trans-Atlantic journey and the two weeks of quarantine in Florida had taken their toll. Jack recalled how poor Golden Eagle II looked: "That son-of-a-buck looked terrible after he came out of quarantine. I'll never forget what Dad said when he saw the horse up at Sportsman's Park. He called Murty up and said, 'If you damn dummies think that is a good-looking horse, you've got to be crazy.' But we worked on him and got him right. He was a nice horse." Golden Eagle II was training in Chicago, and when the turf options in the Midwest ended for the season, Jack shipped him to Laurel Park Racecourse in Maryland, where he won the mile and 1/16 Congressional Handicap.

The French invader was rounding into top form, and Jack knew he needed to keep his horse on the boil—and on the turf. Jack had been itching to give Southern California racing a try, and he knew that his budding turf star would be his golden ticket. Van Berg, his assistant Loren Rettele, and Golden Eagle II arrived in Arcadia, California, in December of 1971, with dead aim on the Santa Anita Park turf stakes. Just a week after King Of Cricket won the Malibu Stakes for trainer Noble Threewitt, Jack sent Golden Eagle II out to win his Santa Anita bow in an allowance race. In his next start he finished just behind the classy and in-form Big Shot II but in front of The Pruner. That game second-place finish in the San Marcos Handicap further validated Van Berg's legitimate presence on the West Coast. Golden Eagle II then finished third in the Arcadia Handicap, followed by second in the San Luis Obispo.

Then Jack's presence and perseverance paid off when Golden Eagle II won in the San Bernardino Handicap on the grass. Jack got 60 percent of the $50,000 purse for the win, but he scored significantly more from a subsequent sale after the win. Throughout the Santa Anita meet, Jack had been entertaining offers to sell Golden Eagle II. Money was not scarce for Sigmund Sommer, one of a few prospective buyers who had designs on Golden Eagle II. The extremely successful New York building contractor structured success in racing, as well. Sommer was familiar with the Van Berg racing operation. He chased Marion and Jack in races-won for a few years and was fourth in the national thoroughbred owner earnings in 1970. He became the nation's leading owner in money won in 1971 (the year Marion passed away) and again in 1972. Sigmund Sommer's pockets and passion were deep. His trainer was eventual Hall of Fame trainer Frank "Pancho" Martin. The Cuban-born Martin was to New York racing what M. H. Van Berg was to midwestern racing. Marion and Pancho were similar in many ways; they were both esteemed horsemen, rigid in their ideas and methods, and respected by many. Many say Martin was unjustly depicted in 2010 film *Secretariat*. Indeed, he was the trainer of Sham (owned by Sommer), but he was not the vulgar and mean-spirited man he was portrayed as in the movie.

Jack knew Sigmund and Pancho were teaming to get their hands on Golden Eagle II. So hoping to get all he could for the now stakes-winning stallion, Jack spun his magic even more. "They thought I was some country bumpkin, and so I just played along," Jack said. "I told Pancho that I didn't know how to train a grass horse and thought maybe somebody else could do better with him." After a ninth-place finish in the San Juan Capistrano Handicap, a deal was struck. As long as there are horses, there will be horse trading, and Jack swapped Golden Eagle II to Pancho for a clutch of cash and a few horses. Jack sold one of the newly acquired horses as a stallion to stand in Europe. Pollution was another horse that he got in the trade. He took him back to New York in the fall and won a few races with him. And then, when Jack ran Pollution in a high-priced claiming race, Pancho Martin claimed him back for $40,000. Golden Eagle II never won again after the trade, but he was purchased by John C. Mabee and became a charter stallion for Golden Eagle Farm in Ramona, California.

For many Americans who experience Southern California for the first time, especially those who have endured a Nebraska winter, a kind of awe of the place can envelop the mind and body. This first toe in the water for Jack Van Berg would lead to a return and, ultimately, a total western immersion.

Aside from Golden Eagle II and the Nelson Bunker Hunt horses that took Jack to the Golden State, Jack also brought with him something homespun from Nebraska. British Fleet was a colt by Sonny Fleet, whom M. H. Van Berg had raced and bred to his favorite mare, Estacion. Although Marion passed away before he could see his homebred run, Jack knew British Fleet would give his dad something to enjoy from up above. Jack ran British Fleet during his first Santa Anita meet in 1972. "I was really high on the colt, but John Sellers rode him, and after he came back he told me, 'Jack, he's just a horse. He ain't much.' Oh that really got me steamed and I didn't care much for John after that. He was wrong! I knew he could run," said Jack. British Fleet had already had a prosperous freshman year at Ak-Sar-Ben prior to his Santa Anita appearance. He had developed quite a rivalry with Aye Jay Aye, whom he beat in both the Futurity and Juvenile Stakes but ran second to in the Laddie Stakes.

By the time British Fleet returned to his home soil in Nebraska at age three, he was primed again for action. In the Good Neighbor Stakes the order of finish was British Fleet, Aye Jay Aye, and Great Commander. In the Breeders' Stakes, Aye Jay Aye countered over British Fleet and Great Commander. In one of his most significant wins, British Fleet was moved out of restricted stakes and defeated open company in the $50,000 Omaha Gold Cup. Then, in an incredibly sentimental race, British Fleet won the inaugural running of the Marion H. Van Berg Stakes in front of an overjoyed and overwhelmed Ak-Sar-Ben grandstand. Marion Van Berg was assuredly celebrated in name and in spirit. It was divine. Hard-trying Aye Jay Aye finished second again. In an encore performance, British Fleet won in the open-company $50,000 President's Cup at the end of the meet. Furthermore, in that summer of '72, British Fleet, the son of Sonny Fleet, won those final three stakes races in Omaha on three consecutive Saturdays. Later that year, Jack Van Berg, the son of Marion Van Berg, led the nation again with a record-setting 286 wins. It was like sire, like son. It was like father, like son. It was thoroughly Van Berg.

21

Trainer for Hire

A s 1972 unfolded, Jack continued what he had done when Marion was still alive. He kept divisions of horses around the country and trained in the same manner his father had taught him. But now instead of striving to keep just his father pleased, often with on-the-job training, Jack was now getting on-the-job schooling in the techniques of dealing with owners. Previously, the only colors under the Van Berg shedrows had been purple and gold, but that changed as Jack began working for other owners. The prism of agreements and disagreements with owners (other than his father) was becoming enlightening. Jack recalls a point of contention that popped up with one of his newfound owners:

> After the Santa Anita meet I shipped three of Bunker Hunt's hors-
> es to New York where I was getting $30 a day, and I shipped three
> to Omaha where I was getting $20 a day. So when I sent in my
> bill, I billed him just like that. When I got my check from Mr.
> Hunt, I only got paid $25 for the ones in New York and $20 for the
> ones in Omaha. Well, I thought that wasn't right, so I called him
> up and told him how I wanted to get paid based on my Omaha
> rates and my New York rates. Well, he told me, "We made a deal
> for $25." I said, "But Mr. Hunt, I only charged you $20 for the
> ones in Omaha." He told me, "That's your hard luck." So that's
> how that went.

By late autumn of 1972, W. O. Bridge, owner of the emerging Shin-rone Farm, adopted the approach of "if you can't beat them, join them." Mr. Bridge approached Jack at Detroit Race Course and made him an offer to buy all 116 horses that were racing and owned by the Estate of M. H. Van Berg. With the goal of becoming the leading owner in the nation, and with an agreement of a universal $25-per-day training fee, the horses transferred in ownership. The Van Berg purple and gold yielded to the Shinrone white and green.

William Oldfield Bridge was a trucking company executive, a successful cattleman, and he more than dabbled in horse racing. In 1971 Bridge had only twelve winners; in 1972 he had eighteen winners. With the infusion of the Van Berg runners and the Jack Van Berg training, the Shinrone Farm numbers were destined to improve. In 1973 Jack won his sixth Detroit Race Course training title with a record eighty-one wins. Many of those winners bore the Shinrone colors. Shinrone Farm concluded 1973 with sixty-eight wins and was ranked eighteenth in the nation in races won, with earnings of $264,132. Jack was not the exclusive trainer for Shinrone, but he did advise and broker the acquisition of a number of horses that won for the outfit, and he trained the majority of the starters.

From 1968 through 1974, the JVB initials began to stand on their own as Jack dominated the national trainer standings; in that span, only trainer Dale Baird surpassed Jack in the races-won category. Baird first took the title from Jack in 1971, winning 245 races to Jack's 190. In 1972, Jack was back on top with a record 286 wins. The exchange continued; in 1973 Baird retook the title from Van Berg with 305 wins and earnings of $416,592. Jack finished second with 281 winners and earnings of $1,401,492.

In 1974, with Jack clearly at the helm, Shinrone Farm began to win races in bulk. The most Marion and Jack Van Berg had won in a year during their reign prior to Marion's death was a record 282 races. W. O. Bridge had already surpassed that mark, and he could almost taste victory in becoming the leading owner in the nation. Bridge was clear of the perennial powerhouses such as Audley Farm, Hobeau Farm, and Sig-

mund Sommer. The only obstacle was owner Dan Lasater. A self-starter
and rapid riser, Lasater went from flipping hamburgers at age twenty to
retiring at age twenty-eight as an executive vice president for the Pon-
derosa Steakhouse restaurant chain. His stable sprouted onto the scene,
and he was the leading owner in 1973. By October of 1974, Shinrone
Farm already had won four hundred races, but so had Lasater. The stage
was set for a battle all the way to the end of the year. Then, suddenly, there
was a dangerous and serious twist to the plot: an important player in the
Shinrone production became seriously ill. Jack got sick. It was during the
Hazel Park meet, which was then a fall race meet. Jack recalls how he was
initially misdiagnosed with leukemia:

> I was staying at the Hilton Hotel in Troy, Michigan, and each
> morning I'd wake up drenched in sweat. I'd soak an entire queen-
> sized bed. We raced at 3:30, so I'd go back to the room at noon
> to take a short nap and when I'd wake up then I'd be covered in
> sweat again. I called Dr. Pantano back in Omaha and he told me
> what medication I needed to have prescribed. Mr. Bridge lined
> me up with a doctor there in Detroit, but he only gave me some
> sample prescription drugs and not what Pantano had suggested. I
> never got to feeling any better so I got on a plane and flew back
> to Omaha to see Dr. Pantano. Frank Kirby was with the horses in
> Chicago, so he met me there at the airport during my layover. We
> discussed the horses in training and I sat there in the coffee shop
> and sweat right through my jacket. It was a bad deal. They ran
> some tests and originally thought I might have leukemia, but it
> turned out it was only encephalitis. It was still serious and it really
> knocked me out for a few weeks.

Benny Ciboron and Diane Alexander, two capable understudies,
served as stand-ins for Jack in Detroit while he was hospitalized. But the
sickness that temporarily put Van Berg out of commission was ultimately

more debilitating to W. O. Bridge. Jack was able to overcome his illness with hospitalization, medication, and rest. Not so for the bug that worked into his barn while he was away.

When Jack was in the hospital, he got a puzzling phone call from W. O. Bridge. Mr. Bridge claimed that Jack had told his people to quit working at the Shinrone Farm facility that was located in Bloomfield Hills, Michigan. Jack had done nothing of the sort. In fact, he learned that when his men showed up to work at the farm, they were turned away per Mr. Bridge's instructions. Jack told his workers from the hospital, "As long as these horses are running under my name as trainer I'll see to it that they are taken care of," and he instructed them to return back to the farm. Bridge was on the attack in his phone conversation, and according to Jack, Bridge told him, "You took the first shot at me, now I'll take the next. . . . You must have been having illusions due to your high fever to tell your workers what you did." The salvo ended when Jack told Bridge, "I sure as hell wasn't having illusions when I entered those horses and we won five yesterday." That battle may have ended, but the relationship was scarred. An end was near. Fortunately, it wasn't long thereafter that Jack's health improved enough for him to return to training.

Jack moved his stock of horses down to New Orleans and prepared for another successful Fair Grounds meet, a meet he had won eight of the previous ten seasons. Throughout December Jack was winning races at the Fair Grounds, and so was Shinrone Farm, and the pair was winning races together beyond New Orleans—but they didn't win enough. Dan Lasater won the 1974 national owner title with 494 wins. W. O. Bridge's Shinrone Farm ran second with 459 wins; roughly 300 of those winners were trained by Jack.

Earlier in the year, Frank Kirby had asked Jack if he would help his friend Bob Scallion with the horses Scallion had stabled in Chicago. Jack obliged and provided useful horse training insight to the aspiring trainer; evidentially, Scallion was also a conspiring trainer. Bob Scallion was close to W. O. Bridge, and the two men spent plenty of time together in the Shinrone Farm box seats at the Detroit race meets. Jack thought they were suspiciously close, and his suspicions held up on the morning of the first day of the next year.

On New Year's Day, 1975, Bob Scallion appeared outside of Barn 12 at the Fair Grounds. It was then and there that Jack was informed by Bob Scallion that he was no longer the trainer of the Shinrone Farm horses. When Scallion told Jack that he wanted to come into the barn to look at the horses, Jack threatened, "If you take one step into my barn, I'm going to knock you into the middle of next week." Scallion backed up, but his horse vans sure didn't back up. Transportation had already been arranged, and truck drivers were waiting in the stable gate parking lot to van the horses away. By the end of the morning, all of the Shinrone Farm horses in New Orleans had been loaded up and were destined for New Jersey. Frank Kirby took over training all the horses for $20 a day. By the end of the day, Van Berg had been relieved of all 220 horses across the nation that he was training for W. O. Bridge's Shinrone Farm.

22

Building and Rebuilding

When Jack lost his father, it was a tremendous emotional loss, but at least he still had horses to train. When the Shinrone horses were taken from him, it stung his pride, but this time the biggest loss wasn't emotional—it was the physical and financial loss of all the horses. The meet was under way in New Orleans and Jack had an empty barn—and it wasn't the only barn Jack had that was lacking horses.

When he lost the work for Shinrone, Jack had been in the process of building a farm and full-service training facility in Goshen, Kentucky, where he had purchased 540 acres in partnership with Dravo Foley. Jack knew Dravo from his days of racing in Detroit. Foley won the training title at River Downs in Ohio many times, and the Foley and Van Berg families had raced against each other in friendly competition for years. Ultimately, Dravo and his family settled into a forty-acre corner of the plot and Jack set out to develop the remaining five hundred acres. Big plans went headlong into big interest rates; nevertheless, the construction and cultivation of the farm's business moved forward against the odds. "I had already made my down payment and ordered all the steel for the new, big barn, and then the country went into a damn recession," Van Berg said. "It was bad timing, so I had to overcome all that." Another frustration—Jack never got any big business from the Lexington horsemen for the project.

I was never accepted by the people in Lexington. I'd done some favors and a little work for some big names there in Lexington and brokered some deals on some nice horses, but I never got business from any of the big outfits. The only person to show any interest in me was Bull Hancock [Arthur B. Hancock]. He sent Doc Harthill [Dr. Alex Harthill, DVM] to come and get me to talk about training for Claiborne Farm. We went to Bull's house there at Claiborne Farm in Paris, Kentucky, and had lunch. Bull told me he wanted me to train racehorses for him, and I told him that I was interested. He told me that he had to go on a hunting trip to Scotland, but we would finalize details when he got back. He got very sick on that trip and died a few weeks later.

Now Jack was trying to build and fill a barn in Kentucky and he was also trying to refill barns at racetracks across the land. What's more, he had a number of men on the payroll for him at the Fair Grounds without much work that needed to be done. "I kept all those men working for me in New Orleans except for the two Catalano boys. Both Wayne and Joe were riding then, too, and I figured it was time for them to go off on their own. I thought they could make it and they agreed," said Jack.

It didn't take long for horses to start finding new homes in the empty Van Berg stalls. Jack began training for Al M. Stall, Sr., who was heavily involved in Louisiana thoroughbred racing as an owner and breeder and served as a state racing commissioner for decades. His son Al M. Stall, Jr., commonly known as "Little Al," worked for Jack as a child, was an assistant to Frankie Brothers, and later went on to become a nationally successful trainer. Little Al trained Blame, the 2010 Breeders' Cup Classic winner and the only horse to have beaten the immortal Zenyatta. Both father and son have been inducted into the Fair Grounds Hall of Fame. The senior Stall placed a young filly by Damascus into Van Berg's care and she got her exceptional career started early. Regal Rumor won the Thelma Stakes in 1975, beating Pago Hop. She raced at Belmont, Monmouth, Keystone, Atlantic City, Hialeah, Churchill, throughout Chicago, Oaklawn, and as far west as Hollywood Park. The fantastic filly went on to win eight stakes at five tracks and won 17 of 36 races, earning $266,321. Regal Rumor was a terrific tonic for Jack's New Year's blues.

For the first time Jack was not training for one main man. Owners from coast to coast were eager for the chance to have Jack Van Berg as their trainer. They had seen what Jack had accomplished training his father Marion's horses and they also saw that he could handle the mass of Shinrone horses. Up until now, the gate had mostly been closed for outside owners who sought the services of trainer Jack Van Berg, but now the gate was open and the bell rang. The soliciting owners rang Jack's phone, but Jack did some of his own ringing and drumming up of business. As a result, new owners and partnerships began to pop up. The 1975 Oaklawn Park racing season was just weeks away when Jack formed an important owner partnership with Thomas Glover, a cattleman from Pine Bluff, Arkansas, along with fellow Arkansans Dan Baker and Jimmy Ford. The men formed a racing stable and named it Ridge Runner Stable. Another partnership came by way of Ken Opstein of Sioux City, Iowa, owner of Destroyer, who won the 1974 Santa Anita Derby and then went on to win the '74 Omaha Gold Cup. His trainer, Monti Sims, retired later that year, so Opstein turned his horses over to Jack. Ten years later, Van Berg and Opstein would team on a horse that would run in the biggest derby of them all, which would also result in one of the most infamous derby runs of all.

At the start of the summer of '75, Jack arrived at Ak-Sar-Ben with an entirely new set of horses. Many of his father's horses were gone or had blended into Shinrone Farm ownership, and of course now those horses were gone, too. But the rebuilding process did not sputter upon Jack's reaching Omaha; it continued to gain momentum as he returned home to Nebraska. What occurred in January seemingly had made no impact by July, as Van Berg successfully retained yet another leading trainer title at Ak-Sar-Ben that year.

At the end of a year that began with him getting fired and left with only thirty horses, Jack Van Berg closed out 1975 finishing sixth in the nation with 982 starts, 206 wins, and earnings of $991,690. In the owner standings, Shinrone Farm finished with 109 wins and $561,234 in earnings—roughly half of what Van Berg had accomplished. Just the year before, with Jack as his trainer, W. O. Bridge had finished with 350 more wins and nearly $1.5 million more in earnings. At least without Jack he could claim he saved $5 a day per horse on training fees.

23

An Omaha Opus

In March of 1975, Jack had a hunch about a nicely bred, under-achieving three-year-old colt at the Fair Grounds. In addition to the gray colt's undesirable habit of bolting in training and in his races, Gray Bar's earnings were equally unappealing—he won only $3,758 as a two-year-old. Nevertheless, Jack offered Dreabon Copeland $5,000 for the colt and promised him another $2,500 if the horse made $7,500. The men agreed, and by the end of March, Jack had a new project in his barn. Jack and owner Thomas Glover partnered up and gambled on what many assumed was simply damaged goods. As it turned out, the goods weren't damaged, but the jewels were.

Jack suspected that the colt's unruly behavior, which involved significantly drifting on turns and spinning sharply at a start (bolting and wheeling), was due to the horse having difficulties with an undescended testicle (cryptorchidism). "Gray Bar was a ridgling, so back in New Orleans the day I bought that son-of-a-buck, we went up there and got that nut out of his belly," said Jack. After the horse recovered from the fairly common surgical procedure, Jack sent Gray Bar to Hot Springs at the conclusion of the Oaklawn Park meet, where they began training him while waiting for the meet in Omaha to begin. Jockey Mary Bacon was getting on Gray Bar despite many other riders shying away from riding him due to what they had heard, or could deduce from his past performances.

On May 6, Jack ran Gray Bar in a modest, $6,500 claiming race at Ak-Sar-Ben; the horse won by two lengths. On May 14, Jack bumped Gray Bar up in class and ran him in a $9,000 claimer; he won that race, too. Then again, on just eight days' rest, Jack sent Gray Bar back to the well on May 22. This time he raised Gray Bar up to the $15,000 claiming level; he won by six. Now what? The gamble on Gray Bar had paid off in just two months. But the connections continued to press their luck. On June 6, with a fifteen-day respite from his string of three claiming wins in just a sixteen-day span, Gray Bar returned to the races in his first-ever allowance race. He broke well, found the lead, but faded to third. Had the gelding reached his glass ceiling? Rather than dropping down a rung on the class ladder, Gray Bar was next asked to climb farther up in class. Off a third-place finish in his first allowance race, and off another eight days of rest, Gray Bar was entered into his first-ever stakes race, the $25,000 Ak-Sar-Ben 4-H Handicap on June 14. He ran third, beaten just a length by Bold Trap. But the winner was disqualified for interference with the runner-up; therefore, Gray Bar was moved up from third to second. His owners, Glover and Van Berg, were awarded second-place money. Easing back on the throttle after the more-than-satisfying result in the Ak-Sar-Ben 4-H Handicap was never an option for Jack. The thirty-nine-year-old trainer knew his hearty horse was still training forwardly; he also knew that Gray Bar might earn him his first-ever $100,000 stakes win. Young Bill Mott was working for Jack at the time, primarily as one of Jack's gallop boys. Jack trusted Bill on all of his horses, but Jack was no less a taskmaster to Bill than he was with any other of his employees:

On the Sunday before the race, I told Billy that I wanted him to gallop Gray Bar a mile and then go the second mile in 1:55 or 1:56. So I'm on my pony at the finish line and he comes by the second time at the same easy gallop as he went by the first time— slow. So I rode out there on the track after him and I said, "Gawd damn it, I told you to go the second mile in 1:55; take him another mile." So he galloped him around there another mile and went the third mile at the same pace he had gone the first two laps. I rode up to him again and said, "Now, damn it, breeze this son-of-a-buck to the 3/4 pole." Billy thought I was crazy. Just ask him.

The concept of what Jack wanted to accomplish was not only a challenge for Bill to wrap his head around, sometimes it was a challenge just to get Gray Bar around the track. "Gray Bar could gallop slow or he could gallop fast, but he was difficult to regulate at an in-between speed. He'd either want to take off with you or he would want to bolt," recalls Bill Mott.

So there I am at top of the stretch, nearing the end of that third mile, and I look up and here's Jack on his pony about mid-stretch near the 1/8 pole and he's yelling and screaming and waving his arms and telling me to work him to the 3/4 pole. I'm thinking this guy is crazy. Plus, this son-of-a-buck that I'm on is gonna want to prop or bolt at the turn, because he's done it before. Gray Bar already had his left ear pointing straight up and his right ear was pinned back down on his head. I just knew something bad was gonna happen. But somehow we made it through the turn and to the 3/4 pole. Oh, I was so pissed at Jack after that. I rode up to him and told him he was friggin' crazy and that he must have lost his mind. I never said much to Jack when he'd make me mad, but I did that time. Of course, come Saturday it's the Omaha Gold Cup. I thought Jack was absolutely crazy.

In the 1975 Grade 3 Omaha Gold Cup, Gray Bar faced both the Preakness winner (Master Derby) and the Black-Eyed Susan winner (My Juliet). Early in the spring, Master Derby had put together an impressive trifecta of wins. He won the G2 Louisiana Derby and beat Foolish Pleasure in the G1 Bluegrass Stakes, but then his connections passed on the Kentucky Derby and instead went on to win the GI Preakness Stakes. After running third to Avatar and Foolish Pleasure in the G1 Belmont Stakes, Master

Derby was then pointed to run in a unique, proposed race at Belmont Park called the Race of Champions. The race was designed to pit the winners of the Kentucky Derby, Preakness, and Belmont Stakes against each other. But when Avatar dropped out of the Race of Champions, Master Derby's owner, Mrs. Verna Lehmann, was then coerced (with $50,000 from the New York Racing Association) also to bow out. In doing so, the brilliant filly Ruffian became a substitute opponent for the Kentucky Derby winner. *Foolish Pleasure vs. Ruffian.* On paper it became a mammoth match race. On the racetrack it became the most fateful horse race run in North America. Master Derby was diverted to Ak-Sar-Ben and primed for the Omaha Gold Cup.

The other graded stakes winner who arrived in Omaha from Baltimore after a marvelous Maryland weekend was the G3 Black-Eyed Susan winner, My Juliet. A dark bay daughter of Gallant Romeo, My Juliet routinely beat the boys in stakes competition from six furlongs to a mile and 1/8th, and she did it from coast to coast. After her win at Pimlico, My Juliet then won the Dogwood Stakes at Churchill Downs. After trouncing over fillies in the Ak-Sar-Ben Princess Stakes, My Juliet was poised for the Omaha Gold Cup.

The pot was on the boil for the big race; a terrific field had been assembled, and a record Ak-Sar-Ben crowd of 30,030 packed the facility in 93-degree weather. More than 8,000 fans took shelter in the indoor coliseum's air-conditioning, a progressive and unique feature of *Aks*. Inside, races were shown on a giant fifty-foot video projection screen hung from the rafters, and reserved table seating was sold. Corn-fed Nebraska beef could have safely hung in the coliseum, too; inside it never seemed to be above 68 degrees. Outside, the heat waves roiled. Beads of sweat appeared on the brow of twenty-five-year-old jockey Kenny Jones. A typically cool customer, the young Texan was feeling the heat of riding in his first-ever $100,000 race—and riding Gray Bar for the first time. In a peculiar twist, the gelding's regular rider, the mercurial Mary Bacon, had flown the coop and taken her tack to Hollywood Park. Jack's instructions to the replacement rider were simple: "Stay close to My Juliet, but don't let anyone else get in front of you." Easier said than done! It was a simple strategy in the mind of the trainer, but countless considerations pinballed in the mind of the jockey. How would the race play out? The field moved closer to the start. Jones wiped his palms of sweat. Gray Bar's neck was shiny wet, Van Berg's shirt was completely soaked, and the fans were dripping with anticipation. The lid was about to blow—then the gates crashed open and they were off!

Gray Bar broke sharply. Moving into the first turn, Jones took a light hold and crouched in behind the rippling gray mane of his eager mount. Past the 3/4 pole, they raced down the pine tree–lined backstretch in the richest horse race ever run in Omaha. Suddenly, all the drama and hype that filled the big race began to leak away. "Shoot," Van Berg remembered, "Gray Bar made the lead going down the backstretch and then he just opened up on them. He won by about six lengths. Those other two never had a chance." Poof! The potential clash of the two touring titans disappeared when the magic of Jack appeared—in the form of Gray Bar. He paid $30.60 to win.

My Juliet's runner-up effort to Gray Bar in the Omaha Gold Cup interrupted her three-race win streak. But she immediately resumed her winning ways, rattling off five consecutive wins thereafter, including the G2 Test at Saratoga, the G2 Cotillion at Keystone Racetrack, and the Next Move at Aqueduct. My Juliet later went on to win the G2 Vosburgh and the G2 Michigan Mile, both against male competition.

In a remarkable coincidence, after Master Derby's third-place finish to Gray Bar, he too would go on to win five straight races, but not until after a half-year of rest. Rejuvenated, his subsequent wins included the G3 New Orleans Handicap and the G3 Oaklawn Handicap. He then was beaten by just a head by the great Forego, when he came in second in the 1976 Metropolitan Mile at Belmont.

It should be said that the Omaha Gold Cup was tough on Gray Bar, too; he did not start again until October of the following year, following surgery to remove a chip from his knee. And he never again ran in a stakes race in his twenty-two subsequent starts. Gray Bar was modestly competitive winning just two of those races, both at Hazel Park. He won an allowance race under jockey Wayne Catalano and his final win came in a $25,000 claiming race, when he overachieved again, winning at 23-1.

Gray Bar, the former $6,500 claimer, sobered the high life of some pretty classy company, and he is one of the many handcrafted jewels on the treasured Van Berg Crown of Claims. His triumph in the '75 Omaha Gold Cup is easily one of Jack Van Berg's greatest training feats. It was a show-stopping performance by the *Merlin of the Midlands*!

24

Merlin of the Midlands

John McEvoy experienced and wrote about Midwest horse racing for decades. Based in Chicago, McEvoy is a former editor and senior correspondent for the Daily Racing Form. He is also an award-winning writer and author of five thrilling horse racing novels. John understood what M. H. Van Berg had done and witnessed what Jack Van Berg accomplished while in his prime. Within his detailed *Daily Racing Form* coverage of the 1975 Omaha Gold Cup, it is evident that McEvoy was clearly inspired not only by the presence and performance of Gray Bar, but also by Jack Van Berg's incredible racing resume. In his July 1, 1975, column, John McEvoy decreed, *"Jack Van Berg is henceforth to be known as the Merlin of the Midlands."* There was nothing bold about that declaration, and it was not merely headline hype.

What McEvoy wrote of his observations in Omaha was a typical cross-section of what Van Berg (both Marion and Jack) had been doing for years. The impression M. H. Van Berg made in the Detroit horse racing record books was essentially the same mark he and his son Jack made in the Ak-Sar-Ben record books. Nebraska was home for Jack Van Berg, but Ak-Sar-Ben was his throne. Horse racing evolved in Nebraska due to a group of Omaha businessmen who first conducted horse racing in 1920 at Ak-Sar-Ben Field in Omaha. The group formed a non-profit, philanthropic organization called the Knights of Ak-Sar-Ben, and aside from racing, hosted 4-H shows, fairs, concerts, and an annual member's ball with a Mardi Gras themed krewe and court.

Jack Van Berg won his first Aks training title in 1959, at the young age

of twenty-three—he then held the title until he was forty-one years old!
Jack was the king of the court and he had an unrelenting grip that lasted
an amazing nineteen consecutive years. Vince Lombardi coached the NFL
champion Green Bay Packers in 1959 and led "*The Pack*" until 1967;
eight years at the helm. Bonanza, the NBC television series, also began in
1959 and galloped through 1973; fourteen years of the Cartwright family
and some Hop Sing on the side. And the launch and splashdown of the entire thirty-four manned and unmanned Apollo space missions was shorter
than the span that JVB was the leading trainer at Aks. All five of Jack's
children were essentially born and raised while Jack reigned at Ak-Sar-
Ben. Throughout their childhood, they only knew their dad as the "Leading Trainer in Omaha." That was the rub. The demands of maintaining
multiple divisions of horses that dotted across the Midwest and stretched
to the coasts occupied all of Jack's waking hours. Often, his only chance
for sleep was a short nap while he was on the road or on the wing. Family
life for Jack was virtually nonexistent.

Late spring was a lively time in the Midlands for Jack; in April he was
typically winding down with racing in New Orleans and Hot Springs, and
in the meantime he was racing in Chicago and powering up for an Omaha
meet. In the mid '60s Marion began travelling less with the horses and
was becoming more selective with his departures from his home base in
Columbus. This made for a much more rigorous routine for Jack. Long
before the conveniences of electronic communication and the comforts
of modern travel became available, Jack embarked on an astonishing approach to training. He was traversing across the plains with the frequency
of a P-I-E freight truck. Jack explains an air travel ritual that he kept up for
a few years . . .

In the springtime I'd fly back and forth from Omaha to Chicago
to help my dad with the horses at Sportsman's Park. Every day,
in at noon, then back out at eight o'clock at night. I'd train in the

morning at Ak-Sar-Ben and then catch the United Airlines noon flight to Chicago to saddle the horses for the races and do some work around the barn in the afternoon. Then fly back to Omaha that night. And then I'd either stay in Omaha or drive back to Columbus that night. Either way, I'd be at the track in Omaha for training every morning. I'd do that five or six days a week. Back then they had those excursion tickets where you had to fly and stay somewhere for at least a week. I bought a bunch of them round-trip tickets for $38 and would just switch 'em out whenever I needed them. When I got on the plane I'd go straight to the back seat and go to sleep, but I'd tell the stewardess to wake me up for the meal. They served from the front of the plane to the back, so that allowed me to get a nap in and eat lunch, then hop off the plane and go to the track. I had one of those early car phones and when I was running late, I'd call the United ticket counter there at Eppley Airfield in Omaha. Those folks were all my buddies and I'd tell them "I'm running tight" and ask them to slow down the loading process. I'd get there, park my car, and then run down that concourse and be the last one to load the plane. I did that a lot of times.

In present day, passengers asking gate agents to hold flights is simply unthinkable; even decades ago it took a special person to command that sort of attention. Jack was that rare and special person.

During the Van Berg era of supremacy at Ak-Sar-Ben, father and son collaborated as owner and trainer of more than forty stakes wins. And the supremacy of Jack Van Berg as the leading trainer was indeed an era, divided only by the years when his father, M. H. Van Berg, was alive, and the years after his death. Within those nineteen consecutive years that Jack was the leading trainer in Omaha, he saddled a total of some sixty Ak-Sar-Ben stakes winners. With special thanks to Space Commander, Admiral

Van, Redbird Wish, Spring Broker, Sonny Fleet, British Fleet, Ramblin Road, Royal Dick, Beira, Gray Bar, Joachim, Switch Partners, and several others.

Don Von Hemel would be the first to crack the Van Berg vise, when the classy Kansan won the Ak-Sar-Ben leading trainer in 1978, breaking the nineteen-year run set by Jack. Then Louis Brandt followed Von Hemel's accomplishment by winning the Aks training title back-to-back years, before DVH won it back for three straight years. By the mid '80s, Jack had begun to refine his national operation, but he still kept a division of horses in Omaha and won the Ak-Sar-Ben training title for the twentieth time in 1984. A win from Gate Dancer in the Omaha Gold Cup helped his cause. The following year, a smooth-talking, sharp-dressed guy wearing sunglasses arrived in a limo at the Ak-Sar-Ben stable gate. He kept a spotless shedrow and raced all his horses with flashy white bridles. His name was D. Wayne Lukas.

It was a heated battle all summer between JVB and DWL. Lukas was whisking away the competition with his California invaders, not the least of which was his talented three-year-old named Imp Society, who had won five straight at Aks and was in the process of sweeping the divisional stakes races. The three-year-old crown at the end of the meet was the G3 Omaha Gold Cup. Jack shipped in his Preakness Stakes winner and the Gold Cup as quickly and cleverly marketed as *"The Mane Event,"* Imp Society vs. Gate Dancer. Off at 1-2, Gate Dancer ran like a heavy favorite and was clear at the top of the stretch; 8/5 second-choice Imp Society ate dust through the stretch and finished second. But when the dust settled at the end of the meet, Jack won forty-two races and Wayne won forty-five. Van Berg left Omaha with a large gold cup; Lukas left town with a sterling silver leading trainer belt buckle.

Jack persisted with his hearty harvest in the heartland, as he continued to collect trophies at Ak-Sar-Ben throughout the '80s and into the '90s.

He reaped dozens more blacktype winners, enjoying enormous success, specifically with the filly and mare stakes. Jack won the G3 Ak-Sar-Ben Oaks with Pima and Fit To Scout; the G3 Ak-Sar-Ben Queens Handicap with Targa, Oriental, and Furtaws Friend; and the Budweiser Breeders' Cup with Oriental and Fappitass.

Van Berg also won the signature Aks races in bulk. He won the G3 Omaha Gold Cup six times (British Fleet, Gray Bar, Joachim, Flare Dancer, Buffalo Beau, and Gate Dancer) and the G3 Cornhusker Handicap four times, including twice with Joey Bob in '72 and '73, then again in '74 with Blazing Gypsey and finally with Gate Dancer in 1985.

But in the years that led to the despicable demise of Ak-Sar-Ben, so lovingly remembered as the "Jewel of the Midwest," Jack's force and forest in Omaha were significantly reduced. The barn of horses he kept under the shade of the maple trees—horses who raced past the plotted pines along the backstretch—was basically the orchard for his third-stringers and an oasis for stakes horses in transition. Truth be told, Jack's minor presence at Ak-Sar-Ben in the final years before it closed in 1995 was due primarily to his love and gratitude to the track forefathers, the dedicated AK employees, and the devoted horsemen and race fans. Numerous times Jack defended Ak-Sar-Ben during its dying days, while attacking its questionable leadership and intentions.

What Jack accomplished was not limited to inside and around the corridors of I-80, I-55, and Highway 71. His band of horses, employees, and owners found their way to the winner's circle beyond the outposts he maintained in the Midlands.

25

The Spirit of '76

In 1976, our nation's red, white, and blue colors were flown with pride across the United States all year long. The entire country prepared to celebrate its two hundredth year of independence, and a colossal birthday party was planned for July 4. There were extensive advertising campaigns with announcers dressed as Uncle Sam. They barked of tremendous savings on furniture, washing machines, automobiles, and any goods and services that could be marketed with a red, white, and blue logo or patriotic pitch. The land that election year was awash with partisan pride and promises that the savings would be great—at least until the back-to-school and Christmas sale ad campaigns began. With the Ford vs. Carter presidential campaigns at fever pitch throughout the year, the red, white, and blue was cover to cover, curb to curb, and tusk to tail.

But the continental color scheme was not ubiquitous; there was a palette of purple and gold that streaked across the nation's racetracks. This color scheme, too, lasted all year, but it was painted in a much heavier coat than seen before. The Van Berg horses and the spirit of JVB were slathered over the competition in record-breaking numbers that year. Jack was everywhere. Or was he?

In 1976 Jack had the broadest span of divisions and horses that he had ever attempted to orchestrate. If Jack was the trainer of all his horses in training, then he needed to prove it by appearing at all the tracks on a somewhat regular basis. In horse racing, there was and is no uniformity from one state's rules and regulations to the next in terms of how often a trainer must appear at the track. In general, the rules of racing require that a trainer may not be away from his horses for an extended period of time. Working seven days a week, and with roughly the same number of barns operating at once, left Jack with an excruciating and eclectic travel schedule. It also meant he relied heavily on his help at the racetracks.

One of Jack's most devoted employees and right-hand man was not a man at all. Dianne Alexander surfaced at the Van Berg barn on a whim, but she stayed because of intent:

> I was in Florida and my college friends and I wanted an adventure. We decided we would explore the United States and we got as far as New Orleans until our money ran out. When I learned that I could get paid to work around horses at the racetrack I thought that was a pretty good idea and worth checking out. I loved horses. I needed money. So I went to the Fair Grounds. I showed up at Jack's barn and I told him I was looking for a job. He said, "I haven't had much luck hiring women," but he didn't say no. So I just stood there and waited and waited and I think he got tired of me just standing there, so Jack finally said, "All right, show up tomorrow and don't be late." So I show up the next morning and the guys told me to grab a shank and a cooler and go down to the end of the shedrow. I said, "Grab a *what* and a *what* and go *where?*" I had no idea what they were talking about. But I figured it out. I really only had plans to make a little money and then move on. I ended up staying with Jack for twenty years.

It didn't take long for Jack to appreciate the hard work and effort that Dianne put forth, and she soon was on the road with the Van Berg horses from one race meet to the next. Her book-smarts, trustworthiness, and level head made her a commodity around the barn. Because she was a woman, she might have been a sentimental favorite to Jack, but she was treated the same as the men: "I was an only child who came from a quiet family, so I never got yelled at," recalls Alexander, "but when you work for Jack, you're always getting yelled at."

During the Oaklawn Park meet the track stewards called Jack into their office to discuss what they would and wouldn't allow regarding him being an absentee trainer. The stewards were wise to Jack's numerous outfits across the land, and they were not satisfied that Jack was actually on the grounds training at OP as much as the rules specified. Affairs around the barn were being conducted with a Van Berg spirit, but Jack was more ghostlike in terms of his actual appearances there.

Dianne was overseeing the Van Berg horses there in Hot Springs, but she was only licensed as a groom. The stewards informed Jack that either Dianne Alexander was to get her assistant trainer's license or that he needed to turn his horses over to another trainer. Alexander recalls the morning when Jack came out of the steward's office and his face was beet red:

Jack grabbed me by the arm and said, "Come with me." We went down to the barn and he took a horse out of the stall and we went over every part of that horse. He remarked about this, that, and the other about the horse. And when he was done, he asked me about what he had just shown me. There were two things that I didn't get correct when he quizzed me about them and he said to me, "If I ever ask you about those two things again, you better not give me the wrong answer." So a few days later I was in the racing office entering horses, which you could do without a license. One of the stewards, Bob Farmer, saw me and told me that I shouldn't be doing that. He said, "You get in there right now and take that trainer's test." Well, I hadn't really studied enough and I didn't feel like I was prepared, but I took the test and didn't miss one question on the written or the oral test. But when you work for Jack you are more prepared than you will know. Later when I called Jack, I told him that they made me take that trainer's test. And he says, "Yeah, how did you do?" When I told him I didn't miss a question he said, "Well that's what I expected." So much for the congratulations, I guess. But it was just what was expected. If you learn to do something from Jack, you better do what you have learned.

What Jack learned from Dianne was that she was very organized, reliable, and loyal. When a race meet would end, Dianne was always the last to leave town because she was kept around to be sure all the horses were properly loaded, that all the equipment was packed and shipped, and that all the details were tidied up. Some of Dianne's most vivid memories involve the transport of horses, the transport of Jack, or her own personal travels and travails with Jack:

Long before we all had cell phones, we had finished at Ak-Sar-Ben and the horses and everything had just been shipped. A few days before, I began asking Jack which division of horses he wanted me to go to, but he kept telling me, "I'll tell ya later, just deal with it." I had cleaned out my apartment and I was waiting for instructions on where to go. I kept waiting and waiting for Jack to call me and he never did. I knew that he would be expecting me somewhere; I just didn't know where that might be. So not wanting to make him mad and keep him waiting, I figured I better start driving—somewhere. Here I am in Omaha, all by myself, not knowing where to drive. All I knew was that I needed to leave Omaha. I guessed that heading east across Iowa made sense. If he needed me in Kentucky I could drop down into Missouri and go that way. If he needed me in Chicago, or Detroit, or farther east, I'd just keep driving. About every hour I'd pull over at a truck stop and try to reach him on a pay phone. I did this for hours until about the time I made it to Chicago. I finally got a hold of him when I was getting close to Arlington Park. He told me to keep driving to Detroit; he needed me there. And he told me to hurry up.

Jack saw that Dianne had good common sense and that she could keep the books to the cent. He began to give her more and more book-keeping chores and allowed her to take on more responsibility with the record-keeping. Ultimately Dianne was in charge of payroll for all of the divisions. At one time she was cutting payroll checks for nine divisions across the nation. The payroll protocol was that Jack's assistants called Dianne on Friday morning and she would then process all the checks that would go out later that day. She often was in a mad dash to rush the payroll checks out to the airport to make a Delta Dash flight. If she wasn't rushing checks to the airport, Dianne was typically in a sprint to get Jack to the air-port. Once while in Chicago, she was in the back seat of the car while Jack was driving. The objective was to get both Jack and the payroll checks to the airport for an on-time delivery. Dianne recalls, "There were four of us in the car, and we were all involved. Jack wanted to drive because he was in a hurry, so I sat in the back and wrote out checks, and he signed them. But he was doing about eighty miles per hour on the Eisenhower Expressway! I would hand the checks to Loren Rettele, and he would give and take the checks to Jack. Tom Griffiths was steering while Jack was signing. He would tell Jack to slow down or speed up because Jack was looking at the checks—not the road!"

Occasionally, Jack would get to the airport with time to spare. On one such occasion Dianne had dropped Jack off at the Louisville, Kentucky, airport and had returned home. She got a call from Jack, and he angrily said, "Hey, come pick me up." When Dianne asked where he was, he yelled, "I'm at the damn airport! I'll explain later." It turns out that as Jack waited for his flight, he had asked a man sitting next to him to wake him up in case he fell asleep. Long story short, Jack never got the wake-up nudge. The only thing he caught at the airport was a nap. And it didn't improve his disposition.

Dianne also remembers a jaunty journey when Jack didn't drive or fall asleep:

> We were in Omaha and Jack wanted to go to a farm auction some-where out in the country. So I was driving, and Bob Posa, who was the driver of the big Van Berg horse van commonly known as "The Blue Goose," was also in the car. Jack was in the back seat reading the *Daily Racing Form*. We were running a little late and Jack kept encouraging me to hurry, so of course I stepped on it and I got stopped for speeding. When the officer came to my window, Jack looked up innocently and said, "But officer, sir, I told her not to go so fast." Luckily, the officer only gave me a warning, but as we pulled away, Jack said, "Kick this thing in the butt—we're late!"

1976 was not only a year to remember for Jack Van Berg, it was one for the ages. It was a year that he accomplished the rare feat of being both the leading trainer in races won *and* in money won. It was a stunning sweep, but these achievements had been billowing on the horizon. In 1973 he had a record 1,749 starts with 281 wins. In 1974 he had a record 329 wins with 1,712 starts. The idea of reaching 400 wins in a year swirled in Jack's head. Around the time of his fortieth birthday in June of '76, Jack Van Berg recorded his three thousandth lifetime win; then he simply stormed on to notch-numbing numbers like no other horseman on the planet. His sheer volume of 1976 starts and wins laid waste to all records, with 2,362 starts and an amazing 496 wins. The record $2,976,196 that Jack's runners earned in 1976 even surpassed leading owner Dan Lasater's money-won mark of $2,894,074. And Jack and his team did it with a significant 21 percent win rate.

Not all of the 496 winners were the work-a-day claimers that made up the bulk of the Van Berg operation. Jack had his share of stakes winners, and their weighty winnings, which came in large lumps, were key in helping Jack lead the nation.

Summertime Promise got the blacktype barrage started early in February and she stayed late, winning her final stakes race of the year in October. Technically, she did not win her first stakes race until April, in the $50,000 Apple Blossom Handicap at Oaklawn Park. Prior to that, Summertime Promise had three consecutive seconds in graded-stakes races, including the G1 Santa Margarita Invitational, when she was beaten by just a nose. After another second in the G3 Gallorette at Pimlico, she won the $50,000 Indian Maid Handicap at Hawthorne and ultimately closed out her year with a win in the Yo Tambien Handicap. Both races were over the Hawthorne turf course and each time she was handled by the classy John Lively. In 1976 Summertime Promise earned $176,720 for her owner, Ken Opstein.

Joachim was owned by Edith Pratt and Jack Van Berg. He became the leading Van Berg money earner for the year, with a '76 record of 22-6-3-4 $229,825. The bay colt by Proud Clarion rattled off three-straight allowance wins at Ak-Sar-Ben before he stepped up to stakes competition and won the G3 $100,000 Gold Cup and the G3 $50,000 Ak-Sar-Ben President's Cup Handicap. Jack then took his three-year-old to Chicago, and Joachim won the G2 $100,000 Secretariat Stakes.

Almost Grown only won one stakes race in 1976, but it was the right one. Jack ran both Almost Grown, owned by Flash III, and Joachim as Van Berg–trained entries in the G2 $100,000 Added Hawthorne Gold Cup Handicap. The two colts were coupled in the wagering; one ran first, the other ran last. The value to the winner was $86,720.

Regal Rumor and Officer's Call also helped the cause in Chicago. Regal Rumor, owned by Al M. Stall, Sr., won the $30,000 Florence R. Handicap the last day in May but also won allowance races before and after throughout the year. The humble South Dakota homebred of Nial and Elaine Tidball, Officer's Call soldiered on all year and won just twice in twenty-one starts. After three consecutive seconds in stakes at Fonner Park in Grand Island, Nebraska, the gelding finished out of the money in eleven of his next thirteen races. The tenacious trooper finally tasted success in the $30,000 Charles H. Bidwill Memorial Stakes at the end of October, but even that was bittersweet; he had to share the win in a dead heat with Dare To Command. One thing is for sure about Officer's Call: he was a mighty *mudder*. The Bidwill stakes win was in the slop, and his only other win in 1976 came at Agricultural Park in Columbus, Nebraska, when the going was rated heavy.

Marathon, Bay Streak, and Lady B. Gay all won stakes, too. Big or small, they all counted for something that added up to something big. Even the six allowance wins at Louisiana Downs for Hebert that year, capped off by a win in the $10,000 Bicentennial Handicap win at LaD, were meaningful. Hebert did his part, as did the aforementioned big money winners, but there were hundreds more horses whose contribution in wins and earnings made for a record-setting season. The stars and stripes shined brightly in 1976, and it was a red-letter year for Jack Van Berg.

26

The Disciples

One trait of a successful businessman is the knack of maintaining a healthy relationship with his employees. M. H. Van Berg would never have enjoyed so much success without designating, and retaining, capable assistants, nor would his son Jack have achieved his greatness. Neither man would have been inducted into the National Racing Hall of Fame if they didn't have confidence in their competent workers. Sure, the Van Berg workers were subject to a chain of command and plenty of strict commands from the top. But the Van Bergs established trust in their employees and had faith that their instructions would be carried out. And there was reciprocal respect, regardless of rank.

Many of Marion's assistant trainers were of an age similar to his own. Jack also had similar-aged or older assistants, such as Mark Wallerstedt, Loren Rettele, and Benny Ciboron. However, Jack grew many of his assistants from seed. Some came to him in a willing and conventional manner, with intentions of wanting to learn about horses, horse racing, and training racehorses. Others were sent to Jack with the hopes and prayers that they would learn something. They all were taught about work and discipline. Those who didn't learn didn't last.

The First Disciple: Frankie Brothers

The first to enter into what evolved into the JVB Subordinate System was Frank Brothers. He was a kid from New Orleans who had a good background with horses. "Frankie," as he is typically addressed, showed quarter horses at age six. He had a bedroom full of trophies and belt buckles that he earned with his fine horses. But as he trudged through high school and wandered into college, he grew aimless. He needed a career. Frankie found the thoroughbreds fascinating, particularly the racing thorough-breds, but his father, Louis Brothers, preferred Frankie not go the way of the racetrack. Mr. Brothers owned a small electrical contracting business but saw that his son had developed a sincere passion for racing, *not* the family business. Louis knew that an interest in something was better than an interest in nothing. So he approached Charlie Touzet, the owner of a tack shop located near the Fair Grounds, and asked Charlie who Frankie might try to work for in the stable area. "If you're going to go back there to learn, there's only one man to learn from, and that's Jack Van Berg," said Charlie. Mr. Brothers made an appointment to meet Jack and the two men agreed that Frankie would begin work as a hotwalker.

This entry-level position on the backside, even before one advances to stall cleaning, involves walking horses around the barn shedrow. When a horse returns from its training on the racetrack, it is typically hot from the exercise and needs to be cooled out before being returned to its stall. A keen hotwalker observes the horse's behavior and cares for it while it is being walked. A sharp trainer observes the hotwalker to see if he or she has any innate horse sense or potential horsemanship. A clueless hotwalker is a danger to himself, others, and of course, the horse. Jack saw that Frankie had a clue.

When the racing season ended in New Orleans in March and the hors-es were vanned away to other tracks, Frankie decided to follow along and Jack was grateful he did. Frankie's previous experience with horses was evident and his desire to learn more was equally evident. In just over a year's time Frankie graduated from hotwalker to groom to shedrow fore-man. He even learned to gallop horses on the track. But despite these pro-motions, as Frankie recalled, "You're always rubbing horses when you work for Jack. You never really leave the stall work." Jack was notorious for working his help to their breaking point and then sometimes pushing them a bit further. "He'd give you all the barbed wire you could eat and somehow you'd end up liking it," said Frankie. "And you wouldn't ever want him to have to tell you to do something more than once. That voice! That was enough incentive—or fear. Jack sounded just like his dad." Jack's voice and discipline made an impact on Frankie, but maybe too much of one. It seems Jack's staunch strictness came back to haunt him. Jack remembers one year at the Fair Grounds when Frankie was frequently firing the hotwalkers for being just a few minutes late for work in the morning. "Hell, we didn't have anyone left in New Orleans to walk the horses," said Jack. "I told Frankie that if he fired one more hotwalker, I'd throw nails down the shedrow and make him walk the horses barefooted." But Jack was proud of how Frankie had developed and he knew he could trust him with any of his divisions stabled across the nation. Frankie became a fine horseman, but not before there was a kind of cultural cleansing. Jack likes to tease, "Frankie drove up in a Cadillac, and when I was done with him I had him driving a VW."

Of course sometimes the assistant can think they know more than the trainer. Jack recalls a time when Frankie had the horses at Rockingham Park. Frankie had developed a habit of scratching horses when the *Daily Racing Form* arrived if it looked like they couldn't win. Well, this annoyed the racing secretary to no end. So the next year when Jack applied for stalls, the racing secretary told Jack, "If you bring that Brothers kid back up here again I won't give you any stalls." So Jack had to remind Frankie who the trainer was and who the assistant was. That steamed Frankie, and he never completely adjusted to the reminder. A few weeks later, Jack had an impatient owner who was getting anxious to have his horse run, so Jack told Frankie to enter the man's horse at a higher level than the previous race in which the horse had run poorly. The horse was fit and sound, but Frankie felt Jack was asking too much of the animal, so

Frankie let his opinion be known. Well, that race didn't fill, but the horse was also eligible for another race against even greater competition. When Jack told Frankie to enter the horse in the more difficult race, that really got him chirping. "Jesus Christ, Jack, you can't do that!" shrieked Frankie. Jack let Frankie squawk and squeal for a while and then reminded him not to scratch the horse. "Hell, the horse won by six lengths. But when you're young, you think you know more than anybody else. I know, I was like that with my dad," said a smiling Van Berg.

Frankie remembers . . .

> Once Jack put you through his system of training, he pretty much let you do things on your own. If he gained faith in you he'd leave you alone. We'd talk on the phone all the time and I would either do what he said to do with the horses, or simply do what he taught me if I didn't get any specific instructions. He was good about that. But when he came to town everything had to be just right with the horses or you'd hear about it. I got my butt chewed plenty of times by Jack, and probably deserved it. But I'll never forget the time I saw him get his butt chewed by his dad. In 1970 Marion was on his way to Saratoga Springs, New York, to be inducted into the National Museum of Racing Hall of Fame, so he stopped by Rockingham Park to check on the horses. I was just a groom then and wasn't responsible for the entire stable, only my four horses. Marion made Jack take all sixty of the horses out and jog them for his review. Jack was in his mid-thirties by then—he was married and a father of his own children—but Marion roared and howled and yelled at Jack as if he was still a child. He scolded Jack for every possible thing imaginable. And Jack just stood there and took it. You know, Jack swaggered around like John Wayne, but when his father was around he'd get as meek as a church mouse. I know that all came from the deepest respect Jack

had for his father. Jack was like a father figure for me, too, and still is. I love him. And he's the most naturally gifted horseman I've ever known.

Frankie worked for Jack for roughly ten years and then, with Jack's blessing, moved out on his own when given an offer to train for Al Stall, Sr. But he would periodically call Jack to pick his brain if he ever got hung up or unsure about something. "I remember I was having a problem with Hansel (1991 Preakness and Belmont winner) that really had me puzzled. I called Jack and asked his advice. Of course he began his response with "ya dumb son-of-a-buck," but he helped me then, just as he always has," said Brothers.

In the 1980s Frank Brothers was the leading trainer at the Fair Grounds for six years and at Louisiana Downs for nine consecutive years. He also won training titles at Keeneland and Churchill Downs.

The Second Disciple: Bill Mott

While some of Jack's disciples were delivered to Jack, others he hand-picked. Bill Mott's involvement in horse racing had already sprouted by the time he reached the Van Berg training operation, but working for Jack Van Berg gave Mott fertile ground to blossom. The son of a veterinarian, Bill was raised in Mobridge, South Dakota, located on the eastern edge of the Cheyenne River Indian Reservation. He got his animal and horse sense from his family and gained his first bit of horse racing knowledge from some fellow South Dakotans. As a young teenager, Bill met Ray Goehring, who trained horses on the dusty half-mile county fair tracks of South Dakota: Fort Pierre, Aberdeen, and Rapid City. At age fourteen Mott got started on the racetrack, working for Keith and Marilyn Asmussen, parents of Cash and Steve Asmussen. Bill got his first trainer's license at age sixteen and ran his parents' horses at Park Jefferson in Jefferson, South Dakota, as well as Atokad Park in South Sioux City, Nebraska.

In 1972 Bill left South Dakota for the first time and brought three horses to race in Detroit. After all three horses got claimed away from him, he not only was out of horses, he was out of money. Bill hooked up with Bob Irwin who had branched out to train on his own after Marion Van Berg passed away. "It felt like I was already working for Van Berg because all of Bob's tack was the purple and gold tack and equipment he got from Van Berg," said Mott. That summer, Bob Irwin sent Bill and a groom to Ak-Sar-Ben to run a horse in the Omaha Gold Cup; the colt's name was The Cutter. Their horse ran third to the Van Berg horse, British Fleet. But in the days surrounding the race, Jack Van Berg was not only assessing The Cutter, he was also sizing up young Bill Mott. "Because I came to town with only one horse I had plenty of free time, so I started getting up on horses and galloping a few. And then a few other guys asked me to get on their horses, and I was even going out to a small training track west of town to gallop some," said Mott. "I'll never forget the first time I met Jack—he asked me to start galloping for him and he said, 'Now listen, I pay all these guys $2 a head to gallop; I'll pay you $2.50 but you can't tell anybody.' It was in Omaha where I started working full-time for Jack, for a 50-cents-per-horse incentive."

Bill knew he had the fundamentals of racing and training, but as a teenager, he also knew he was just getting started and had tons more to learn. Young Mott was a South Dakotan savant.

I learned an awful lot from Bob Irwin. He had time to teach me and I asked him a lot of questions. So when I went to work for Jack, that put me in a good position to have that much more ex- perience and knowledge. Working for Bob and working for Jack was like two versions of working for Marion Van Berg. I guess you might say that I already had my primary education. When I was working for Jack I was getting my graduate degree. But boy, I did work for him. Even when I was an assistant trainer, that was just a title; I was still out there galloping ten horses a day, and there were always three or four horses that I was grooming at the same time.

Billy, as Jack calls him, was being put to the fire, and Jack knew he was forging a genuine horse trainer through all the blood, sweat, and tears. "Jack worked me, worked me, and worked me, but sometimes," jokes Billy, "he would only work me a half day; that's when I would only work from 5 A.M. to 5 P.M." The hard work and effort paid off for both parties and Van Berg began to develop faith in Mott. Billy knew his place in the scheme; he did his job and he did it well. But Jack was frequently unwavering in his demands and unruly in his routine. Mott remembered:

Jack would frequently call and wake me up at night. And if I wasn't instantly alert when he called, he'd accuse me of partying too much and goofing off. He'd say, "What the hell are you doing up there if you don't know what's going on?" I'd say, "Well shit, Jack, I was sleeping—what the hell do you think I was doing?" Now eight o'clock at night might not seem too late to call, but hell, I'd busted my butt all day and I was zonked out. That phone would ring and it would scare the crap out of me. Jack would start right in with the questioning about the horses: how did they run, who's in tomorrow, how are they training? Shoot, I had to provide a forty-horse report popping out of a dead sleep! It got so that I had to keep a clipboard of the overnights and results right next to my bed because if I didn't have all the answers instantly he'd start yelling at me.

All the yelling and training was worth it when at the end of 1976, Team Van Berg had their record-setting 496 wins. But in 1977 Jack was forced to make changes in how he managed his various divisions of horses across the land when the stewards cracked down on him. Mott explains:

Frankie and I had the benefit of being down as trainer for the entire year with every string we were running. Now nothing really changed; we were training as we had been, but it just relieved Jack from having to show up every six days. They began to enforce that rule, which made sure trainers were actually at the track training their horses. Jack had such a demanding schedule he finally agreed to put our names down as the trainer. That had a lot to do with Frankie and I both getting our names out there as trainers. I was winning all these races—they were all Van Berg horses, but I was down as the trainer. Frankie and I were doing all the day-to-day training, but Jack was making all the big decisions as far as where the horses went and who got what horses. He had some horses that he put on a particular schedule and he would definitely let you know how he wanted things done and you definitely had to do it that way. When he would come to town he would look over the horses and tell you what you should be doing. But by that time I think he felt Frankie and I had enough experience. We would do the regular stuff and confer with him on the major stuff. If we had a question, we'd go to him, and if we thought we could get it right on our own we might—or might not. But Jack was always in charge.

Of course, there is always a time when the student thinks he is smarter than the master. To this day, Bill still cringes at the butt-chewing he got from Jack when he thought he knew better:

There was a gray filly named Roman Hat that I had for Jack up in Chicago. She developed a fistula on her withers that had gotten very inflamed. So after talking to my vet about it, I took it on my own to drain the swollen area and inject some cortisone into it. There is a strong risk of infection with that technique, and the effort to help can really go the wrong way with an injection. At the time I wasn't aware of that, but Jack sure let me know about it. And he let me have it! He told me that if I was going to start acting like I was the trainer he'd take every damn one of the horses away from me. I'd never made him that mad before. Damn, he was hot! As it turned out, no harm came to the filly, but that didn't matter. The point was that I did it, and I didn't ask first.

But life for Billy under the Van Berg shedrow wasn't all under draconian law. Mott recalls a side of Jack that he enjoyed and appreciated:

Jack was a lot of fun to train with. We would talk and laugh and tease and we had a good time training. If you did a good job, Jack would pretty much let you know. There's always those Gray Bar types out there—the kind of horses that you watch train and that run off and do things wrong in the morning, and you think you can improve them. Jack and I liked to look for those horses, and we'd go in together and claim horses in partnership. We had a good time together doing that and we did very well claiming horses together.

As a matter of fact, one of the horses owned by Mott and Van Berg and trained by Van Berg (when Jack was in town) was a gelding named Bold Escapade. They claimed him at Arlington Park for $8,500 at the start of the summer of '76 and won three races with him before he was claimed away from them. Mott and Van Berg claimed him back again for $6,500 at Hawthorne in October and won again with him. Then, on the final race of the year in Chicago, in the ninth race at Sportsman's Park, Bold Escapade won by a nose to give Jack Van Berg his 496th win. Obviously that single win didn't push Van Berg over the world-record mark (the record was broken several weeks before), but it was a nice way to ring in the new year. And a short "good job" from Jack is always much better than a scolding that you can't walk, or gallop, away from.

Billy wasn't like one of those renegade horses that he and Jack used to scout. He was already good to the core—a class act. Jack drilled down into that core and helped release all of Mott's class and ability. Bill Mott didn't come from a rich, blueblood heritage; he didn't need to. Class has nothing to do with money. Class is consideration, sacrifice, knowing right from wrong, and then showing the strength to do right. It was the class and ability of Bill Mott that caught the attention of Jack Van Berg. Jack tapped it and exposed it, and the result has been an endless flow of pure horse racing splendor: Cigar, Royal Delta, Theatrical, and Paradise Creek are but a few of his Eclipse Award champions. Mott is a three-time Eclipse Award champion trainer himself. He has won nine training titles at Saratoga, ten at Belmont Park, nine at Gulfstream Park, and five at Keeneland. He is the all-time leading trainer at Churchill Downs, and he has trained more than four thousand winners. Bill Mott, following the path of M. H. Van Berg and Jack C. Van Berg, is a Hall of Fame trainer. Class, like cream, rises to the top.

The Third Disciple: Wayne Catalano

The tack shop on the racetrack is much like the water cooler at the office: if you hang around it long enough, you'll catch the news, hear the latest rumors, and listen to a lot of bellyaching. Because Charlie Touzet, the tack shop operator at the Fair Grounds, knew his clients and many neighbors, he saw that a very distressed Bernadine Catalano was searching for solutions for one of her problematic sons. Charlie had the answer: send him to Jack! It worked with Frankie Brothers, but a Catalano boy would be a far greater mission. Bernadine was raising five children on her own; she was short on resources and short on options. Near the end of the Fair Grounds meet, she approached Jack, desperate for him to give her sixteen-year-old son, Joe, a job. Jack remembers:

Here comes Mrs. Catalano, and she said, "Mr. Van Berg, I've got a son and I'm having a lot of trouble with him, and Charlie Touzet said you could straighten him out. He said I could bring him to you and have him go to work for you." I said, "Mrs. Catalano, I got a secret to tell you—I won't take any crap off of him. I will shake him out of his boots. I want you to know that. And he's gotta be sixteen years old so he can get licensed." So she brings him out and he's just a little bitty shit. But he keeps showing up and working for me, but he won't bring his birth certificate to get licensed. I keep telling him if he doesn't bring that damn birth certificate, he can't work here. So Mrs. Catalano comes out again and she's crying up a storm. She says, "Mr. Van Berg, I lied to you—he won't be sixteen for another two weeks." Well, my hands were tied, but she was bawling and pleading with me to keep him on. So I decided he could work for me, but not back in the stable area. We had all of our tack boxes and storage trunks that needed to be painted, so I had him out in front of the stable gate scraping and painting for me for about two weeks. I remember one morning I was coming off the racetrack on my pony, and I saw that one of my workers, Burdette Brandt, had Joe throttled around the neck, pinned up against a horse trailer, and he ready to punch him in the mouth. I hollered, "Burdette! Don't you hit that boy! What the hell are you doing?" Burdette looks back over at me with these big wild eyes and says, "He ain't gonna call me Buck Teeth." I told Burdette to put him down, then I told Joe to keep his damn mouth shut or I'd shut it for him. I said, "I already got permission from your mother, and I will do it." So, anyway, he gets licensed just before the meet is over, and I took him to Chicago with me and I taught him to gallop. And I ain't shittin' you, he could gallop some of the toughest horses. I taught him how to take a hold and I told him how to talk to the horses and not fight with them. He ended up being a top apprentice when he started riding.

Meanwhile, back in New Orleans, young Wayne Catalano was following in his brother Joe's footsteps and straying off the path. Independence Day had come and gone, but Wayne still had some festive firepower
that he was itching to use. He used it in school. What was supposed to be
just a big bang in a locker resulted in a big bomb. The entire locker, and
other lockers, got blown to smithereens! It was Wayne's first attempt at
indoor pyrotechnics, but it wasn't his first blowup inside the principal's
office. With the shockwave came the aftermath, and Wayne got kicked out
of school. Poor Bernadine: another of her boys had driven her to the brink,
and Wayne was destined for the clink. So she had Wayne get some of his
clothes, told him to get in the car ,and drove him up to Chicago to be with
his brother.

Wayne didn't necessarily end up in Mister Rogers' neighborhood. He
became friends with a few riders at Sportsman's Park and began running
bets for the jockeys. He was having an incredible time for a teenager:
no school, little supervision, and plenty of easy money. "I was walking
around with two pockets full of cash and my hard-working brother Joe
was making $38 a week. Joe and I were staying in a tack room and party-
ing and fighting and drinking. It was some crazy stuff," said the wildcat
Wayne Catalano. Wayne had become legal age to work on the racetrack,
but work was the farthest thing from his mind.

The backstretch has eyes, and none of Wayne's behavior got by Jack.
He didn't like what was developing. So Jack called Mrs. Catalano down
in New Orleans and asked her to sign Wayne over to him so that he could
work and have Jack as his guardian. She gratefully did. Wayne was a ripening renegade until Jack caught up with him. Then, Van Berg abruptly
alerted Catalano that the party was over when he said, "Now look, you
little bastard, you're gonna stop going over to that jock's room, and you're
gonna stay here at the barn and work for me." Wayne knew Jack meant

business, but he had an agenda of his own: "I told Jack that I wanted to be a jockey, so Jack promised me that if I came to work for him, he'd help make me a jockey." Jack made good on his promise, but the aspiring rider had to put in his time and work hard like everyone else. Van Berg made a jockey out of Wayne—and a whole lot more.

> Jack started me out like he starts out everyone else: he taught me how to walk a horse, then how to groom a horse, then how to gallop a horse, and how to be a jockey. After a few years I rode my first winner and when I did, I was wearing the purple and gold Van Berg silks. Before long, Jack had me just short of a full-on assistant trainer. He sent me to Keeneland and I was watching the shedrow and trying to be a jockey at the same time. I was winning races, too. Then we went to Churchill and I was half-ass watching the shedrow there, also.

But when Catalano committed to the saddle, he simply tore up his competition, repeatedly winning riding titles throughout the Midwest. He shattered jockey Larry Snyder's record at Hazel Park, riding 176 wins at the meet. In 1977 Wayne was the second-leading jockey in the nation and strung together a remarkable forty-one consecutive days of riding at least one winner. Wayne's exuberance shows when he recalls his early days with Jack:

> I was so proud to have won my first race for him. Jack was more than influential for me—he was everything to me! Jack was there to school me and scold me and tell me what I did right and wrong. But oh, how I hated to see his face when I'd come back after I screwed up in a race, or even on the track in the morning. I'd see that stare and think, "Oh shit, here we go." Whether it was your fault or not he could make you feel an inch tall. Jack was hard, but he had a good heart. He can come off as a real John Wayne, but

inside he's a sweet man. More than once I've seen other trainers go to him with their horses when they couldn't figure out what was wrong with them. Jack would bark out, "Jog 'im down the road," and he'd look at the horse and tell them what was wrong with the horse and what they needed to do for it. He was amazing! And very helpful to other horsemen. He's changed a lot of lives and he's an unbelievable person.

In the midst of a nine-year career as a jockey, Wayne "The Cat" Catalano won close to two thousand races. One of his biggest days in the saddle came in late December of 1976, when he rode five winners in a day—all of them for Jack. "I could have won six, but I got away from the gate bad on one of them," said the competitive Catalano. "Five wins in a day for JVB!"

Wayne had to quit riding in 1983 due to a knee problem that he developed. He began training and scored his first win as a trainer that same year at Arlington Park. Early on, Wayne had just a few horses, but Jack saw to it that Wayne got some of his horses from prominent owner and breeder John Franks. "I had some good luck with that first handful of horses from Mr. Franks," Wayne remembered. "Next thing I know he sent me another van full, and I was on my way. I quit school in seventh grade, but I graduated from Van Berg University."

Wayne Catalano graduated with honors! And not only did he blow apart some school lockers in grade school, he exploded the Chicagoland racetrack training records, often breaking records he set himself. Catalano has won three Breeders' Cup races, with the fillies Dreaming Of Anna, She Be Wild, and Stephanie's Kitten.

27

A Road to a Renaissance

While he didn't train as many winners as the aforementioned disciples, Scott Wells has earned tremendous success on the racetrack. He has a profound pedigree for horse racing, and he definitely *knows Jack*. Raised in Osage County near Pawhuska, Oklahoma, Wells is the son of Ted Wells, Jr., a Quarter Horse Hall of Fame trainer who trained the 1965 All American Futurity winner, Savannah Jr. Scott had a fine foundation of horse sense from his father before he met the blunt force of Jack Van Berg. With an intrinsic sensitivity for arts and passion, and things that are artful through passion, Scott Wells has evolved into a true Renaissance man. His experiences with horses and horse racing have awarded him with incredible opportunity and accomplishment.

Wells has managed racetracks in New Mexico; Texas; Mexico City; and Montevideo, Uruguay. He is currently the president and general manager of Remington Park Racetrack and Casino in Oklahoma City. Scott is articulate and eloquent in his speech and has written countless literary works and video pieces expressing his passion and knowledge of horse racing. He has also authored books that have cleverly captured both the raw and refined essence of horse racing. Wells has the innate ability to reveal the characters of horse racing and the blood and guts of those characters—and horses—which have provided race fans with so many priceless memories. Scott himself has suffered, sacrificed, and succeeded at all levels of horse racing. He has seen it and seen through it.

What follows is an essay from Scott Wells, describing his personal enlightenment of the sometimes dark and dire road he was made to take with Jack Van Berg, and what Jack Van Berg made of him along that road.

VB

When I met Jack I was just a twenty-five-year-old kid who thought I could train a horse just because my father had been a good trainer. I'd worked around the barn forever and I'd been Dad's assistant when I was a teenager, and then I'd worked for Wayne Lukas and we had really good success with quarter horses out in California. I'd broken off from Lukas and gone out on my own and had trained a mixed stable of quarter horses and thoroughbreds in New Mexico when a good friend of mine, Jim Bayes, went to work for Van Berg shoeing horses. Jim was already a great farrier, but then he learned even more from Jack Reynolds, the legendary horseshoer. They took to each other and Jim got his foot in the door with Van Berg. He knew I wanted to switch to training a straight thoroughbred stable and he called me and convinced me to come to Hot Springs and he'd get me a job with Jack Van Berg as an assistant trainer. "After working for Jack for a while you can write your own ticket," he told me.

"Are you sure he'll hire me?"

"Why sure! He'll love you!"

In hindsight, Bayes was right. Jack did love me. It just took a couple of decades for him to get to that point. Encouraged and assured as I was by Bayes, I gave my owners, my horses, and my livelihood to other trainers and headed for Hot Springs, Arkansas. I had it all figured out. I'd work for Jack for a year or two, then leave him and recruit my own big stable and become a big-time trainer. But I had a surprise or two in store.

When Jim Bayes introduced me to Jack Van Berg, all Jack did was ask me, "Well, what can you do with a horse?"

I'll never forget that. I really hadn't ever thought about it like that. I'm usually pretty quick with an answer, but I stammered a little and finally told him I could do about anything but float teeth—and I was willing to learn that, if necessary.

"Can you gallop a horse?"

"Sure. It's been a while, but I've galloped plenty."

"Can you groom a horse?"

"Yes, sir. I've groomed . . ."

"Be here at five in the morning."

"But Mr. Van Berg, I was hoping to be your assistant trainer. My dad was a trainer and I've been training horses on my own for quite a while."

And I'll never forget what he told me next.

"Listen, son, I've got a million of you young guys wanting to pick my brain. Let's see what you can *do*." Then he walked away and that was that! I was pretty deflated, I can tell you. He hadn't mentioned me being an assistant or anything like that. He wanted me to groom horses! I thought I was an all-star! I'd given away my stable and my self-employed status in trade for a job rubbing horses! There was no mention of pay or anything. That would be a surprise for later, and not a good one.

I started school at the Van Berg Academy early the next morning and the lessons came fast and furious. For one thing, I'd never seen a trainer inspect so many horses so thoroughly. Jack watched each horse jog, he felt for heat in every leg, he palpated each throat, he examined the skin on the necks and shoulders to evaluate hydration, and he checked each horse's hooves, all the while issuing instructions for each horse to an assistant standing by who wrote everything down. The instructions might include everything from changes in the horse's feed mixture to shoeing instructions right down to the most minute details of his daily leg and hoof care. What I didn't realize until months later was that Jack didn't need to write any of it down. He had the most amazing ability I've ever seen to keep every horse straight in his head, down to the tiniest detail. And that wasn't just with a string of forty head. He could do it with all of his divisions and without a note in front of him.

And I didn't know the half of it yet! Because he bought and sold and claimed so many horses, Jack could stand by the rail in the morning and identify nearly every horse that worked or galloped by. For most of them, he could tell you what kinds of old injuries or problems they might have and how they were getting along with them at any given time. That's what made him such a great claiming trainer. If a horse ever showed true racing class, Jack never forgot it. Often, when that horse showed up in the lower claiming ranks, Jack would claim him and work his magic. And in his case, the "magic" didn't come from under-the-radar designer drugs. The Van Berg Magic came from nonstop attention to every little aspect of each horse's life. For instance, one day we claimed seven horses. I think we lost two or three that day, too, but the point is, we had more horses than we had stalls in our barn, so I had to put them in empty stalls elsewhere in the barn area there at Oaklawn Park. After the races, when Jack wanted to inspect them, I took him over to see the nearest one, and as soon as Jack stepped into the stall to feel that horse's legs, he lit into me like an army sergeant! The ground underneath the straw bedding was uneven!

"Here. Come here and stand right here," he told me, positioning me on the edge of the depression in the stall's center, putting one of my legs a couple of inches higher than the other. "Now how comfortable is that? How would you like to stand on that uneven ground for hours at a time? It'd make your back and your hips hurt, wouldn't it?"

"Yes, sir."

"Well, then get the hell in there and fix it! And don't you ever put a horse on uneven ground like that again!"

There were scores of such lessons, one of the main ones being that it wasn't at all worthwhile to try to take any shortcuts. True, Jack travelled from outfit to outfit and you never knew when he would show up. He might be gone for two weeks at a time in some cases. So some of the grooms would eventually let their guard down and take a shortcut on some specific task. They quickly learned the risk was not worth it. No matter how long Jack might have been gone from one's own division, he was bound to show up just about the time you tried to cheat the system. The first signal was always that big, booming voice. Right after you heard that, you'd see grooms tidying up around their areas or maybe ducking into their stalls to try to cover up some shortcut they might've taken. Then here'd come Jack, going over each horse, each stall, with a fine-tooth comb. He'd rub his hand inside each water bucket and he'd know whether or not that bucket had been thoroughly washed out that morning. He'd check every bandage to make sure it had been applied correctly. He'd even take a hoofpick and pull the mud out of a horse's hooves. By examining the mud and the hoof, he could tell whether or not the hoof had been properly washed or not before the mud was applied. If you got caught once, you got an ass-chewing and a warning. If you got caught twice, you were fired. The message: it's easier just to do it right the first time!

As regimented as the Van Berg Way was on many things, it was still based on the individual needs of each horse. There were lots of standard operating procedures for specific ailments, but there was always enough room to adapt the treatment to the particular horse. I know every person who ever worked for Jack Van Berg or for his father has carried with himself or herself many of the Van Berg responses. There are still certain liniments I occasionally smell when walking through a stable area which remind me of a Van Berg stable.

I could go on and on about the specific little things that I learned from Jack, but at the time I didn't realize how much he was shaping me as a man, not just as a horse trainer. For one thing, he piled work on me like no one ever had or ever has since. And there wasn't a pat on the back or a kind word, either—good work was expected. I learned years later that Jack really did appreciate it when someone did a good job for him. But he wasn't one to openly praise you. He'd ride you hard and expect your best effort, and I learned that should be enough. It was while working for him that I learned that sometimes the only satisfaction you were going to get was being able to look at yourself in the mirror at the end of a long day and being satisfied that you'd done a full day of high-quality work.

We won 496 races that year, a world record that stood for twenty-eight years until Steve Asmussen broke it. I have no idea how many horses passed through our hands in that time, but some of them I remember as clearly as if it were yesterday. Summertime Promise was one of our stable stars. She was a pretty bay daughter of Nijinsky II and could really run on the turf, but she had a terrible habit of hitting herself on her hocks and pasterns until Jim Bayes corrected her shoeing under Jack's guidance. After that she won numerous stakes races, made more than $300,000, and eventually produced Blushing Promise, the mother of the good sprinter and sire Carson City. We had Destroyer, who won the Santa Anita Derby when Monti Sims trained him. We had Gray Bar, but he was a little past his prime by the time he came to my division. But of all the horses we had during my time with Jack, Regal Rumor was my favorite. She was unbelievable. I think she won ten stakes that year. She was such a gallant, determined mare. Jack had learned the key to her was to train her mostly at a jog. It kept her loose and fit without pounding on her. He'd sometimes have us jog her three or four miles every day for weeks at a time, and whenever he entered her in a race, she was the horse to beat. She ran the same way every time, too. She'd track the leaders and then make a huge move on the turn for home, taking the lead and nearly always holding it to the wire. She had an enormous amount of talent but even more courage.

I guess I never behaved myself better than when I worked for Jack because at the end of any given day I would be so tired I sure as heck didn't feel like going out—and I didn't have much spending money to throw around anyway! I remember looking at those paychecks and wondering for a moment what the hell I was doing working for such wages. And then I'd think of all I was learning and I'd tell myself that this was like getting paid to go to graduate school. I was getting instruction from the best professor possible, so the real payoff wasn't in the paychecks—it was in those lessons I was learning. Perhaps one of those would make a nose or a head difference in a race someday in the future and my payback would come instantly. And that did come to pass. In the fourteen years I trained horses after working for Jack, I'm sure 75 percent or more of the races I won were due to the on-the-job training I got working for the Van Berg stable.

One thing I never did again afterward, though, was to ice a horse's testicles! Talk about miserable duty! Jack bought a group of four South American horses, all of them four or five years old and all very rank, entire males. One of them was a horse named Joachim and he was a handful but he could really run. But his testicles were very large and they really did bother him, even when he jogged or galloped. So when he raced, as part of his prerace treatment, someone would have to hold an icepack on his scrotum for an hour and a half before he went to the paddock to be saddled. By that time I was Jack's foreman, meaning I oversaw all the operations at the barn including overseeing the grooms and hotwalkers. The ice duty was supposed to be the groom's responsibility, but we didn't have a groom or a hotwalker who was willing to risk his life holding that icepack on Joachim. Naturally, it was unpleasant for the horse, and he'd kick and stomp and wring his tail. Try it sometime if you're into pain and danger. You have cold water running down your elbow and a mad horse is kicking at you and stomping in the puddle that's forming at his hind feet. Ninety minutes seemed like ninety days. But, I couldn't argue with the results. We won the Grade 1 Secretariat Stakes with Joachim one afternoon at Arlington Park and he paid a bundle to win. As we were leaving the test barn, Jack handed me a hundred dollar bill and told me to buy fried chicken and beer for the crew. I was astonished! He'd never done that before. He even told me to invite some of my friends from other stables if I wanted to.

Now in 1976 you could buy quite a bit of chicken and beer with a hundred dollars and I spent every penny of it. As I was returning to our barn I hollered at some friends in other barns and pretty soon there were about twenty of us gathered at the Van Berg stable celebrating. Well, just before we got to the bottom of the buckets of chicken, here came a dump truck backing up to our shedrow and it dumped a full load of sand.

"All right, boys, grab some wheelbarrows and some shovels and help us out," bellowed Jack. Of course he rolled up his sleeves and led the way as he gave out the orders. Within minutes he had the biggest crew on the racetrack spreading that sand a wheelbarrow at a time all the way around that forty-horse barn! We worked until after dark but we had the prettiest, most level shedrow in town and Mr. Van Berg probably got a hundred man hours of hard labor for his hundred dollars worth of chicken and beer! Another lesson well-learned.

Many times back then I would have other trainers ask me, "What does Jack run those horses on?" and I'd always tell them, "the racetrack." I wasn't trying to be a smart-ass, though many of them accused me of it.

"C'mon, he's giving those horses something," they'd say.

The straight truth is, those horses got the regular permitted medications in the regular permitted doses. What they got special was tremendous conditioning and great shoeing. Jack knows more about a horse's hooves than almost anyone and he's made hundreds of successful claims by picking out horses with hoof problems and then correcting them. He also made sure to run a fit horse. We trained 365 days a year. We didn't take off Christmas or Thanksgiving or New Year's. There were days in Chicago when it was snowing and miserable and nearly every other trainer on the grounds would walk their horses or maybe jog them in the shedrow for a few days until the weather got better. Not so with the Van Berg stable. Our horses didn't miss a day of exercise. And when the races were run, if it came down to a driving finish as it so often does, we always knew our horses would have that little edge of extra fitness.

When I finally got another chance to train on my own, it was tough to leave Jack because I was still learning so much. But I had a chance to improve my station in life so I took advantage of the opportunity. A decade passed before the next time I saw Jack in person. Of course I'd seen him on TV with Gate Dancer and then with Alysheba, and I remember I had tears roll down my cheeks when I heard Jack speak of his father after the Kentucky Derby. I was stabled in Maryland at the time and I was just leaving the racing office at Pimlico one morning a couple of weeks later and I saw Jack surrounded by reporters and TV cameras. I wanted to say hello but figured I'd catch him later when he wasn't so busy. But, to my surprise, he saw me and got up and came over and grabbed me and gave me a rough hug and said, "Come on over and see my colt." So we walked over to the Preakness barn and he showed me Alysheba and gave me some more advice I've never forgotten.

"I've been watching you in the *Form*, you know. You're doing real well with the stock you've got. But wait until you get one like this! I'm tellin' you, you keep doing things the way I taught you and when you get one like this, you'll be ready. I'll tell you one thing—they're a helluva lot easier to train than those cheap ones."

Well, I never did get a horse anything remotely like Alysheba. But Bill Mott did and Frank Brothers did and Wayne Catalano did and so did many others who learned their lessons the Van Berg way. And I know for certain that those lessons they learned from Jack came in handy many, many times along the way.

28

The Inspiration of Laurie Bale

The Junior Jockey Club at Ak-Sar-Ben is likely a lasting memory for anyone who attended the horse races in Omaha, whether they saw the club or experienced it. There was no dress code, nor was there any palming of money to a maître d' to gain entrance into the club. The JJC at Aks was an institution, or at least a convenient daycare for parents wanting to leave their kids during racing hours. If the youngsters didn't already have a grip on horse racing based on a family member or friend's interest, racing invariably gripped them thanks to the JJC's prime position between the paddock and the outer rail; their playpen was just an arms-length from the horses, jockeys, and the racing. The JJC was marketing magic. And so was Ak-Sar-Ben.

One child who was quickly smitten by horse racing was young Laurie Bale. However, she wasn't running wild and racing the other kids and mimicking the race-riding jockeys under the Omaha sunshine. While she was surrounded by all the kids in the JJC, her observations of horse racing came while seated in her wheelchair. But Laurie's vantage point did nothing to sway her from shouting and cheering for her favorite horses and jockeys, just like all the other kids—and parents.

Laurie became a keen horse racing fan, and her parents, Robert and Joan Bale, became keenly aware of the joy it brought to what was often a very difficult life for their dear daughter. To no surprise, the against-the-odds story of Gray Bar resonated with Laurie and the gray hero was her immediate superstar. For an early thirteenth birthday present, Robert Bale arranged for Laurie to go to the Ak-Sar-Ben stable area and meet Jack Van

Berg. When the two met, that loud, brusque, impatient giant, Jack, quickly became a kitten in the little girl's hands. That's Laurie Bale! The bright young girl visited for a while with the temporarily tamed, gentle giant, and when she finally came face to face with Gray Bar, Laurie told Van Berg that she recently had a dream that Gray Bar would win the Omaha Gold Cup. Jack said, "If that gray horse wins I want you in the winner's circle." On June 28, 1975, Gray Bar won the Omaha Gold Cup and just before the gray underdog stepped into the winner's circle, big Jack Van Berg waded out into the crowd and wheeled Laurie into the winner's circle for the win photo. That's Jack Van Berg!

The following year, Jack arranged for Laurie to go to the 1976 Kentucky Derby. Prior to her trip, there was a special gathering at the Stockade Restaurant in Millard, Nebraska, just west of Omaha. It was a popular hangout for many racetrackers, and it was there that Laurie met jockey Sam Maple through trainer Hoss Inman. Sam took Laurie under his wing, and he even took her under her arm, as a chaperone at her eighth-grade high school dance.

Jack, Laurie, and Sam Maple would become good friends in the years that followed. Laurie, just a young teenager at the time, credits both Jack and Sam as having an outstanding influence on her life. "I would not be the person I am today if it wasn't for those two," said Bale. "When you are disabled as a child, you really get bullied a lot and kids have a tendency to make fun of something they don't know. I was a pretty shy kid and Jack went out of his way for me. He just made me more confident in myself, and because of him and Sam I discovered that there are some really good people out there. The racetrack has an amazing sense of community. To be invited into that world, even on a very small scale, and to be accepted for who I was, is just absolutely tremendous."

Laurie Bale was also the name of a talented filly who was a multiple stakes winner. Technically, her name was Miss Laurie Bale and she was a homebred of Van Berg. Jack co-owned his Nebraska-bred filly with an

Iowan named Don Bruce. Jack thought so much of the filly that, aside from naming her after Laurie, her first start was in the 1977 Ak-Sar-Ben Lassie Stakes. The maiden miss went off at 6-1 and finished third in the thirteen-horse field. She injured herself and she did not make her next start until her three-year-old year. It was at Oaklawn Park in March of 1978 where Miss Laurie Bale raced to her first-ever win, and she won with Sam Maple in the irons. She raced in the domain of Jack Van Berg, so the name of the trainer of record varied. Bill Mott trained her at Oaklawn and when she ran in Omaha the trainer line in the program read Frankie Brothers; both budding trainers were still taking orders from Jack at the time. It was a summer to remember for Laurie Bale, as Miss Laurie Bale won an allowance race, en route to a win in the Countess Stakes, which led to a seven-and-a-half-length romp against the boys in the Ak-Sar-Ben Breeders' Stakes. Miss Laurie Bale was a favorite in each race that summer and won each dash under the hands of Sam Maple. In her fourth attempt at victory that summer, she was soundly defeated in what was her first attempt at two turns, and she finished out of the money in her next two starts, which included an allowance race at Santa Anita as her final race.

Twenty years after her first Kentucky Derby, in 1996 Laurie Bale returned to Louisville to enjoy the run for the roses. When she was there, Dan Johnson, the horse racing reporter for the *Des Moines Register* newspaper, waved Bill Mott over to come say hello. Laurie was flattered when Bill remembered her and she was even more impressed when Mott recited the pedigree and race record of Miss Laurie Bale from memory. "I guess successful trainers have a memory and attention to details like that," said Bale. Class and determination can shape and create success. And so can inspiration.

29

A Cavalcade of Stakes

Jack began setting and breaking national training records for races won
in the '70s, so he obviously had quantity, but he also acquired quality
along the way, and plenty of it. After a stunning season in '76, Van Berg
proudly pressed for more. Summertime Promise was there for him again
in 1977 when she won the G3 Gallorette at Pimlico, but Jack didn't win
his next $100,000 stakes race until 1978, when Landscaper won the 1
3/8th-mile G1 Century Handicap at 17-1. Van Berg won four other stakes
in '78, all in Southern California. In 1979 he won the $50,000 G2 Los
Angeles Handicap with the speedy Hawkin's Special, and then Jack won
four more stakes at Ak-Sar-Ben, including the $75,000 G3 President's
Cup with Switch Partners.

After four consecutive wins in Louisiana with Frankie Brothers overseeing the Van Berg operation, Jack knew Nell's Briquette was good
enough to win elsewhere. "She was a little straight-legged thing who
could really run. She raced for Triple L Stables, some brothers from Dal-
las. I brought her to California and she was tougher than nails," said Jack.
On the final day of 1980, the Cal-bred won the $75,000 Cal Breeders' Filly
Stakes at Santa Anita for her owners Triple L Stable. She and Jack began
brightly in 1981, winning the Pasadena Stakes and then the G1 Santa Su-
sana Stakes. Nell's Briquette then got beat by a head in the G1 Fantasy
Stakes at Oaklawn and was defeated by the same margin that summer in
Omaha by the quintessential queen of Ak-Sar-Ben, Bersid, trained by Lyman Rollins. The sting of narrow defeats eased a bit with the development
of Targa. The Cannonade filly would win a division of the Matinee Handi-

cap at Hollywood Park and then be shipped to Aks to win the $75,000 Queens Handicap.

Most trainers would be pleased with just a few stakes wins a year, or two, or even just one. Five years after his record 496 wins in 1976, Jack had recorded a total of twenty stakes wins. But that collection of stakes wins in a five-year span was a relatively light tremor of tallies, which would quickly rumble from a simmer to a boil, and then to a full-on stakes eruption. In 1982 Jack trained fifteen stakes winners. In 1983 he had thirteen blacktype winners. In 1984 he won another fifteen. And in 1985 he recorded yet another fifteen stakes wins.

Jack got his first taste of the Triple Crown in 1981, when he took over the training of Bold Ego. Bred by J. D. Barton, the New Mexico–bred was transferred into Jack's name just before the Kentucky Derby. He'd already won 7 of 10 races for trainers Cliff Lambert and Dennis Werre. He was voted the Champion Two-Year-Old in New Mexico, and the speedball had won all of his races in sprints and on the lead with jockey John Cushing. Werre was running the barn for Jack in Hot Springs at the time and had already won a sprint stake at Oaklawn before Jack showed up to see him. As Jack remembers:

> I worked him a mile one morning and that little clocker named Scatch came running down and said, "Jack, that horse will go a route of ground." So I decided to run him in the 1-mile Rebel Stakes. The owners thought I was crazy running him in a mile race, so they didn't even come to town for the race. Hell, he won that race for fun and he won the Arkansas Derby, too. He won three in a row there in Hot Springs with John Lively up, and we just beat Top Avenger, so I figured we'd go to Kentucky.

In the build up to the race, Jack recalls a point-blank, if not rude and ignorant question asked him by famed ABC television broadcaster Howard Cosell. "Jack," Cosell said, "why would you bring a New Mexico–

bred to the Kentucky Derby?" To which Jack replied, "Howard, he can't read and he don't know where he was bred, but he can damn sure run."

Jack had a clear view of his first-ever Kentucky Derby runner when he saw his speedy Bold Ego on the front end for much of the race. Bold Ego had locked horns with Top Avenger again and the pair zipped through the fastest-ever opening quarter (21.4) and the fastest-ever half-mile (45.1) in the race's 107-year history. Nearing the 1/8th pole Jack watched Pleasant Colony take the lead and power home for the win. Bold Ego finished tenth of twenty-one for owners Double B Ranch and Dr. Joseph Kidd.

In the Preakness, Bold Ego had better luck with the pace. The early fractions were 23.4 and 47.3. J. L. Lively was able to rate his colt more effectively in the middle jewel of the Triple Crown, but Pleasant Colony came swooping again. Bold Ego was second, beaten by a length. Jack was not very eager to run Bold Ego in the final leg of the Triple Crown, but he did nonetheless. Bold Ego ran last; Pleasant Colony ran third.

After Bold Ego's last-place finish in the Belmont, he didn't race again until October, but he did win his final career start a year and eighteen races later, after a mix of small stakes and allowance races. His final five wins connected: Churchill, Ak-Sar-Ben, Ruidoso Downs, Albuquerque, and Hollywood Park. He made about a five-thousand-mile loop in 1982 alone. And his connections sure got their kicks on Route 66. Back in the care of trainer Cliff Lambert for those final New Mexico wins, Bold Ego was retired to stud after his four-year-old season and went on to be a popular stallion in New Mexico, siring a number of horses that earned more than $200,000.

Targa won big again in 1982, taking the G2 $100,000 Santa Maria Handicap at Santa Anita and then the $150,000 Sixty Sails Stakes at Sportsman's Park for owners Ken Opstein and television actor John Forsythe. The star of *Dynasty* and the voice of *Charlie's Angels*, Forsythe was active in thoroughbred racing and served on the Hollywood Park Racetrack Board of Directors for many years.

Rich And Ready bounced around with a few owners and trainers with modest success before he arrived to the Van Berg barn, after a running third as a beaten favorite in an allowance race. With a new owner, E. C. Hurlock, and a new trainer, Rich And Ready promptly popped up and won the $100,000 Fair Grounds Classic. Later that year he won the G3 $150,000 Louisiana Downs Handicap.

Bold Style was a Kentucky-bred who began modestly at Turf Paradise in Arizona. But the Len Mayer homebred found his way home and broke his maiden with Jack at Churchill Downs. In 1982 Jack had him primed in Hot Springs, and Bold Style won the $75,000 Rebel Stakes at Oaklawn Park. Bold Style then ran third in the Arkansas Derby, sixteenth in the Kentucky Derby, fourth in the Preakness, and ninth in the Arlington Classic before eventually getting a half-year's rest. Bold Style would return boldly. Brindy Brindy and Dave's Friend both emerged in '82 and won a few stakes for Jack, but their best was also yet to come.

Brindy Brindy occupied a soft spot in Jack's heart. He trained the precocious filly up to her first start, which was a maiden special weight win at Ellis Park with Wayne Catalano up. She then won an allowance race at both Ellis Park and Keeneland, before concluding her two-year-old season with a win in the '82 Pocahontas Stakes at Churchill. In 1983, after a mixed bag of results at Oaklawn early in Brindy Brindy's three-year-old season, Jack's belief in her rang true when she hushed a packed grandstand on April 9, by winning the G1 $250,000 Fantasy Stakes at 57-1. At that point, it was the richest race Jack had won in his career. It was also the start of what would become a memorable week in April for Jack C. Van Berg, at the1983 Oaklawn Park Racing Festival of the South. Later that summer Brindy Brindy crossed under the wire first in the $100,000 Ak-Sar-Ben Oaks. But she was ultimately placed second after the steward's decision to disqualify her was upheld in court. The purse money dwindled from $60,000 to $20,000, then became even smaller after legal fees and court costs. Evidently Jack didn't rule everything in Nebraska.

It should be noted that by today's standards a $25,000 stakes race is a *stakes* race in name only. Presently, allowance races routinely have higher purses. But in the early '80s, there was nothing small about winning a stake of $25,000. That money then would be equivalent to roughly $75,000 now. And there is no inflation converter for the joy, celebration, and pride of winning a stakes race any year; that value is always gauged as *priceless*. That said, there's always a price to pay with the bar tab and a hangover—blacktype can have you seeing red.

Dave's Friend was a beast! In fact, he was "The Beast from the East." His lifetime record was 76-35-16-8 $1,079,915. Imagine what it could have been if just a few of those sixteen second-place finishes had been wins. Dave's Friend didn't surface in the Midwest until he had already won 26 races in 44 starts, which included seven seconds. By the time he arrived in Omaha for the '82 Ak-Sar-Ben Speed Handicap, he had already won the Bold Ruler Stakes at Aqueduct Racetrack *twice*, along with four other Aqueduct stakes. Dave's Friend had also previously won stakes at Pimlico, Keystone, Meadowlands, and Bowie. In the Aks Speed Handicap he finished in a famous dead-heat win with Ogatual. Bob Holthus was training Dave's Friend at the time, but Bob developed some heart problems and Dave's Friend and a few other horses were turned over to Jack.

John Franks purchased Dave's Friend in the spring of 1981 from trainer Robert Beall and utilized a few trainers until the iron horse came into the care of JVB. When Jack picked up Dave's Friend in July of 1982, they headed east and immediately won stakes at Detroit and Thistledown before turning west and rattling of three straight seconds in stakes at Hollywood Park and Santa Anita. Jack has fond memories of a real war horse:

Dave's Friend had some ankles on him but he was a pretty sound horse for an old horse. And he had some foot problems but we worked on him a lot. Mark Wallerstadt had him in Oaklawn those years he won all those races. But horses are just like football players or basketball players, you've got to work on their ankles and knees and sweat 'em and rub 'em and do them up and use machines on them. There are different kinds of machines for therapy on horses like ultrasound and vibrators and whirlpool machines and tubs just like they use for many athletes. Most horses have little problems, but you have to look out for them. We looked after Dave's Friend like all the rest, but boy he was a hard-trying son-of-a-buck. We ran him anywhere over any surface against any competition. We once ran a good second to Chinook Pass in a turf stake at Hollywood. We even ran him over the turf at Beulah Park back when that track was named Darby Downs for a few years.

When Dave's Friend arrived at Oaklawn in 1983, he won a $50,000 sprint handicap as the favorite, ran fourth in another sprint handicap as a favorite, shipped to Turf Paradise for the G3 $100,000 Phoenix Gold Cup and ran second as the second choice, and then returned back to Hot Springs. Making his eighteenth start at ten different tracks in the span of twelve months, with never more than a few weeks' rest, Dave's Friend won the $100,000 Count Fleet Handicap by five lengths. It would be the second Racing Festival of the South stakes win for Jack in just five days.

The very next day Jack would win his third Racing Festival of the South stakes race and his second $250,000 race, when Bold Style took the G2 Oaklawn Handicap. In six days Van Berg's three horses won stakes races totaling $600,000 at Oaklawn Park. Jack won seven more stakes in 1983; Hur Power won the $75,000 Round Table Handicap at Bay Meadows in San Francisco and Hail To Rome won the $75,000 Fairmount Derby in St. Louis. Jack would record roughly 250 additional wins across the land that year and reclaim the national leading trainer title from Dale Baird. In 1983 Jack led the nation with 258 wins.

1984 was essentially the same. Van Berg won another national training title with exactly eight fewer total wins, but with exactly $950,800 more in total earnings. Dave's Friend won another $100,000 Count Fleet Handicap—at age nine. It bears repeating, Dave's Friend was a beast! Jack also started a pair of homebreds who made him proud—and made him money. Charging Falls ran sixteen times in his first season of racing at age three, and earned more than $113,000. His lone stakes win came in the $15,000 Sophomore Handicap at Albuquerque; the $9,845 earned for the win was half as much as the third-place money he later earned in the $100,000 National Sprint Handicap at Hollywood Park. And Jack's filly, Foggy Nation, also had a sparkling beginning. After wins at Hollywood and Santa Anita, she too found her way to New Mexico and won the $15,000 Fair Queen Handicap at Albuquerque. Young jockey Marty Wentz was astride for the stakes wins of both Foggy Nation and Charging Falls. The following year, hall of fame jockeys Bill Shoemaker, Pat Day, and Laffit Pincay, Jr., would win graded stakes races with the horses. Without a doubt, the best of the bunch in 1984, and arguably the best horse Jack had trained to that point, was a much-maligned, masked marvel—Gate Dancer—who became so infamous that he is worthy of his own chapter.

In 1985 Charging Falls won the $50,000 Hillsdale Handicap, the G3 $75,000 Los Angeles Handicap, and the G3 $100,000 Phoenix Gold Cup. Foggy Nation won the G3 $60,000 Las Flores Handicap. Flare Dancer won the G3 $150,000 Omaha Gold Cup. Gate Dancer carried on. And then the cavalcade reached a crescendo.

1986 became a cavalry charge of stakes races and graded stakes wins like Van Berg had never experienced before. Jack won twenty stakes races with purses of $50,000 or more; he won with fourteen different horses at eleven different tracks.

Wheatley Hall never won a stake for Jack, but after finishing second to Rampage in the Arkansas Derby, he earned a trip to Louisville a few weeks later. Jack's fourth starter in the Kentucky Derby ran sixth.

Incredibly, Charging Falls was at it again another year. Jack chose his spots wisely with the now five-year-old chestnut horse. He ran him just five times in 1986, but Charging Falls won three races: a pair of $50,000 stakes at Oaklawn Park and then the $100,000 Mutual Savings Life Handicap in New Orleans.

Obviously there were several more stakes winners that year, but the new, big star to come onto the screen was a well-bred bay colt named Herat. Woody Stephens trained the son of Northern Dancer before Jack took over the training. Herat won the bulk of his races early while with Stephens; they consisted of two main track sprints and four wins over the turf, including a division of the $75,000 Buckpasser Stakes at Hollywood Park. Despite Herat's two consecutive bad races back in New York, John Franks became interested in purchasing the colt from W. W. Hancock II. It was not uncommon for Mr. Franks to spend big money on a *made* racehorse. John Franks was a self-made millionaire; the Shreveport, Louisiana, oilman had the money, and he wanted to have Herat. As Jack remembers:

> John Franks called me up one night after I had just gotten home from the races. He said, "Jack, can you be in New York in the morning?" Well, I said, "Yeah, if you need me." He tells me, "There is a horse up there [Herat] that Woody Stephens has that I can buy for a million dollars, but I won't buy him without you looking at him." So I caught the redeye that night and arrived at JFK the next morning at six o'clock and drove over to Belmont and looked at the horse. He was a little thing but he was very well balanced. So Woody galloped him for me and he went really well. So I called Mr. Franks and told him that Herat was sound and clean-legged and looked great, but "he's very small, I want you to

know that. But when he gallops, he looks like a giant out there." Mr. Franks asked me, "Do you like him?" I said, "Yes, he's just small." "Well, go ahead and buy him," he said. So I bought him.

Jack first shipped Herat up to Bay Meadows and he ran a disappointing seventh in the Ascot Handicap. In his next start he ran second at 24-1 in the $100,000 Hollywood Derby. "Al Stall, Sr., and his buddies bought a horse from France, Charming Duke, and they sent him out to California for the Hollywood Derby," Jack said. "He was a hittin' son-of-a-buck, so I helped them with the horseshoer to get him shod right so he'd stop hitting himself when he ran. We got him right all right; that son-of-a-buck is the one who beat me in that damn Hollywood Derby."

Herat followed that game effort with four poor starts (tenth, eighth, tenth, and fourth), all in graded stakes company, either over the turf or muddy going. "Herat was a little hyper at times and he'd shut his air down if everything wasn't just right. We had to keep him relaxed. We had to learn about him, but Mr. Franks was patient through all those races," Van Berg said. "John Franks was a very good man! And I never charged him any commission for any horses we sold."

Then, off of a fair fourth at 39-1 in the G1 San Antonio Handicap, Jack got the notion to run Herat in the $1 million G1 Santa Anita Handicap.

I told Mr. Franks that Herat was really getting good and I think we should run him in the Big Cap [Santa Anita Handicap]. He says, "Do you want to use him as a rabbit [pacesetter] for Gate Dancer? And I said, "Mr. Franks, everyone is going to think that, but I'm telling you this horse is just as good as you can make one right now. He's popping out of his skin. Gate Dancer don't need no rabbit, but I don't want you to think that's why I want to run him." The morning of the race I was walking around with a carrot and I showed it to Chris McCarron, who was riding the favorite

Precisionist, and asked him if he wanted to go feed my rabbit. Pat Day was supposed to ride him but instead Rafeal Meza rode him. Herat went to the front and that little son-of-a-buck never stopped.

At 157-1, over a fast main track, Herat led every step of the way in the G1 $1,000,000 Santa Anita Handicap—well, *almost* every step of the way. In the final yards of the 1 1/4-mile race, he was caught by the mighty Greinton in the final strides. In post-race comments, referring to the ultra longshot Herat, Greinton's jockey, Laffit Pincay, Jr., asked, "Who was that horse, anyway?" Herat was a quirky fella. Mr. Franks could have earned $600,000 for the win; instead he only won $200,000 for second place. But after the race, Allan Paulson, aviation entrepreneur, Eclipse Award Outstanding Breeder, and owner of the memorable Cigar, bought a half-interest in Herat for $2 million. The decision to buy that little horse for a million dollars just paid off.

Striking while the iron was hot, or so the connections hoped, Herat was shipped to the Fair Grounds for the G2 $200,000 New Orleans Handicap. As the 9/5 favorite, Herat sailed home, an easy-winning favorite over the fast, main track and equaled the 1 1/4-mile track record of 2:01 4/5. Despite his low odds, it was a rare, positive, repeat performance. But soon Herat was back to his discouraging ways; he ran out of the money in four straight graded stakes races. Convinced he had a horse that could still win, Jack then convinced Franks and Paulson to send Herat to Laurel for the $200,000 Budweiser Maryland Classic.

We shipped him to Maryland, and on the day before the race, my assistant up there, Chris Tooley, called me and said, "Jack, this horse can't put his foot down." There was a guy there by me at the barn when I got the phone call. He had a machine he was using there on the backstretch in California. It was a TENS unit like they use in dentist offices. They use it for nerve-related pain.

He wanted to come along to see if his machine could help. So we caught a plane and flew up there that day. I pulled his shoes off myself to have a look to see what was wrong. We used that machine on him, and I did him up with poultice and I called Jack Ballenger, the horseshoer I used up there. I called him and said he had to get to the barn by five o'clock the next morning. Now this horse was dead lame and everyone in the barn had seen it. I trimmed his feet and Ballanger came and reshod him. In the meantime I called Mr. Franks and explained what was going on and that I would jog him at eight that morning and we'd see how things went. He told me that he would be waiting at the airport to see how things went. I took him to the track; he moved like a well-oiled machine, and I called Mr. Franks and told him to catch that plane. There were people that swore up and down that I gave that horse something. But I figured he had a nail come out of position in his shoe and it was hitting on a nerve in his hoof. You get a broken toothpick caught up in your gums and see how good that feels.

Sent off at even money, Herat, with Jerry Bailey wearing the green, orange, and white silks of John Franks, won comfortably, by more than five lengths. Retired to stud two starts later, Herat, a son of Northern Dancer, went on to produce a number of stakes winners over the main and turf.

While the surge of stakes wins in 1986 surely is a high-water mark for Jack Van Berg, the intense horseman continued to win races from coast to coast in a yeoman-like manner. Jack commanded divisions of horses and horsemen who commanded respect over their rivals. With 1,841 starts in 1986 he won 266 races. For the ninth time, Jack led the nation in wins.

In mid-September of 1986, Van Berg won a fairly cheap race with a very expensive horse. He won the third race at Turfway Park. The horse earned $5,750; the horse cost $500,000. The two-year-old colt was named Alysheba.

To say things were business as usual for Jack C. Van Berg in 1987 and 1988 would simply not be true. Alysheba was Jack's number one horse, but he still had more than one hundred horses in training. Aside from Alysheba, Jack won twelve blacktype races with eight different horses in 1987. But beyond Alysheba, Vilzak was the only other G1 winner Jack had in '87 and '88. The Cal-bred won two races in Europe; however, stateside, Vilzak was a one-trick pony. In 1987 Vilzak ran an amazing eighteen times from California to Chicago to Kentucky to New York and back home to California. He tormented his trainer and the bettors with one disappointing race after the next. He lost when he was a favorite, and his only U.S. win came when he was a long shot. But on that day, December 13, 1987, Vilzak got in the mood. At 14-1 in the G1 $500,000 Hollywood Turf Cup, against a very nice field of turf stars, it took him all year and every yard of the 1 1/2-mile circuit to pull out the win. But at the finish, Vilzak prevailed by a neck and earned $275,000. What a grind!

Jack's youngest son, Tom, joined Team JVB (though he was technically born into it) after he graduated from Arizona State University. He was involved with Hill Pass, who won the 1994 G2 San Pasqual at Santa Anita, defeating Best Pal at 15-1. Tom was also with Bossanova after Jack claimed Bossanova for the Kenis & 3+U Stable. The gelding went on to win five races, including two allowance races and the Rising Market Handicap at Santa Anita. Bossanova even ran fourth in a four-horse blanket finish in the G3 Cornhusker Handicap in 1994.

Tom, his brother Tim, and their father Jack put on a stakes spectacular in the '93/'94 Santa Anita Park racing season. Jack won the training title with thirty-three wins, and the Van Berg runners were in the money in sixteen stakes races, winning eight of them. It was a Van Berg trifecta of triumph. "I remember Dad won the '93 La Canada with Alysbelle, Alysheba's full sister, and was third in the Santa Anita standings that year; then 1994 got even better," said Tom. "Mamselle Bebette won four G3 stakes that meet at Santa Anita and upset Desert Stormer at 20-1. And we beat Cool Air, that nice Gary Jones filly, in the Las Cienegas Handicap. Dezibelle's Star got on a roll, too, and we won three straight, including the La Habra Stakes. And Dad ran second in the Breeders' Cup Juvenile with Blumin Affair at 42-1; then he closed strongly and ran third in the '94 Kentucky Derby at 14-1."

JVB & Sons was really hitting on all cylinders in '93 and '94. Tom and Jack were working hand in hand at Hollywood Park, while Tim Van Berg ran the barn for his dad across town at Santa Anita. There was a satisfying closeness between Jack and his sons that went beyond geographic proximately. The operation was humming along, and it felt good. Of course, in true Van Berg fashion, Tom Van Berg went out on the road just like his father and grandfather. He operated a division in Maryland, based at Pimlico, mostly of John Franks–owned horses. "It was a pretty exciting time back then, and I don't think Dad and Tim and I realized how well we worked as a team," said Tom Van Berg. "The machine never ran the same after we split up." Both of Jack's sons remain involved in horse racing with their individual enterprises.

The dozen or so years that went by after Jack's astonishing, record-shattering 496 wins in 1976 were heady stuff. They would be heavy stuff, too. He had heaps of important wins, and was faced with massive personal and professional decisions. The days, weeks, months, and years simply streaked by. But within that span there would be a special set of years that would expose Jack in ways he'd never dreamed. The double-edged sword of success was drawn.

30

On the Road with JVB

If you were living or working with Jack, you were lucky to have a home base—most staffers didn't, and only a few family members did. When Jack was married to Helen, his second wife, she kept a home in Hot Springs, Arkansas, to serve this purpose. Then, it was up to her to simply try to keep up with Jack as best she could. "I usually stayed home for two weeks with the kids and then was on the road with Jack for two weeks," said Helen. "My father, Bill Murphy, and his wife Maureen lived outside of Hot Springs, and when I would leave town, they would come to town and stay at the house with the kids. They gave my daughter the care that she needed when I was away. When I would return, they would then go home themselves. That was the routine."

With the mechanics and routine established of taking care of the precious valuables, such as children and a home, now all Helen had to do was take care of herself, Jack, and their clothes. For years, the two lived nearly a Bonnie and Clyde lifestyle, minus the bank heists and tommy guns. Helen remembered:

> My luggage was my chest of drawers. We were constantly on the go and I needed to be ready to go at the drop of a hat. We lived in hotels and it was off one plane and on to another. We might fly directly to one destination, but we might visit many other destinations on the path of returning back home. And we'd show up at racetracks at night to check horses—it wasn't always in the morning during training. It was whenever we would arrive into town, because wherever that was, we generally weren't staying

there long. And Jack used to only wear Levi's. I tailored them for him, and he wouldn't let anyone touch them but me. And he would ship his laundry back to me on the plane. He would fly it back on Delta Dash and I would drive up to Little Rock, bring it home, and do his laundry, then drive back with a box full of clean clothes. All the guys back there in Little Rock knew him and they never charged him to put his clothes on flights even if he wasn't on the flights himself. They all knew it was his dirty laundry.

The grind of all the travel would take its toll even on the most nimble, but when you try to accomplish what Jack did within a marriage, it was expectedly too much at times. Helen recalls a specific occasion when they were living in a hotel suite near Hollywood Park that they called home:

Jack and I were at a point where I was having issues with wanting to have some one-on-one time with him instead of going out with a group of people to a restaurant after the races all the time. He was just growling and not buying my complaints. I pleaded with him that we, just he and I, go to a movie and to dinner. So one day, in classic Jack Van Berg style, he took me to a movie, but we didn't see just one movie. After it was done, then we went and saw another and then another. We saw three movies in one day. I guess in his mind he figured that, "Well, I've fulfilled; we covered a lot of ground."

Jack and Helen once made a trip south of the border; in fact, they went south of the equator, all the way down to Chile. The two spent some time together sightseeing in the beautiful capital city of Santiago. Then Jack met some Chilean horsemen for an arranged daytrip to visit some of the horse farms south of Santiago. Day turned into night and Jack had not returned. This was in the early '80s, and Chilean dictator Augusto Pinochet had enacted a curfew. Jack was out past bedtime—his wife knew it, and so did the national police, known as the Carabineros de Chile. All Jack knew

was that his passport was in the hotel and the stone-faced Carabineros had
him at gunpoint. Helen was more mad than scared when she got a confus-
ing phone call:

> Jack left me in that hotel all day by myself. No one spoke English
> and I sure didn't speak any Spanish. I'd been stuck there all day
> with no word from Jack and then late at night the hotel staff gets
> me on the phone. Jack was on the other end and he was speaking
> very softly. He wanted me to get his passport and read him the
> identification numbers. Well, I was angry at him as any woman
> would have been at the time. I told him no, I wouldn't give him the
> number unless he told me where he was. But Jack wasn't allowed
> to mention where and why he was being held. I didn't know that,
> so I wasn't giving in. We went around and around like that for a
> while until Jack slowly whispered to me, "Helen, give . . . me . . .
> the damn . . . passport number." I could tell he sounded desper-
> ate, so I gave it to him. When he finally got back to Santiago, he
> didn't have many kind words to say to me, but of course I didn't
> have many nice words to say back to him. We got over it and now
> we can have a good laugh about it. But it sure wasn't funny at the
> time. Oh, that Jack!

You can never be too sure where and when you'll be somewhere if
you're on the road for Jack. Bill Mott, like so many other Van Berg employees, knows all too well about sudden and long-term displacement.

> I was down at Hialeah one spring and Jack said he wanted me to
> go to Chicago for a week or so to look after things, because he had
> to replace his nephew Chuck Karlin, who he needed to put in a
> truck to move some horses around. Now Jack had already told me
> I was supposed to go to Omaha for the summer, so I had someone
> drive my car packed with all my clothes ahead of me. I had a bag
> with enough clothes for about a week. I figured I'd get to leave

Chicago as soon as Chuck got back. Hell, I didn't leave Chicago until December 31st.

Jim Bayes was a horseshoer from Arkansas who started working for Jack in 1974. He and Jack linked up at Oaklawn Park and were tacked together for nearly twenty years. They are still friends today. Van Berg considers both Jim Bayes and Jack Reynolds as two of the best shoers in the nation. "I was a horseshoer and the horseshoers were on strike. I don't believe in unions, so I went to work," said Bayes. "I'm a scab and I don't mind saying it; I've shod horses all over the world." Jim was shoeing horses at all of his outfits across the nation. He was on a plane bound for a Van Berg barn several times a month, and Jack wasn't his only client.

I remember one time I was in Omaha and I had been shoeing horses all day. I got cleaned up and needed to catch a plane to Chicago that night to do the same thing the next day. On the way to the airport, Jack tells me about some special dessert at Mr. C's restaurant. He says, "You got to try this dessert before you go." Well, I tell him, "No, I've got to catch a plane." "I'll get you there, Big Boy," he says, and we wheel into the restaurant. We sit down and the next thing I know Jack starts ordering food. Now, I can't enjoy a bite because I keep looking at my watch. So we finally get in the car and I say, "Jack, I've got to catch this plane and we ain't gonna make it." He says, "Relax, Big Boy," and gets on the phone and calls the United counter there in Omaha and says, "This is Jack Van Berg and I'll be at the airport in seven minutes and I want you to hold that plane . . ." and I'm thinking to myself, this is the biggest load of crap I've ever heard. Well, I'll tell ya, when we got to the airport there was a guy waiting for me at the curb and he grabbed one of my bags and we went straight to the plane. I stepped on, they closed the door behind me, and off we went. That was the damnedest thing!

Jack would make a point to try to be there when any of his horses were being shod, regardless of who was doing the shoeing. He had a keen eye for horse's feet and an equally keen eye on the person handling the horse's feet. Anyone who worked for Jack had to know that Jack was going to tell you how to do your job, and with Jim Bayes, it was no different. "I guess Jack and I got on so well because I used to let him use my knife. He loved to cut on feet!" said Bayes. "He'd say, 'Gimmie that knife, Big Boy,' and then he'd bend over and go to work. And to be honest, when he was done, all I had to do is put the shoe on. Yeah, he did a really good job."

Jack and Jim carried on like that for years. Jim Bayes shod both Gate Dancer and Alysheba. The power of persuasion in Jack's voice was not lost on Jim.

Jack had the ability to get people to do things that they really didn't want to do. I've seen him get lazy people up and working and enjoying the work as Jack worked right alongside them. Once he called me and needed me to fly from Hot Springs to New York to shoe Alysheba. I had just broken my ribs the day before and I told Jack I didn't think I could. He said, "Get on a plane, I need you here tomorrow." And somehow he was able to get me to decide to come. I got to New York and rented a car and drove to Belmont Park, but I was hurting so bad I couldn't lift my shoeing box out of the trunk of the car. But I did it for Jack and I'm glad I did.

Jim Bayes is retired from horseshoeing now and farms hay in southwestern Arkansas. A recent drought devastated his crop yield and the insurance adjuster was on his way to assess his land. Jim was worried about the size of the check that the adjuster would cut. "I could sure use some of that JVB magic today," Bayes said. "Jack's got a silver tongue and the balls of a brass baboon."

Mike Willman has been part of the media scene of Southern California racing for decades. He is passionate about his role in horse racing.

When he and Kurt Hoover and Jon White conducted their insightful racing analysis from Santa Anita, Hollywood Park, Del Mar, and Fairplex, track announcer Trevor Denman would describe their teamwork as "poetry in motion." Currently the director of publicity at Santa Anita, Mike understands horse racing and he relishes the many important individuals he has met along the way. One of his favorites is Jack Van Berg. Mike tells one of his favorite Jack Van Berg stories:

> This story is regarding Jack's residency at the now-imploded Airport Park Hotel, which used to be on the northwest corner of the Hollywood Park parking lot, directly across from the Forum, where the Lakers and Kings played for many years. Jack had a deal whereby he lived on one of the upper floors, and he lived there for about six years, I believe. Anyway, it was no secret that the hotel was in deep financial trouble. Perhaps coincidentally, a number of tenants fell behind in their rent. The day finally came when Southern California Edison pulled the plug on the place— no kidding! They just shut the power off. Well, Jack had been over at the racetrack training and came back to discover the lights were out and, obviously, the elevators did not work. He quickly assembled a group of backstretch employees and began the arduous task of carrying all of his belongs down the stairwell. I later asked him about getting out of the hotel, which was blown up shortly after the power outage, to make room for an as-yet-unbuilt football stadium. Jack replied with a smile, "Let's just say I left there well in front."

PART III

31

Gate Dancer

The first time I saw him was at Ak-Sar-Ben; he had just stepped onto the racetrack from the gap near the 1/2-mile pole. The morning sun danced on his glistening, light bay coat as he eagerly strode into a simple jog. But his jog was far from simple. The exercise rider was already feeling the pull; he was anchored in, ankles buried deep into the irons. The rider's hands were up close on the horse's neck; he took a very short hold of the reins. I could see all of this with my naked eye, and I was in the grandstand near the finish line. And then the radiant horse transitioned into that unmistakable canter, coiled and as though he could shoot to the moon with a release of the rider's grip. His neck was bowed and tucked down almost to his knees. His forehead was angled down and in, virtually parallel to the ground, yet his eyes shot up and out. He was springing forward and intensely focused. He looked ready to explode out of his skin, yet he was moving fluidly and in a controlled, methodical bounce, bounce, bounce . . . I had never seen a horse move like this. I thought to myself, My God, he looks glorious. I asked out loud, "Who is that horse?" *He* was Gate Dancer!

As the author of this book, a book I agreed to write when Jack asked me in June of 2010, I must say I actually wrote that opening paragraph back in the summer of 1984—if only in my head. I have such a vivid memory of what I witnessed, that I feel the impression it left on me is now *in* me. It is an image that defines the way I think and feel when I see a racehorse—an inner impulse derived from purposeful propulsion.

That horse, that glorious creature—Gate Dancer—was owned by Ken

Opstein of Sioux City, Iowa. Opstein had been in horse racing years before Jack Van Berg became his trainer. Ken and his trainer, Monti Sims, were winning races, and the pair enjoyed sweet success with Destroyer, who won the 1974 G1 Santa Anita Derby and '74 G3 Omaha Gold Cup. But when Sims retired in 1975, Opstein needed a trainer. At first he divided his horses up between three trainers, but when he won his first five races with Jack Van Berg, Ken, without much more persuasion, moved all of his horses into the kingdom of JVB.

"I'd like to think I'm a good judge of a horse," said Opstein. "I made a pretty good study of it and I knew I could spot what's good and what I like in a horse. Between me and my farm manager Dean Johnson, we were doing okay picking and buying horses." But then Opstein discovered a key ingredient in his recipe of racehorse assessment and acquisition—he added a few scoops of Jack.

> I realized that I could use Jack to help me spot the negative aspects in a horse. He and his father Marion had made a lifetime of claiming horses that they could patch up and win with at a higher level. Jack could spot problems that were happening or getting ready to happen. What I'm saying is that most anyone can train a horse if nothing is wrong with it. But I've seen lots of trainers come to Jack looking for assistance when they didn't know what was wrong with their horse. Van Berg could and would spot the problem and help these guys. So I learned that I could use Jack to help me spot the defects in a horse that I might initially like. The three of us did quite well as a team buying horses.

In a bit of foreshadowing, Opstein saw early on how Jack could be resourceful in his attempts to resolve a problem. His filly Summertime Promise had a problem of *running down*; she would skin her heels through the top-surface of the racetrack when she ran. In mid-July of 1976, Ken and Jack were driving to Aqueduct in New York to run Summertime

Promise in the G2 Sheepshead Bay stakes. Along the way they drove by a lingerie store. "Jack says to me, 'Hey, pull over into this store,'" Opstein recalled. "I blinked my eyes a few times and raised an eyebrow, but I pulled over. Next thing I know, Jack comes out with some padded bra inserts, hops back in the car, and simply says, 'Let's go!' Along the way Jack explained to Ken that the shape of the bra inserts was ideal for using as an ankle cushion in the leg wraps for Summertime Promise. It was too good of a story to keep quiet. "I can recall reading newspaper headlines that read 'Filly Runs with Falsies' and another one read 'Summertime Promise Wears a B-Cup,'" Opstein said. A few years later, he would see his most prized horse run with even more creative equipment.

Ken Opstein developed a horse farm in Ocala, Florida, and he became interested and impressed with Sovereign Dancer, a stallion who stood at stud at a nearby farm. Jack was already aware of Sovereign Dancer and how good-looking his foals were. Jack, being Jack, went big again and told his assistant Bill Mook to buy as many Sovereign Dancer foals as he could, which resulted in the purchase of nine weanlings. Later, in 1982, Bill discovered two more yearlings in Ocala that were for sale. One was out of Sun Gate, who was from the last foal crop of Bull Lea. The foundation sire of the famed Calumet Farm, Bull Lea was the North American Leading Sire from 1947 to 1953 and the Leading Broodmare Sire from 1958 to 1961. The asking price for the pair was out of range for Jack; however, an important part of the deal whereby Jack didn't have to pay for the colts until the following spring got lost in translation. Not wanting to lose the chance to train the colts, Jack knew Opstein was there in Ocala at the time and thought he may want to buy the horses, so he told Mook to have Ken go look at the colts. Opstein recalls the negotiation process that followed after he saw the pair of Sovereign Dancer yearling colts bred by William R. Davis.

I immediately fell in love with the yearling colt out of Sun Gate, who I was informed was priced at $65,000. When I told Jack that I planned to buy him, Jack says, "Hang on, I'll take the one they want $15,000 for, so let's offer to buy both the horses as a package deal and ask if he'll knock off $5,000 for the pair." I agreed to ask, but I told Jack I was going to buy the colt I liked regardless. Well, I asked, and the deal was accepted. So I got my colt for $62,500 and Jack got his colt for $12,500. Jack's colt was named Sovereign Star; my colt was named Gate Dancer.

Both colts began to train well in Omaha at age two. Jack was getting glowing reports back from Ak-Sar-Ben from his assistant Mark Wallerstadt, who galloped many of the Van Berg horses, including both of the Sovereign Dancer colts. "Mark told me that Gate Dancer was going well and that Sovereign Star was training even better," said Jack. "But his shins started to get sore on him, so I sent him back to my farm in Kentucky and figured we'd save him for the next year and have him ready for Hot Springs."

Meanwhile, Gate Dancer continued to train forwardly leading up to his two-year-old debut. The betting public may not have been convinced on June 29, 1983, but when Gate Dancer left the starting gate at 6-1 in the first race of his career, Ken Opstein was just as prepared as his two-year-old colt. Gate Dancer won by eight lengths under jockey Kenny Jones. "I always bet on my horses," said Opstein. "It's sort of an act of support for the horse, I guess." Harry Farnham, the longtime Nebraska horse racing commissioner, once asked Ken if he ever felt that betting on his horses was just plain greed. "I said, 'You're right. But I never bet enough to win more than the winning purse,'" replied Opstein.

After his romping debut, Gate Dancer then ran second to Izapappa, who was no shrinking violet. Izapappa was a popular homebred of the Kemling Brothers (Paul and Orville) from Aurora, Nebraska. He was a genuine two-year-old racehorse who would go on to win the Aks Futurity, the

Columbus Futurity, and both the Freshman Stakes and Juvenile at State Fair Park in Lincoln. And he evolved into a prodigious Nebraska-based sprinter who won twenty races and more than a quarter-million dollars.

With the first stage of expectations confirmed, Gate Dancer was then sent west for the next challenge. But not before a few months off to allow for some typical two-year-old growing pains, not unlike those that Sovereign Star experienced. Under the care of Jack's son Tim Van Berg, who was overseeing Jack's California-based horses, Gate Dancer made his third lifetime start in an allowance race in December of 1983 at Hollywood Park. "Chris McCarron rode him and he won under a stranglehold, but after the race, McCarron said to me, 'Don't ever put me on that horse again.' During the race it looked like Chris was trying to pull the horse up, but Gate Dancer was actually just pulling Chris around the racetrack for the win," said Tim Van Berg. "If you see the win photo of the race, I think Chris's face is as white as a ghost."

With that win, Gate Dancer earned a trip into stakes competition and finished second in the Los Feliz Stakes at Santa Anita. Commemorate, the race winner, went on to win the Kings Bishop Stakes, the Hollywood Express Handicap, and to finish second by a nose to Eillo in the G1 Breeders Cup Sprint. At the stroke of midnight on December 31 on any year, all racehorses turn a year older (despite their actual birth date). And with that final gong of the clock, Gate Dancer graduated from his futurity year of racing into his derby year, so it was up to Bay Meadows in San Francisco to test the waters to see if Gate Dancer might be Kentucky Derby material. At this point, the prospect of him being a *Derby horse* was more conceptual than visceral.

In the El Camino Real Derby, Gate Dancer had another erratic trip. "He broke well, but then dropped back going into the first turn," said Tim Van Berg. "Going down the backstretch he made a big move and ran right up close again, but then he dropped back going into the far turn. Then they come out of the turn and here he comes again and he gets up for second. I remember after the race Dad asked his jockey Steve Cauthen what happened and Steve simply said, 'I don't know.' He was puzzled." And horses didn't typically puzzle Steve Cauthen. He had already won the 1978 Triple Crown with Affirmed, was voted an Eclipse Award for Outstanding Jockey, and was en route to becoming a three-time British Champion Jockey.

After the Bay Meadows race in San Francisco, Gate Dancer returned home to Los Angeles where he was dropped back into allowance competition and won again, this time under jockey Eddie Delahoussaye. Gate Dancer had now run six times and had won half of those races, but thus far, he only had stakes-placed finishes, no stakes wins.

Nevertheless, Gate Dancer continued to train like a monster. "I remember Dad would always call and chew me out. He'd say, 'What the hell are you doing working him so fast?' and I'd have to tell him, 'Dad, we can't hold him; he just works that way. He could go a lot faster if we let him,'" said Tim Van Berg. Gate Dancer proved that he trained nicely; he just didn't race nicely.

The grand-looking colt was developing a bad reputation of not running straight in his races and racing with his head up high. Jack tried a number of things to correct his destructive racing habits, including using a bit he called the Ramblin Road Bit. It was a special bit devised by his father Marion, which helped his horse Ramblin Road race to his potential. But the bit was not the least bit effective with Gate Dancer. Nevertheless, on February 20, 1984, Gate Dancer won an allowance race at Santa Anita; it was his third win in six lifetime starts. The fans loved seeing their favorite win a 1 1/16-mile allowance race at Santa Anita by a commanding eight lengths. And despite the efforts of jockey Eddie Delahoussaye, Gate Dancer really was in command, as he lugged in badly through the stretch. It was nearing springtime, and Gate Dancer still had many questions and behavioral issues to answer.

Was he a Derby horse? Was he a contender? And why wouldn't he run straight? Opstein and Van Berg had questions. They still had plenty of hope, and Gate Dancer still had plenty to learn. To get the answers, he was targeted for a series of three-year-old races that lead up to the Santa Anita Derby.

Off Gate Dancer's big allowance win, and with partial confidence restored, Van Berg and Opstein ran the horse in the Santa Catalina Stakes. He was the third choice and he finished third. After the race, Delahoussaye informed Van Berg that he thought Gate Dancer was listening to the crowd in the stretch run and not paying attention. Jack paid attention to what Eddie said and immediately his mind went to work. "I'd seen how they trained and raced horses down in Argentina when I went down there to buy horses. Many of those horses wore hoods that covered the horse's ears," said Van Berg. "I wanted to make a hood out of blinkers and keep foam rubber in place in his ears. I hated cotton in my ears as a kid so I didn't want cotton in Gate Dancer's ears. I designed the hood, and Terri at Rainbow Racing Silks and her mother made me a hood."

On March 25, 1986, Gate Dancer debuted a new look. In the post parade of the G1 San Felipe Handicap, he now wore a big gold shadow roll on his noseband and a conspicuous purple hood initialed with a gold "V B." Some may have mistaken his headgear as blinkers but they were not. While they looked like blinkers with rabbit ears, there were no eye cups whatsoever on either side. They must have helped—he almost won. Gate Dancer still lugged in and he laid on Fali Time in the run to the wire, but he was improving. Maybe some questions were getting answered. "He used to run with his head up high like a turkey running through a field," said Van Berg. "The earmuffs might be funny looking, but they sure didn't seem to hurt him any."

The plans were to run Gate Dancer in the Santa Anita Derby but he got sick and a 103-degree temperature knocked him out of the race. So instead of running in the Santa Anita Derby, he was sent to Oaklawn to train for the Arkansas Derby. Gate Dancer had some first-class traveling companions in his plane ride from California; alongside in the flight were Dave's Friend and Brindy Brindy. All three were headed to Central Avenue in Hot Springs for an assault on the Racing Festival of the South.

Gate Dancer picked up at Oaklawn Park where he left off at Hollywood Park and was proving a handful in Hot Springs. After seeing the work tab and a fast 5/8 work of :58 2/5 for Gate Dancer, a son gained an opportunity to tease his father. "I called Dad up and gave him the business and asked what the hell he was doing letting that horse work so fast," Tim Van Berg said.

Winless in four stakes races, Gate Dancer may have proven that he couldn't win a stakes race, but he left no doubt that he was a *Derby horse*. Gate Dancer not only convinced Ken and Jack of his Derby potential, by the afternoon of April 21, 1984, he had also convinced every Tom, Dick, and Harry; the betting public sent him off as the 8/5 favorite in the G1 Arkansas Derby. Althea was the second choice in the wagering. She was the Wayne Lukas-trained Alydar filly who had routinely dismantled her male rivals in Southern California stakes competition her two-year-old season and just a week earlier had run second as the beaten favorite in the G1 Fantasy Stakes at Oaklawn.

The filly beat the boys in the Arkansas Derby and Gate Dancer was seven lengths back in third; his lugging-in problems were still not cured.

Plans were made and tickets booked for a trip to Louisville for the Kentucky Derby. Unfortunately, the cloud of bad luck that was synonymous with Gate Dancer followed him and settled overhead at Churchill Downs. Not only did he draw the extreme outside post position number 20, he stumbled badly leaving the gate. Gate Dancer lost three lengths at the start and then dropped back to last, more than twenty lengths behind. Delahoussaye steadily advanced with the 18-1 long shot, and as they turned for home the Cajun jockey bravely guided the purple-hooded wild child through a narrow gap between horses. But despite Eddie doing all he could, Gate Dancer found his old pal Fali Time and bumped him a half-dozen times through the final furlong. Then, the dark cloud of misfortune showered down on horse, owner, and trainer. Gate Dancer was disqualified from fourth and placed fifth, becoming the first-ever horse to get disqualified for interference in the Kentucky Derby. What's more, in 1984 Churchill Downs still only paid purse money down to fourth in the Kentucky Derby. The only thing Gate Dancer earned for his rough trip in the Derby was the title of being named a rogue.

Jack looked through the din of being disqualified and set his sights on the second leg of the Triple Crown. He saw that Gate Dancer had cleaned up his food and was playing and bucking after the race. The Derby may have kicked his connections in the heart—or lower—but Gate Dancer was ready for more.

The duration between the Kentucky Derby and the Preakness is only two weeks—precious few days to prepare a horse for such a significant race. But Jack learned that the bulk of the prep work needs to be done before entering the Triple Crown. "If you have a horse ready going into the Derby, you really don't need to do much with them in between those Triple Crown races," said Van Berg. True to his words, Jack didn't put much more training into Gate Dancer, but he did make a change. When entries were taken for the 1984 G1 Preakness Stakes, there was a surprise jockey change, to Angel Cordero, Jr.

After the Kentucky Derby, not only did jockey Eddie Delahoussaye suggest that the noise of the crowd still may have cost Gate Dancer the race, Eddie suggested that he himself might have been an issue. He then said something to Jack that was professionally classy, but personally costly. Delahoussaye recalls, "I also told Jack that maybe he ought to look for a different rider. I said that he has a great chance to win the Preakness with

Gate Dancer, but me and the horse just aren't getting along." Jack appreciated Eddie's insight. He tried the hood and Gate Dancer seemed to accept it, and Jack was willing to accept Eddie again as his rider. But ultimately, Jack says his reason for the change was based more on frustration with Delahoussaye's agent. "I kept calling his agent and he'd never call back. And when I left him a message on his answering machine all I could hear was some damn reggae music going on in the background," huffed Van Berg. "So I changed jockeys and got Cordero."

In the middle jewel of the Triple Crown, Gate Dancer was the 9/2 third choice; Taylor's Special was the 7/2 second choice. Taylor's Choice had run thirteenth in the Kentucky Derby at 6-1, but before that he had won the G1 Bluegrass Stakes and the G2 Louisiana Derby. The heavy favorite was the Derby winner, Swale. Jack had confidence in his new rider and his horse remained cool in the waves of the intense Baltimore heat. The gates opened and Gate Dancer settled back off the pace and into a comfortable stride. Swale was in perfect position several lengths in front of him. But when the field turned for home, not even the frenetic fanatics fazed Gate Dancer. Despite an embargo on keg beer in the infield that summer at Pimlico, the horse with the hood behaved himself much more than many of the rowdy fans. He raced a straight path to the finish line and raced straight into the history books. Gate Dancer's time was 1:53 3/5; he set a stakes record for the 1 3/16-mile Preakness Stakes. At age forty-seven Jack Van Berg scored his first Classic win.

Following the race, winning jockey Angel Cordero said, "I think he could have run faster if someone challenged him. I'd hate to see a horse like this get a bad reputation. He's got a lot of ability; if he puts his mind to something, he'll do it." As fate would have it Gate Dancer would maintain both his ability and his bad reputation. Cordero has a reputation himself; the jockey is known to be a fierce competitor on the racetrack and a jovial clown otherwise. A longstanding tradition of the Pimlico Racecourse is that the metal figure of a jockey astride a horse is immediately painted after the Preakness. As owner Ken Opstein's racing silks of forest green with a black keystone were being painted on the weathervane fixed atop the infield cupola, Angel Cordero, in his own colorful vein, and with a thick Puerto Rican accent, said, "Hey, paint that jockey a darker color, please." Needless to say, the mood was much brighter in Baltimore than it was in Louisville two weeks prior.

After a string of determined efforts, Gate Dancer ran his first poor race in twelve lifetime starts when he ran sixth, beaten by nearly eleven lengths in the Belmont. Swale rebounded to win the race and give trainer Woody Stephens his third of five consecutive Belmont Stakes wins. Presently, trainers in the United States struggle to get their horses to win races at distances of 1 1/8 miles. Stephens seemingly did it for fun and accomplished a feat that is likely never to be improved upon.

In pure Van Berg style, Jack brought his star to race at Ak-Sar-Ben, replete in his gaudy purple hood and gold shadow roll. But the D. Wayne Lukas-trained Imp Society had already been waltzing over his three-year-old foes in Omaha, so a marketing promotion was launched to generate interest, or at least stir a rivalry. The interest was already there, as was the rivalry between Jack and Wayne. Van Berg brought in Laffit Pincay, Jr., to ride, and Lukas gave Joe Steiner the return call. Ak-Sar-Ben named the 1984 Omaha Gold Cup "The Mane Event." But by the time they reached the 1/4 pole, as the saying goes, "If it was a fight they would have stopped it." Gate Dancer rolled to a five-and-a-half-length win over Imp Society.

Sammy Alvarez was the dedicated groom of Gate Dancer and he said the horse was never mean or wild like people said he was: "He was very smart and he always had that eye on you." Of all the races run by Gate Dancer, Sammy's favorite was the Omaha Gold Cup. "He beat that good horse of Wayne Lukas (Imp Society). I remember how they made a big deal about a rivalry between Lukas and Jack. Lukas had two in the race and we ran three. It felt good to win. It was like the Van Berg team beat the Lukas team," Sammy said.

In his next start, Gate Dancer was sent to Louisiana Downs, another former Van Berg fortress, where he was involved in photo finish in the G1 1 1/4-mile Super Derby. However, there was more to the finish than met the eye, or at least the naked eye. After reviewing the videotape, the Louisiana Downs stewards concluded that Bill Shoemaker, the jockey astride Precisionist, had struck Gate Dancer with his whip numerous times in a snug battle to the finish. If Precisionist outran Gate Dancer, surely he would have been disqualified from first place into second place. But Precisionist wasn't disqualified—because Gate Dancer beat him at the wire, and on the square. Maybe the stigma of bad luck that hovered over his head had finally lifted? The hood, however, would remain in place. Gate Dancer, though faultless in the Super Derby, was still involved in controversy, and that reputation proved to be destructive fodder. His next race would become one of the most talked-about races in modern North American thoroughbred racing.

On a picture-perfect day in Los Angeles on November 10, 1984, the Breeders' Cup unveiled their revolutionary collection of seven races worth $10 million. The intent of the horse racing extravaganza was to attract the best collection of horses in the world and to showcase the thoroughbreds on a four-hour NBC telecast. The inaugural Breeders' Cup races conducted at Hollywood Park culminated with an unquestionably dramatic Hollywood ending, but with very questionable results.

The world's richest horse race, the G1 $3 million Breeders' Cup Classic, attracted a fine field of three-year-olds and up. The race favorite was Slew O' Gold. The giant dark bay son of Seattle Slew came into the Classic off six consecutive wins; his last four were a sweep of the New York G1 headline races: the Whitney Handicap, the Woodward Stakes, the Marlboro Cup, and the Jockey Club Gold Cup. Gate Dancer, Desert Wine, and Precisionist were the second, third, and fourth choices behind the 3/5 favorite. Swift fractions were set; the opening quarter was run in 22 3/5, and the half-mile in 45 3/5. Mugutea was in the race to ensure a fast pace for his stablemate Slew O' Gold; after brisk fractions, he had done his job and dropped off the lead. Wild Again and Precisionist then had the lead to themselves, Desert Wine was a few lengths off that pair, Slew O' Gold was a few lengths behind him, and Gate Dancer had settled back to last, a good fifteen lengths off the pace. Nearing the far turn, Angel Cordero, Jr., launched early with Slew O' Gold and made a sudden rush to the leaders; this quick move left Gate Dancer nearly ten lengths behind the attacking Slew O' Gold. At the top of the stretch, Wild Again continued to show the way but Slew O' Gold had advanced to be just a half-length off him in second. Despite being left in the dust down the backstretch, Gate Dancer mustered an incredible response when asked to run by Laffit Pincay, Jr. In only a matter of seconds, Gate Dancer had joined the fray and a three-way battle to the wire was imminent. Pat Day routinely saves plenty of horse for the stretch drive and this race was no different. He had nursed Wild Again through fast fractions and his courageous runner still had more to give at the rail. Slew O' Gold, with his ears pinned, was now only a neck away from Wild Again. Gate Dancer had now chugged all the way up to be alongside that pair. Approaching the final furlong, Wild Again drifted away from the rail; Gate Dancer was still parked to the outside, with Pincay preemptively working on him left-handed. Slew O' Gold was in the middle of the pair, being roused to keep fighting.

Track announcer Tom Durkin called it like this . . . "Wild Again, Gate Dancer, Slew O' Gold in between them! Those three in a dramatic finish! And here's the wire, Wild Again does it! I believe it was Wild Again, an upset winner." The 31-1 odds of Wild Again was surely an upset but there was much more tumult to follow. Gate Dancer was the unofficial second-place finisher and Slew O' Gold was a half-length behind in third. In the epic tussle to the finish line, there was some bumping and crowding and a general exchange that involved all three horses and jockeys. The ever-shrewd jockey, Angel Cordero snatched up Slew O' Gold just before the wire as it seemed his mount might not have enough to win. Justifiably, the Hollywood Park stewards reviewed multiple angles of videotape replays and did so several times before making their decision. When the smoke cleared, Wild Again was declared the winner, but Gate Dancer was disqualified from second place to third place and Slew O' Gold was thereby awarded second place. Gate Dancer could have won $1.3 million for the win, or $675,000 for second place; instead, owner Ken Opstein's controversial colt earned $324,000 for being placed third. The stewards' decision seemed to only sit well with the connections of Wild Again and the relatively few bettors who had made win bets on him. There was immediate outcry from the press suggesting that an injustice had occurred. The cry from the East was that both Wild Again and Gate Dancer should have been disqualified. Out in the West Jack Van Berg was screeching another tune.

The stewards said the tractor harrow marks helped them determine which horses maintained their paths, but I say who the hell knows if the guy was driving the tractor straight. After the media and some other folks got a chance to see the videotape that night, a special conference with the stewards was called for the next day for the stewards to explain their decision. Hell, they had thirty reporters down there acting like a lynch mob. I was stupid to just let it go and not take it to court to appeal their decision. But I didn't want to create any more turmoil given it was the first Breeders' Cup and I didn't want it to become a big stink. To describe it, it's like a guy had robbed some banks a few times, but did his time and went straight. But later he was walking by a bank that had been robbed, and because they didn't know who to blame, they pinned the crime on him.

Jack may not have the same demeanor as Perry Mason, or the evidence of Sherlock Holmes, but he sure can present an interesting case.

As a four-year-old, Gate Dancer ran in many of the great races at "The Great Race Place" in the winter of 1985 at Santa Anita Park (San Fernando, Strub, and Santa Anita Handicap), and he finished third in all three. Jack even gave him a shot over the turf, when he ran sixth, beaten by less than five lengths in the G1 San Luis Rey Stakes. Gate Dancer got some much-deserved rest and relaxation after that taxing meet at Santa Anita. Freshened up, he resumed his training in Omaha, where Mark Wallerstadt oversaw Jack's operation. Mark was a trusted employee and good friend of Jack's; when Gate Dancer was in his barn, he galloped him almost exclusively. Even in his simple morning gallops, he went to the track, dropped his head, bowed his neck, and trained like a champ. Gate Dancer was on the muscle and waiting for his racing orders. He got them on July 27 at 5:12 P.M. when midway down the backstretch Chris McCarron gave him a little rein near the half-mile pole in the G2 $150,000 Cornhusker Handicap. The 1985 Cornhusker was billed as "The Re-Match" based on the title given to the 1984 Omaha Gold Cup when it was Gate Dancer vs. Imp Society. It might have been a rematch on paper; it was assuredly a repeat on the track. Gate Dancer won for fun.

After the races, McCarron, Opstein, and Van Berg had their own fun, when they savored their Cornhusker win with some corn-fed beef. They left the racetrack and turned right onto 72nd Street, and then one block later turned right again into the parking lot of Ross' Famous Steak House to enjoy their famous Omaha Strip prime-cut steaks. Later, the celebration spilled over into the restaurant's Cleopatra Lounge, where a few Crown Royals were raised to salute their hooded hero. Then some regulars and revelers from nearby Clancy's Pub stumbled into the post-race party and the Falstaff began to flow freely. Gate Dancer won the Cornhusker Handicap and was treated to a sweetened grain mash, while his connections and fans imbibed in some fermented grain mash.

Even though he was unplaced in his turf debut before the Cornhusker, Van Berg and Opstein agreed to try Gate Dancer over the grass after their achievement at Aks. All they had to do was load Gate Dancer into a trailer and haul him east on I-80 to Arlington Park; then all they had to do was win the G1 Arlington Million. The van ride across Iowa was the easy part; *the race was difficult.* Gate Dancer finished tenth over the yielding turf course.

Onward east on I-80 with sights set for another try at the Breeders' Cup Classic in New York. But before his second attempt in the BC Classic, there were two key races in Long Island. In the G1 $500,000 1 1/4 Marlboro Cup, Gate Dancer was second, beaten a neck by Chief's Crown. Then three weeks later he was second to Vanlandingham in the G1 $750,000 1 1/2 Jockey Club Gold Cup. His form was holding; he just wasn't winning.

The Breeders' Cup got their Hollywood opening and ending when they staged their showcase of the thoroughbred racehorse at Hollywood Park in 1984. One year later, through all the smoke and stars of the inaugural Breeders' Cup Classic, only one horse returned for the 1985 Breeders' Cup Classic. He was Gate Dancer. The buildup was an event promoter and television producer's dream. Both race fans and television viewers got all the drama of the first Breeders' Cup Classic, complete with a favorite who was scorned, shrouded, and a sentimental selection: he was Gate Dancer.

He went into the race as the tepid 3-1 favorite. All year long he ran head and head with the top older handicap horses: Track Baron, Turkoman, Vanlandingham, Bounding Basque, Geinton, Carr De Naskra, Lord At War, and Precisionist. He had no archrival, though most of the time he was his own worst enemy. Loaded with energy, ability, and accomplishment, Gate Dancer was a real workingman's horse: rugged, though sweet to the core. But his core was always his biggest pitfall. Containment of what boiled inside that caldron of a core was often the biggest challenge for him and his rider. In a second attempt at the Breeders' Cup Classic, Gate Dancer erupted again.

Before the '85 BC Classic, Jack told Chris McCarron, "Gate Dancer can make up ten lengths so fast it will make your head spin. So don't let him go too soon!" "Well, Gate Dancer settled back, but he began to pass horses much earlier than normal," recalled Ken Opstein:

> Coming for home, by mid-stretch we already had a length-and-a-half lead. I was surprised that we were out in front. Chris had so much horse he just had to let him run. Evidently he let him go too soon, because the John Veitch horse, Proud Truth, caught him at the wire. But the next jump right after the wire Gate Dancer was out in front again. He responded just that quickly. You never know, hindsight is 20/20, but we did emphasize to Chris to not go too soon.

Easier said than done.

After another tough defeat in the Breeders' Cup Classic, Gate Dancer ran four more times before the conclusion of his race career. He was fourth of four in the G3 Native Diver, fifth of thirteen in the G1 Santa Anita Big Cap (when Herat was second), third in the G1 Widener, and second in the G2 Oaklawn Handicap. He was not the favorite in any of those races, but his order within the wagering was equal to his order of finish.

Gate Dancer developed into a dependable and dutiful worker on the racetrack, though not without some bittersweet races. He won 5 of the 7 races when he was the favorite, but he left so much more on the table—hundreds of thousands of dollars to be sure. "They had a lot of fun in Omaha with the two promotions they did at Ak-Sar-Ben with Gate Dancer versus Imp Society. And I have those two boxing-style posters they made hanging in my office ('The Mane Event' and 'The Re-Match'), but really, it was no contest in both races," quipped Ken Opstein. "Gate Dancer won easily."

In complete reflection, Opstein is more pragmatic than bitter when it comes to the Kentucky Derby and Belmont Stakes defeats, and the two gut-wrenching Breeders' Cup Classics defeats. "I had plenty of good experiences with him, but I can't help to think, 'Oh what he could have been!'" *He* was Gate Dancer.

32

Montages in Print

In 1984 Helen Van Berg commissioned Hot Springs, Arkansas, artist and photographer Gary Simmons to create a pen-and-ink portrait of her husband Jack. Simmons's choice of pen and ink allows him to produce remarkably realistic looking pieces of art, and his protocol to intensely interview his subjects enables him to passionately implant life into his art.

Over the course of many months, Simmons shadowed Jack for weeks at time. He witnessed Derby defeat, Preakness joy, and drilled down into Jack like no one had before. Both parties accepted mutual involvement in all things "Jack." As a result, Jack had Gary moving gates at his training farm in Goshen, Kentucky, and also travelled to Jack's parents' home in Columbus, Nebraska, the hallowed grounds of Jack's birthplace. Throughout this process, Gary asked questions, shot photographs, recorded interviews, and otherwise just tried to keep pace with Jack, dutifully chronicling the remarkable routine of a legendary man.

What follows are excerpts of passages and explanations written by Simmons, who, through his innate gift of awareness and skills in psychoanalysis, compiled his observations of Jack in a multipage report. He presented his findings along with three individual hand-drawn montages depicting Jack Van Berg ("Personal Life," "The Trainer," "The Farm"). Later, after Jack was awed by the art, he commissioned Simmons to create a fourth montage of his parents and siblings. The pen stroke of Simmons is brilliant, but the formulation of his words that accurately depict the person he illustrates is astonishing . . .

Jack Van Berg is all horse—it's a total love of the animal and of the horse business. It is what he knows, where he gets his strength, and what provides his wealth. As a person he is consistent with his business. He looks, sounds, and acts like a mixture of cowboy and midwestern farmer. He is similar to male athletes and soldiers who abuse one another as tokens of affection. Instead, they state their love through teasing, slaps on the back, firm handshakes, and friendly nudges.

The personal Van Berg seems very consistent with this. His likes, dislikes, politics, and activities all seem an obvious extension of his rearing and of his business. He is the classic male figure who is fascinated with big trucks, fast cars, cattle, farms, making a deal, and doing things his own way. He likes male company, likes female attention, and doesn't let either one prevent him from reaching his goals. Even his family falls back when he pushes— and sometimes he doesn't seem to notice until he finds they are behind him instead of beside him. They seem to respect and love him anyway—a testimony to his intentions even when his actions fail to meet their expectations. Jack Van Berg is bigger than life, in size, sound, and behavior. He is the pied piper of trainers; trailing, is a wake of owners, employees, media people, and admirers. He roars through these people like a large truck coming through a field. He stirs up clouds of dust, insects, and leaves, which finally settle again after he is gone. His personal energy is contagious and legendary, and affects those who participate in his life.

The following are fragments of the descriptions Gary Simmons wrote of his pen and ink montages. They are an explanation of the key elements drawn into the montages, and the descriptions are written directly to Jack. The complete, unaltered essays can be found in the appendix of this book. The montages can be found in the photo gallery. If you look hard enough, you will see an image of John Wayne burnished into the illustration of a knothole in a wooden door. It's worth a look.

Montage no. 1. Personal Life: The general theme is a life crowded with people and influences and a theme of smiles that laugh at life. More often than not you are expressing some kind of humor or jolly demeanor even at the most intense times of your career. I drew Marion as an almost smoky figure, not quite real. He is a man so consistently revered that it is hard to find out anything about him other than glowing praise. His studious pose and pensive stare seem consistent with the stories about the effect this man had on those around him. As the apple of his eye, it's no wonder you were influenced as you were. Viola Van Berg is almost part of the same person of Marion. She flows from him, and so it was in life apparently. And they bonded a family tie. Behind you is the Columbus Sale Pavilion as it is today, the place you talk about with great nostalgia. The homeplace sits next door. The knothole harkens back to the barn and the mischievous Jack. The views of you auctioneering, talking on the phone, and taking a five-minute nap make up their own sequence. You remind me of a high-powered engine fouling out for a second due to heat and overuse, only to sputter twice, catch, and again roar into motion. I saw the love between you and the kids at Churchill Downs and at Columbus. I saw Traci cry when she almost missed being in the paddock with you. I heard Tommy say he wanted to be like his dad. I saw Tim help you saddle Gate Dancer and sit with his hand on your shoulder after your loss. I saw Tami and Tori watch you with pride before the race and I saw you walk with both sons to the barn to check Gate Dancer after the heartbreaking loss in the Kentucky Derby. The sharing is there despite any of the other struggles, which come from their not seeing you often enough, or for wanting more than you can give. That sharing helped me understand more about you and who you are under that terrible mass of people and business which surround you. The main figure of this portrait panel is one typical of the more engaging Jack Van Berg. When you smile, you break into a laugh; it is so engaging that you diffuse any tension you may have set up when chastising a late employee, or snapping at someone who has nagged at getting a place in your busy schedule. It's the best side of Jack Van Berg I have spent time with. It's the side I think makes hometown folk want to pay you respect, makes workers try a little harder for you, and which helps the world step back and give you room.

Montage no. 2. The Trainer: The Preakness trophy stands for the pinnacle of your career and new confidence as a winner in the Triple Crown competition, but it also represents the support you have from Helen and her sense of what is important to you. Below the trophy is Gate Dancer at Oaklawn. You with Mark and Gate Dancer epitomizes your direct involvement in the training, your staying tuned to the horse in spite of your travelling and concern with other horses. Gate Dancer is featured in this drawing as the premium horse in your immediate career. It's not just a matter of performance. I have the feeling you admire this horse for his unorthodox performances and his ability to back up his eccentricities. With his earmuffs, blinkers, special bits, and tendencies to run from behind, he represents your own willingness to buck the odds, to experiment, and to run in the face of established ideas. In this same horse is your confidence and willingness to risk ridicule. I've seen you take the wisecracks about it, add your own humor about it, and diffuse the remark while capturing the moment for yourself.

Behind the running Gate Dancer in the drawing is the training center in Kentucky. As a trainer you have created a physical plant which expresses and uses the ideas of someone who really understands the elements of training and the soul of the horse.

The main figure of the portrait gives the look which stops those who dare to go too far with their challenge of you. I've seen this look—I've even received it in a glance. Combined with a large body and booming voice, this look will get results from anyone within its range. The most important thing about the look is that it is always temporary. Within seconds it will revert back to a grin or a kindness which reassures the victim that he hasn't been sentenced to permanent disfavor.

The mounted figure of you above the dates is a favorite of mine. Again, it's one of those images which show the Jack Van Berg I've seen at work. I like the statement it makes of early morning light, cool temperatures, hot coffee, gloves, jacket, and fidgeting horses. This is the image of a man who loves the business. There is a patience about you in this situation which I fail to see in you in other parts of the business. I think you savor the time on that horse, perhaps because you are most comfortable with yourself at that moment?

Montage no. 3. The Farm: We walked out on the balcony overlooking the training track and you looked into the evening sunset with the look of a man more peaceful than any other time I had seen you. The schematic of the hotwalker symbolizes your creative thinking, which comes when a man really knows which problems he is solving and knows the satisfaction of seeing it work. The white frame farmhouse is shown with its big porch, shade trees, fireplaces, and rolling lawn. It's the only place I've seen you in that you really treat like home. It seems to fit you a little better and you feel like you own it. In the other places I've seen you, it's obvious you're just passing through. The farm's racetrack and the barns in the background are also a view of the training center. The deep-sand walker is obscured, but the whole view involves the nurturing part of the farm—the layup barn, the foal barn, and the walker. The view of you looking over the farm with radio in hand deals with your active direction and participation in the farm's functions.

The drawing of the running horse is recognition of your philosophy about healthy and happy horses. Keep the horses healthy and happy and they'll do their best for you.

The view of you as a rider is a tribute to your willingness to work like your help does, probably more. But it is also intended to recognize the image you perhaps dream of when you think most warmly about yourself. I think it's a natural projection of a Nebraska boy who grew up in the saddle. It's also apparent from the posture that this is someone who is in charge. I've never been around a more forceful personality than yours. Everything you say, every move you make, suggests control and confidence. I don't think in my time with you I have seen anyone successfully resist you. This strength is your virtue and your vice. It impels people to follow you while it exasperates those who want to object. I have a suspicion that if you never won a race, you would still have people following you.

Montage no. 4. Marion and Viola Van Berg: The two central figures show them near the seventy mark, a time of financial security and success, well past crying babies and hot-rodding teenagers. I like the peacefulness in their faces and the confidence with which they look at the viewer. Each displays their own evidence of success. Marion is typically understated in his suit, sweater, and hat. Viola displays the manifestations of his affection and success, but the jewelry and fur don't hide her earthiness and warmth.

Neither person looks pretentious. It's no wonder they continued to gather respect from the people they grew up with.

Marion is universally characterized as a genius with horses, as a man of principle, someone generally kind to others, and as a man who spoke softly and carried a big stick. He was, however, someone who must have used the stick sparingly because he is also considered a gentle man physically, if not always verbally. He is idolized by the thoroughbred racing world and seems to be remembered more for what he stood for than what he did on a daily basis.

Viola is remembered mostly by her kids. Perhaps that is the tribute she would have chosen. She is characterized as gentle, understanding, artistic, and sensitive. She seems to have been nurturing above all else. She is the symbol of a devoted wife. There is not much physically which reflects who she was. The piano is perhaps the only tribute to her artistic sensibility. Her children are her monument.

Prior to procuring Gary Simmons for this project, Helen Van Berg told her husband, "Jack, I want to know what makes you tick." When the project was complete, what she got was a telling toll that booms like Big Ben. Big, like Jack.

The summer that followed the unveiling of the Gary Simmons collection, Jack C. Van Berg was inducted into the National Museum of Racing Hall of Fame. Dan Cattau, a correspondent for the Omaha World-Herald newspaper was in Saratoga Springs, New York, to cover the prestigious event in August of 1985. The room was filled with past, present, and future Hall of Fame inductees and the kind words about Jack gushed from many respectful colleagues. In his story, Cattau made a point of emphasizing the incredible travelling that led to Van Berg's Hall of Fame induction. "He wears those big boots and those jeans and he just goes. He works hard and he rides those planes day in and day out," said Woody Stephens, a fellow Hall of Famer.

The time and effort Jack spends on planes and dissecting a path through traffic, to and from airports, is simply mindboggling. It's truly more than one man—or twenty—should attempt. Jack earned his induction into the Hall of Fame due to years of hard work and dedication. That week, his specific path to Saratoga Springs took some of the same perseverance. Cattau wrote, "On Tuesday, Van Berg was in Omaha, looking after the forty horses he has stabled at Ak-Sar-Ben. That afternoon he was at Canterbury Downs in Shakopee, Minnesota, checking on thirty more horses. On Wednesday he was at his home near Louisville, Kentucky, looking at eighty of his horses. Wednesday afternoon he flew to Saratoga for the Fasig-Tipton Yearling Sales."

At the induction ceremony, the esteemed *Daily Racing Form* columnist Joe Hirsch said, "Examine him while he is sitting, awaiting the ceremonies; that may be the last time you see him in the repose." Hirsch continued, "How can a man do justice to 130 horses?" The turf writer then abridged what it is to be Van Berg: "His work is his vocation, his avocation, his leisure time, his life." Dan Cattau included a few more nuggets from some notables in attendance. Frank Wright, the former trainer and host of the WOR-TV New York horse racing broadcasts, said, "Hey, this guy (Van Berg) has been doing this with horses for years. His induction was almost a horsemen's demand." And Mr. Whitney Tower, the president of the National Museum of Racing Hall of Fame, said, "Van Berg was piling up wins in places that were less well known. He's like a manager who does a terrific job with a major league baseball team in Texas or Milwaukee instead of New York, California, or Chicago." That's true, and he truly piled up a lot of wins in those places.

33

Alysheba
A Classic Name

What's in a name? In the case of Alysheba—plenty! He was a colt blessed with a regal name and the rich bloodlines to back it up. The names of Alysheba's ancestors, his breeders and the ancestors of his breeders, collaborated in one of the most beautiful masterpieces ever to compete on the American Turf. Many names were in the background; one pure name became their mantle.

Sired by Alydar, the colt was out of the Lt. Stevens mare Bel Sheba. Alydar, of course, was the runner-up to Affirmed in the 1978 Triple Crown, but he became far more accomplished at stud than his rival was on the track. He was the nation's leading sire in 1990 and from 1986 to 2000 was among the leading sires and broodmare sires.

Lt. Stevens, by the incredible Champion Grass Horse–award winner and top stallion T.V. Lark, was the sire of Alysheba's mother, thereby making him the maternal grandsire of Alysheba. He had a knack of running second, like Alydar. Lt. Stevens earned more than $240,000, but that was with eight second-place finishes in stakes competition. While he did win three stakes on the East Coast, he also had a string of seconds in 1964, including the Jerome Handicap, the Arlington Classic, the American Derby and the Discovery Handicap, among others.

Bel Sheba, Alysheba's mother, was a bay mare bred in Kentucky by Preston Madden. She was out of Belthazar, the final foal sired by War Admiral. Bel Sheba won five races and finished third in the 1972 Adirondack Stakes at Saratoga. She was raced by Madden's friend Dr. Ernest Wright. At the end of Bel Sheba's career, Dr. Wright told Preston that he was in the racing business, not the breeding business, and asked him what he should do. Preston promptly responded, "You can take this Nodouble filly I have and race her and I'll take back Bel Sheba." Bel Sheba returned to Kentucky to make babies. As a broodmare, she did produce some winners prior to Alysheba, the most important being Port Master, by Raise A Native, who earned more than $175,000 and won four stakes races in Canada at Woodbine and Fort Erie.

And so with that, Bel Sheba had proven enough on the track and as a broodmare to be led into a breeding barn painted in the devil's red and blue colors of the famous Calumet Farm. She was bred to the great Alydar. But her first foal by Alydar was not Alysheba; it was a 1982 colt dubiously named Titanic. The forgettable bay colt won 2 of 11 races and only $33,920. Bel Sheba was bred back to Alydar, but was barren in 1983 and did not produce a foal. But on March 3, 1984, another bay colt by Alydar was born, and he would receive a far nobler name than the questionable christening his full brother received two years before. So then, by Alydar, out of Bel Sheba, came Alysheba. And the third time was a charm.

Alysheba evolved brilliantly and was the subject of a very popular four-word question heard frequently at Hamburg Place in Lexington, Kentucky; the common query was, "Who is that colt?" Prior to being sold, he was simply known as "that Alydar colt." The youngster was developing into a fine lad and when Preston Madden asked the famous Kentucky veterinarian Dr. Robert Copelan what he thought of him, Copelan responded, "He's the best colt I've seen all year."

July rolled around and it was showtime: go time for the prestigious Keeneland July Yearling Sale. The sale was well under way, and there were about a dozen hip-numbers remaining before Alysheba's, when Patrick Madden, Preston Madden's son, leaned over and asked his father what he had set the reserve price for on Alysheba. When Preston said $195,000, Patrick asked, "Don't you think you ought to raise that limit?"

To which the elder Madden responded, "Listen kid, I'm trying to keep your family inheritance intact for you." After a swift and serious discussion, Preston approached the sale office and increased the reserve sale price to $300,000. A few horses sold through the ring, then *that Alydar colt* stepped in. The first asking bid was $200,000, then the bids jumped to $225,000, then $250,000, and before long the bidding was well above the established minimum sale price. When the hammer fell, the colt had sold for $500,000.

Renowned Kentucky breeder, owner, and trainer John E. Madden bred five Kentucky Derby winners and all five were foaled in the same barn at his Hamburg Place farm near Lexington. His winners were Old Rosebud (1914), Sir Barton (1919), Paul Jones (1920), Zev (1923), and Flying Ebony (1925). His grandson, Preston W. Madden, has operated Hamburg Place for decades since then and has carried on a prestigious breeding institution. "My grandfather bred five Derby winners; my goal was to breed at least one," said Preston. "I'm told the foal-crop in 1984 was 35,000, so the odds were 35,000-1 against me breeding the Kentucky Derby winner of 1987. Honestly, winning the Kentucky Derby is largely a function of luck rather than genius." Then, the blueblood raised up his glistening amber spirit and gave a toast to, and with, a legendary Kentucky tradition.

34

Alysheba
Glowing Pride and Growing Pains

Quarter horse connections and thoroughbred tradition led to the purchase of a classic American racehorse—Alysheba. Jay Pumphrey—who for many years ran the horse division of the famed 6666 Ranch in Guthrie, Texas—was a very good friend of Clarence Scharbauer, Jr., an oilman, rancher, and cattleman from Midland, Texas. Anne Burnett, commonly known as "Miss Anne," owned the vast 500,000 acres of the 6666 Ranch and the Triangle Ranch in north-central Texas. She was also a good friend and partner in quarter horse ownership with Scharbauer. In time, Jay Pumphrey, Clarence Scharbauer, and Anne Burnett (and her daughter Anne Marion) would all be inducted into the American Quarter Horse Association (AQHA) Hall of Fame.

Clarence's wife, Dorothy, was quite the bluebonnet herself. She was born into a rich cattle, quarter horse, and West Texas lifestyle, but she also acquired a taste of Kentucky when her father, Fred Turner, Jr., won the 1959 Kentucky Derby with Tomy Lee. It was a sweet memory Dorothy wouldn't forget and an experience she would crave, hoping to savor again.

In 1980 Dorothy began suggesting to Clarence that she wanted to get involved with thoroughbred racing and to try to win the Kentucky Derby, just as her father had done. It was a lovely thought, and she had the financial backing to buy most any Derby hopeful, but she lacked equal enthusiasm from her husband. One year passed, then another, and then another. Not only did Dorothy not have a Derby hopeful, she didn't own a horse and hadn't even gone to a horse sale. So her daughter Pamela jumped in and said, "Mom, I'll go with you and I'll partner with you on a horse if you like." Dorothy grinned with approval. In September of 1984, Dorothy Scharbauer quietly, and rather uncharacteristically, *informed* her husband that she would love to have him come along to Kentucky and be a partner in buying a thoroughbred, but if he didn't want to come, she and Pam would go buy a Kentucky Derby horse without him. Clarence set down his *Permian Basin Oil Report* and the Scharbauers flew to Lexington, Kentucky.

The trip to Kentucky was not a spur-of-the-moment impulse; some preliminary action had already taken place. Clarence and Dorothy had previously enlisted Ken Carson to act as an adviser in their horse search. Carson was a graduate of Texas A&M who had been living in Lexington, Kentucky. He was persuaded to move back to the Lone Star State to be a part of the development of a new thoroughbred racehorse magazine. Ben Hudson and Jerry McAdams had already established *Track* magazine, the widely and wildly popular quarter horse racing periodical. Now they had Ken working for them. Carson was familiar with quarter horse racing, but through Hudson and McAdams he was becoming familiar with many of the fine folks who frequented Ruidoso Downs, not the least of which was AQHA past president Jay Pumphrey. A connection was made in the piney mountains of New Mexico and soon the Texans were off to the Bluegrass.

While the ladies were extremely ready to buy, they were not reckless. After examining a number of horses at the 1984 Keeneland September Yearling Sale, Dorothy and Pam spent $100,000 on one horse. They bought a son of Cox's Ridge and named him Ridge Review. Now they had a horse they hoped could win the Kentucky Derby, but they would have to wait a year and a half to find out. As time passed, the Derby bug that had bitten Dorothy continued to nag and nip away at her. She knew that her chances to win the Kentucky Derby were a long shot—exponentially longer with just one horse. More horses provide more chances. Before long she had Ken Carson poring over sale catalogs and beating the bushes on the trail to buy more horses. The next summer, the Scharbauers—along with Jay Pumphrey; his wife, Betty; and Ken Carson—headed back to Keeneland. This time it was for the 1985 July Yearling Sale.

Prior to the Texans' departure for Kentucky, Clarence Scharbauer had a lengthy phone conversation (the only kind when Clarence is on the line) with Jack. The call was prompted by Dr. Bill Lockridge, DVM, who helped found Ashford Stud in Versailles, Kentucky. Lockridge had met Scharbauer in his previous trip to Lexington, and he thought Clarence would appreciate meeting Jack when he returned to buy horses. Dr. Lock-ridge arranged for Clarence and Jack to meet over the phone before the sales.

Ken Carson recalls Jack and Clarence's first encounter:

We met Jack Van Berg in Lexington just before the big yearling sale in July and we all hit it off immediately. I remember Jack told Clarence that the freckles on his hands reminded him of his father Marion's hands. Then Jack told the story of how his dad stuck his finger through the knothole and Jack pinged it with the hammer. At the sale, Jack and Jay and I would go to the barns in the mornings and develop a short list to show to Clarence and Dorothy for later in the afternoons.

Finally, the men narrowed their list down to four horses. Jay and Ken tilted toward the side of pedigree, while Jack relied more on his eye for young horses. As a result, it took some convincing for the two men to trust Jack's eye and to allow Alysheba onto their short list. Truth be told, Alysheba was easier to overlook than to look over. He was skinny and wasn't showing much muscle, but Jack didn't mind buying a horse that had room to fill out and to grow. As Jack said, "Alysheba looked like he was in his everyday clothes. That didn't bother me—I've had a lifetime of buying horses that have room for improvement." Before the sale, Jack watched the colt get shown numerous times to interested shoppers, and of course he ran his hands over Alysheba once or twice himself. In Jack's eyes and mind, Alysheba was *the* colt. The Scharbauers also had their eyes on another Alydar colt. But their interest faded as bidding quickly climbed over a million dollars and settled at $1.9 million. The colt, named Gone West, went on to have a fine racing career and an outstanding history at stud.

Pam Scharbauer had gone in on half ownership of Ridge Review the year before, but she was not willing to get involved with too much more than that. "Pam told her parents that she would share in ownership again, but only with one horse. All Clarence wanted was for his daughter Pam to be involved with the best of the chosen four," said Carson. After the sale the entire group was together at the Columbia Steak House. Van Berg said, "Clarence leaned over to me and asked me which one I thought was the best. I said, 'Hands down, it's the Alydar colt, Clarence.' Then Clarence got up from the table to call Pam." He informed her that she was now part of a half-million-dollar chance to win the 1987 Kentucky Derby.

Alysheba, the Alydar colt, developed as well as Jack had expected. "Before the sale I told folks that Alysheba looked like a diamond in a rock pile," said Van Berg. When he went to the track to train, it's hard to say who was more radiant—the horse or the trainer. "We broke him at my farm in Goshen, Kentucky, and when we'd take the two-year-olds out in sets to train, Alysheba would gallop out in front by nearly a hundred yards," Jack said. "He just had that big of a stride; he would always be clear of the other horses." Dean Flatland worked for Jack in Goshen and was key in teaching Alysheba the fundamentals of becoming a racehorse. "Dean was an excellent hand on a horse, and he was really good with the babies," Jack said.

Things could not have been going any better for Alysheba and the manner he was gearing up for his racing debut. He glided effortlessly across the ground in the morning; in the meantime, Jack was having difficulty keeping his own feet on the ground. The day before Alysheba was to make his first start, Stalwart Sal, a filly Clarence bought in the same sale as Alysheba, whistled dixie in her debut to win by five and a half lengths at 26-1. On his way to the winner's circle, Jack told a group of people, "If you think she ran well, wait until you see the son-of-a-buck we lead over here tomorrow. You can bet your money on him, too, because he easily outworked this filly." The next day they led over Alysheba and that son-of-a-buck finished fifth..

As is so often the case with young horses, training in the morning is a whole different kettle of fish than racing in the afternoon. Jack was disappointed by Alysheba's debut, but he hung his hat on the hope that his colt simply needed racing experience in order to show his true colors.

The Hollywood Park meet had come to a close by mid-July, so Jack opted to ship Alysheba to Chicago along with Stalwart Sal, who was to race in the Polyanna Stakes at Arlington Park. The plan was nearly a complete success. Stalwart Sal won comfortably; Alysheba ran second. He beat the favorite comfortably, but he lost the six-furlong race by just a head. Continuing to push east and growing increasingly impatient for Alysheba's first win, Jack then sent him to Turfway Park in Florence, Kentucky. John Cherry had worked for a number of trainers in a number of capacities before he began working for Jack Van Berg. He was an assistant to Gordon Potter in New Jersey and he worked for Willard Proctor in California. After moving back to the Midwest, John worked for J. J. Pletcher (father of Todd Pletcher) at Oaklawn Park before Jack's assistant, Joe Petalino, asked him to come help him with the string of Van Berg horses in Kentucky. A soft-spoken, reliable horseman, John quickly found his niche under the Van Berg shedrow at Turfway Park. "Joe told me, 'There is gonna be a pretty nice horse arriving here about eleven o'clock tonight,'" said Cherry. "'You're gonna have to be here to unload that horse,' he said. So at about midnight a horse stepped off the van. That was Alysheba." As horse and groom, Alysheba and John would eventually become inseparable.

Sent off at 1/5, Alysheba waxed would-be rivals in a 1 1/16-mile maiden race at Turfway. With blinkers on and Don Brumfield up, he won by eight lengths. Then at 2-1 he stepped into his first-ever stakes race. He finished second as the second choice in the $100,000 In Memoriam Stakes at Turfway. Alysheba was coming to hand. In his next start, the G2 $150,000 Breeders' Futurity at Keeneland, he faced the Wayne Lukas–trained 8/5 entry of Pledge Card and Sooner Showers. Orono, a long shot, won at 15-1 and Alysheba ran second as the third choice. Alysheba had yet to win in $100,000 and $150,000 stakes races, but Jack knew he had a special horse, and he was convinced that he and Alysheba could prove it. In the 1986 G1 $1-million Breeders' Cup Juvenile, Capote was the winning favorite for Wayne Lukas, but Alysheba put in a solid run from off the pace to check in third at 33-1. Eyebrows were raised after the race. Alysheba caught some attention back in the SoCal sunshine, but Jack calmly contained a warm inner smile. In the last big-money stop for two-year-olds of '86, a full field assembled in the G1 $1-million Hollywood Futurity. It was a thrilling finish, with Charlie Whitingham's Temperate Sil a neck in front of Alysheba, who was a neck in front of Masterful Advocate. With just 1 win in 7 starts, the first year of racing for Alysheba was not a complete loss; he earned $359,486. But he still had some work to do to recoup his purchase price of $500,000.

"I never had to do anything special with Alysheba although throughout the summer we were fighting his shins," said groom John Cherry. "Most two-year-olds get sore shins and you have to stop on them. We never did any severe treatment with *Sheba*. Jack just took it slow and easy with him in the mornings."

Jack was the trainer, and he had his share of sharp assistant trainers; he also had some sharp grooms. Sammy Almarez was to Gate Dancer what John Cherry was to Alysheba. But when Alysheba left Kentucky to complete his two-year-old campaign in Southern California, his groom stayed behind in western Kentucky. Van Berg was aware that John Cherry was a key integer of the Alysheba equation; he didn't want the two separated by more than two thousand miles. Despite the promise Alysheba held, it took some convincing for John to travel west to be with the Derby hopeful, as he explains:

> Joe Petalino came into the barn one morning in January of '87 and he says that Jack wants me out in California to rub Alysheba. And I told Joe that I didn't really like California. I said, "There's too many people out there for me and I'm pretty countrified." So a few weeks go by and Jack shows up in the barn in Kentucky. It was cold and he just stepped off the plane wearing a windbreaker jacket. He's growling and grumbling. "It's too damn cold here. You ought to come out to California, John," he says to me. I told him that I didn't particularly like California. Then he says, "I know, but I need you out there." So I told him I'd think about it. Now a few more weeks go by and we've shipped from Turfway to Hot Springs for the Oaklawn meet. Here comes Jack the first week of the meet and he asks me, "You coming out there with me to rub that horse?" I told him I'd been thinking about it and that it might be a pretty good deal. He's a pretty nice colt. So I told him, "Yeah, I'll be out there," but if something went wrong, or if Alysheba got hurt, I wasn't staying. Jack says, "Don't worry, everything will be okay."

As it turns out, everything wasn't okay. In 1987, Alysheba made a humble return to racing as he began his three-year-old season in a March allowance race at Santa Anita. Despite having already earned well over $300,000, Alysheba was still eligible for a nonwinners of two, conditioned allowance race. The race may have been a modest target, but Alysheba wasn't bet modestly; understandably, he went off at 4/5. His disappointing fourth-place finish that followed was not understandable. Puzzled by the performance, Jack requested that Alysheba be scoped after the race. Dr. Herb Warren, DVM, used the endoscope on Alysheba and informed Jack that his colt had an entrapped epiglottis. He told Jack that there was a minor procedure that could be performed but there was a risk that he might lose some training time. Jack understood but thought he might try another option before they attempted the surgery. He decided to run Alysheba on Lasix, a legal diuretic approved in horse racing. Little did Jack know that his attempt at a simple solution would later cause Alysheba to become a Lasix lightning rod of media attention.

Jack and Alysheba pushed on, and two weeks later they lined up against Temperate Sil again, this time in the G1 San Felipe Handicap, the final prep for the Santa Anita Derby. Alysheba beat Temperate Sil, who was the 8/5 favorite, but he ran second to Chart The Stars. Jack was convinced Alysheba should have run much better, so he had Alysheba scoped again. The results showed more of the same. Jack explains:

> We got the report that Alysheba had an entrapped epiglottis, which is like a flap located at the base of the trachea. When that thing isn't working right a horse can't breathe. Alysheba was having difficulty catching his breath and I think that's why he scoped like he bled. I don't believe he ever was a bleeder; it was his damn epiglottis. I asked Clarence (Scharbauer) if he was willing to take a shot with performing a small throat surgery on Alysheba and if it worked, it would still allow him to recover in time for the Kentucky Derby. He said yes, so we had the vet, Dr. Scott Merrell, come out and perform the procedure on Alysheba right there in my barn at Santa Anita. They sedated him and gave him some local anesthesia and then went down one of his nostrils with that scope and down the other nostril with a little hook knife. Then he cut the membrane that was causing it to stick. It took a couple hours to complete the procedure, partly because Alysheba was

not too willing at the start, but he settled down okay and came out of the procedure okay, too.

Alysheba was forced to miss the Santa Anita Derby due to the surgery, but the surgery and sacrifice were a success. Jockey Chris McCarron was on the road to recovery, too, due to a nasty, five-horse spill he was involved in during the Oak Tree Meet in October of 1986. Although Chris had never ridden Alysheba in a race, Jack and Chris both knew that if Pat Day ever took off Alysheba, Chris would be named to ride. After Alysheba's second-place finish in the San Felipe, Pat Day informed Clarence Scharbauer that he intended to ride Demon's Begone, not Alysheba, in the Kentucky Derby. At the time, Demon's Begone had just scorched his foes in both the Southwest and Rebel Stakes at Oaklawn Park and was the heavy favorite to do the same in the Arkansas Derby. Day chose the more certain of the two mounts.

Following a string of steady gallops after the surgery, Alysheba was ready for his first work. It was roughly one month until the Kentucky Derby, and thus far two riders who had previously ridden Alysheba opted for another horse as their likely Derby mount. Scharbauer and Van Berg had already agreed to name Chris McCarron. But the day before Alysheba's scheduled work, Chris McCarron pulled a muscle in his leg and regretfully informed Jack that he wasn't well enough to work him and do the horse justice in the work. So Jack then gave Gary Stevens a leg up into the saddle. After the very fast, yet very easy five-furlong breeze, Stevens didn't want to turn over the reins. When the horse glibly neared Jack after the work, a very giddy jockey said, "Jack, I've never had a horse throw me back behind the saddle like he did when I chirped to him and asked him to run. I'll sign a contract right now to ride this horse whenever and wherever you like. I don't care what my agent tells me." Jack broke the news to Stevens that he had already given his word that McCarron would be the jockey. Once fit, McCarron rode Alysheba in his remaining seventeen lifetime races.

With all favorable opportunities to run at Santa Anita exhausted, Jack inched Alysheba closer to Louisville by basing him in Lexington at Keeneland. Roughly two years earlier, Alysheba had sold for $500,000 at Keeneland but had won only once. His race record was 9-1-5-1 and he was still roughly $100,000 shy of earning as much as his purchase price. His epiglottis was fine; his real problem was *seconditis*. Still eligible for an allowance condition that would have made him a walkover winner, Alysheba was targeted for such a race, until a small infection requiring the treatment of penicillin closed that door. It was now April and the Kentucky Derby was less than a month away. The race options, stakes or otherwise, were becoming sparse. Jack discussed a final Derby prep race for Alysheba with Keeneland racing secretary Howard Battle, someone Van Berg considers one of the best in the field. Battle was also an excellent illustrator of racehorses, and his work is often seen displayed at racetracks to this day. He informed Jack that in recent decades, the Bluegrass Stakes had become the most successful springboard for landing in the winner's circle at the Kentucky Derby. Battle assured Jack that the Bluegrass was the right spot for Alysheba. In his final work leading up to the Bluegrass, Alysheba was brilliant again. He worked so well that when the clockers came down out of the clocker stand, they said they hadn't seen a horse work like that in decades.

On April 23, 1987, in the G1 Bluegrass Stakes at Keeneland, Alysheba left the starting gate as the 4/5 favorite against a short field of just four other foes. At the start, he bumped into his inside rival, Valid Prospect. Then moving through the first turn, he was rank and was caught in a tight pocket. Alysheba ran up on the heels of both War and Valid Prospect, while Avies Copy had him hemmed in from the outside. He finally settled into stride down the backstretch, and when they turned for home, McCarron slipped to the inside of a tiring Valid Prospect and then rolled right up right up to War, the longtime leader. Meantime, Leo Castelli had launched from last. Inside the final furlong it was three horses racing to the wire: War at the rail, Leo Castelli was on the outside, and Alysheba between them. The three horses hit the wire necks apart and it was Alysheba who went under the wire first. But just as the preliminary order of finish was posted, the stewards' inquiry light also switched on. The numbers of the first-place and third-place finishers were flashing on the tote board. The replay showed that there was some bumping that took place near the 1/16 pole and that Alysheba was definitely involved. Jack looked to the sky and recalled all the turmoil he'd suffered with Gate Dancer, and exclaimed, "Good God, not this again!" Some people standing by Jack recalled a slightly less angelic exclamation. And when Alysheba was disqualified from first to third, Jack howled again. At the very point of the track where the starting gate had been positioned, and the point of the race with an awkward camera cut, the stewards determined that the bump Alysheba gave, and also received, warranted a change in the order of finish. Alysheba would go into the Kentucky Derby with just one lifetime win.

There's nothing like seeing a major sports event in person. The 130,532 in attendance at Churchill Downs for the iconic spectacle on May 2, 1987, assuredly have vivid memories of the race—whether they viewed the race in its entirety or not. When done properly, a television broadcast can genuinely enhance a sporting event. The ten minutes of TV that immediately followed the 113th running of the Kentucky Derby were professionally produced and deliciously divine.

A transcript follows of the ABC television broadcast involving the post-race interviews conducted in the winner's circle with Jack Van Berg and Chris McCarron, hosted by Emmy Award–winning Hall of Fame broadcaster Jim McKay. For those of you without a VHS tape player, enjoy the ride . . .

McKay: Jack, last October the 18th you looked me in the eye and you said, "Jim, I'm gonna win the Kentucky Derby." I said, "With what?" And you said, "With Alysheba." It looks like you were right. Congratulations!

Van Berg: Thank you, Jim. I had an awful lot of confidence in him from the start. A lot of confidence. He was a good horse from the start. We had some problems but he came around good for us. I just want to thank everybody who has ever helped me. The Scharbauers for giving me the chance, my mom and dad, everybody, my family, my wife, everybody. Thank you.

McKay: I remember when you won the Preakness (with Gate Dancer) you told me you were thinking of your dad, and I think you are right now? Congratulations, Jack. We'll see you in Baltimore, right?

Jack mouthed the words *thank you*, but no sound seemed to come from his lips. Jack was moved by the experience, and the decades of dedication, primarily to his father, started to quake and flow from his body. He nodded his head in agreement to McKay's questions and graciously backed away.

When winning jockey Chris McCarron had his opportunity to speak in the post-race interview with Jim McKay, he emphatically said, "I'm really, really happy for Jack Van Berg. I've never ridden for a more deserving horseman to win the Kentucky Derby. He's the hardest-working horseman I've ever been around. And I'm really very, very happy for Jack."

Then, while still on-air in the winner's circle, McKay and McCarron looked to a TV monitor and reviewed a complete, live replay of the running of the Derby thanks to an isolated camera shot that ABC had assigned to Alysheba as part of their television production. The replay rolled and Chris McCarron explained the trip he had right from the start and expressed his observations during the running of the race. As the field flowed through the far turn, the broadcast showed a revealing shot of Alysheba's progress, originating from the rail, to his steady move between horses, and then to a clear, advancing position on the outside. From midway through the far turn, the winning jockey then provided detailed insight to a remarkable ride . . .

> As you can see, he is really moving nicely now. I felt I had a ton of horse; my concern was that I didn't want to hit the front too soon because he has a little bit of play in him. He's still immature yet, and he doesn't know that he is out there for business only. He got to these horses very comfortably, and right now I don't want to go by Bet Twice too quickly. But by the same token I want to be ready to pounce on him at any time.

Then an aware producer in the broadcast booth slowed the replay just prior to when the leader, Bet Twice with jockey Craig Perret, shifted to the right and into the path of Alysheba and McCarron.

With the field at the top of the stretch in the replay, McKay interjected by saying, "You thought you had his measure right now." McCarron responded, "I thought I had his measure, but when Craig (Perret) asks his colt to run, Bet Twice responded very well. But as you can see right here he ducked out in front of me and I clipped heels." Just then, the replay precisely shows the contact and quick reactions from horses and riders. "Watch my colt, look at that! That is unbelievable." At that very second, the slo-mo replay revealed that the contact from Bet Twice nearly knocked Alysheba to his left knee. In getting knocked off stride like that, Alysheba's right hind leg paddled outward in an effort to maintain balance. At one frame in the replay, Alysheba's head drops below the plane of where Craig Perret's boot is positioned aboard Bet Twice. But the horse wasn't the only athlete trying not to get dropped to the track. The sudden jolt compromised McCarron's position in the saddle and for one stride Chris popped up awkwardly. Jim McKay's remark at that point was a raw

"Eww! Oh, boy! You almost went down!" McCarron resumes, "I thought I was gone! How he recovered from that and beat that colt is beyond me." McKay offered an answer in his remark: "Maybe a good rider helped?" McCarron modestly shrugs off the compliment and resumes his analysis of the replay just at the point where Bet Twice has shifted over in front of Alysheba for the second time, this time without contact. "Again he ducked out in front of me again. At this point I thought that if Bet Twice would have beaten me he would have come down (in disqualification). But right here I certainly wanted to beat him fair and square anyway." Then McKay poignantly said, "A few of the more caustic critics were saying this horse is crazy—he's not going to win a big race." Chris McCarron, clarifying what millions of people had just witnessed and would be privileged to witness in the evolution of Alysheba's career, very organically said, "Oh, he's not the least bit crazy. All he is, is a kid. He's just a three-year-old and he's probably a younger three-year-old in his head than the other colts in the race were." The race might have been ugly, but the recap was eloquent. Alysheba had won the Run for the Roses. His beauty was just beginning to blossom.

There were plenty of rosy cheeks and noses back at the barn after the Derby, too, as groom John Cherry recalls: "When I came back from the test barn with Alysheba there was a large, plastic garbage can filled with ice and champagne. It had been delivered to the barn where Alysheba was. Jack had already been by to check on the horse, but when he came back again later that night after dinner, he saw that there wasn't much champagne left. So he sent one of the guys at the barn to go across to the liquor store and buy four more cases of champagne. Heck, it was 10:30 at night and Jack says, 'We ain't done yet, boys.'"

There was no time for a Kentucky Derby hangover—in just two weeks Alysheba was expected to carry Chris McCarron at the Preakness in the blue and white Scharbauer silks, and also to convey the colors, and weight, of being a *Derby winner*. All the colts were assigned 126 pounds, though Alysheba would shoulder a bit more. Onward to Baltimore!

Jack knew that Alysheba was in peak physical performance in the buildup to the Kentucky Derby, so he required nothing more than routine training, or perhaps even less. The colt gave less; the trainer received plenty:

> I was afraid since he ran so hard in the Derby that he might have knocked himself out for the Preakness. I flew in my exercise rider Steve Bass, who worked him in Kentucky and worked him before the Bluegrass. I warned Steve not to go too fast with him. Well, he went too slow. Hell, he went a half mile in :52 or :53 seconds. All the reporters were on me about how slow he went. Well, I told them that was exactly what I wanted. But he went too slow, actually. Alysheba slept on the plane all the way to Pimlico. Although he always fell asleep easily on a plane, just like me.

All week long Jack caught flak about Alysheba being flat, but he was the 2-1 favorite on the Pimlico tote board. Cryptoclearance, who ran fourth in the Kentucky Derby with a rough trip, was 5/2, and Gulch, who ran sixth, went off at 7/2; Bet Twice was fourth choice at 9/2. Jack remembers what occurred on the walk up to the paddock for the Preakness:

> The crowd started cheering his name and chanting *Aly-sheba, Aly-sheba*. His eyes got big as saucers then and he started doing a little dance up and into the paddock. If he was flat or tired he sure as hell woke up. Craig Perret told me later that he looked over to Jimmy Croll [trainer of Bet Twice] and said, "If you think that horse is tired, you better take another look." Alysheba knew when he was going to go into action; he was a smart son-of-a-gun. He only won the Preakness by about a length, but he won it within himself, and he sure woke up Bet Twice when he ran by him.

Bringing a horse up to any leg of a Triple Crown race is important stuff for any thoroughbred trainer, and winning any of the Classic races is likely to be their career highlight. But preparing a horse for the Belmont Stakes with the Triple Crown still available to be won is a horse of a different color. Trainers, aside from their horses, are often the ones who need special conditioning to handle the pressure. It so happens that in 1987, Triple Crown Productions was formed and a special points system was created that offered enticing bonus money. Any horse that runs in any of the three legs of the Triple Crown earns 5 points for first place, 3 points for second place, and 1 point for third place. The point leader at the end of the three-race sequence wins $1 million. What's more, should a horse actually win the Triple Crown, a $5 million bonus would be awarded. There was plenty to calculate for the connections of Alysheba heading into the Belmont. Specifically, the 1 1/2-mile race equated to approximately $14,000 per stride for Alysheba—but only if he won. No pressure.

The days leading up to the final leg of the Triple Crown passed quickly for jockey Chris McCarron, primarily because they were so eventful:

I caught the redeye from LAX to New York on Thursday. My plans were to be at Belmont Park to ride the Friday card before the Belmont Stakes on Saturday. When we took off I noticed the plane had done a 360-turn and I thought that was strange. Just then the pilot announced that we were returning to the airport because our number three engine had caught fire. We landed okay, but I didn't get out of L.A. until the next morning and that meant there was no way for me to make it to New York in time to ride on Friday. I didn't mind that much, because from the day after we won the Preakness I was getting hounded by the press. It was not uncommon to do two and three interviews a day, and I was conducting phone interviews in the jock's room in between races. It was a three-week blur.

It's always nice if, prior to a big race, a jockey can arrive and ride at the track the day before, or at least ride a few races the day of the big race. That was McCarron's intent, but the delayed arrival to the East Coast prevented him from having that luxury. He landed in New York and then went straight to his room at the Garden City Hotel in Long Island. It may or may not have been a blessing in disguise; Chris didn't see Jack until he walked into the paddock to ride Alysheba.

When I got to New York I knew it was going to be even worse with the media, so I wanted to be secluded. I was seeking refuge from the track. I didn't want to be distracted anymore. The reporters were starting to ask me all kinds of crazy questions that I didn't want to let influence my thinking. So in the paddock Jack said to me, "If he comes out of there running, and wants to go to the lead, don't worry about it. He can gallop faster than most of these horses can run." But what he said basically went in one ear and out the other, because he'd come from behind in all of the races he'd won up to that point. And he did break well, but I reached up and grabbed ahold of him and I tucked him in and I was on the rail most of the way. We were in about the middle of the far turn and I was starting to move with Alysheba and we were following Gone West who was also moving up. But then Gone West started to stall and I now had Cryptoclearance right alongside. I couldn't get out of there and they stopped me. Meanwhile Bet Twice is already going to the front and widening, but I had to check off his heels and come to the outside. We got up to almost second but Alysheba started tiring and we got nailed for third money and we finished fourth. I admitted straightaway after the race that I cost him second-place money and I cost him the bonus. I just had to be as contrite and regretful as I could possibly be. I did hear that the Scharbauers were looking to find another rider to replace me after that, but Jack went to bat for me. Although Jack will never let me live it down—every time he has a chance to throw that dig at me he does.

McCarron still grinds his teeth about the trip Alysheba had in the Haskell Invitational Handicap at Monmouth Park, the race that followed the Belmont defeat. Once again, Chris is willing to shoulder the blame—some of it.

> We should have won the Haskell for sure; I did not ride a very good race. I will say that I was following Jack's instructions. He told me to stay in behind Lost Code because he had a habit of lugging out in the turn. So that's where we were going down the backstretch. Lost Code was in front of me and Bet Twice and Craig Perret were parked right alongside of me. The three of us were clear from the others, and as we were going into the far turn, Gene St. Leon on Lost Code looked back and Perret yelled, "He's right behind you." And so with that, St. Leon moved Lost Code even closer to the rail. That's the way we went through the turn. Nearing the quarter pole, I still couldn't get through because Perret has Bet Twice laying on Lost Code, keeping him on the rail. I had to take ahold of Alysheba and swing him to the outside, and when I did, I took him out too far. I overreacted and the colt overreacted and it cost us about a half length and we lost by a neck.

After the Haskell, Bet Twice and Alysheba raced against each other three weeks later in their subsequent starts in the Travers Stakes at Saratoga, but the pair was soundly beaten in the slop by Java Gold. They wouldn't cross paths for another nine months, until they met again for the Pimlico Special Stakes at age four.

When the question of Lasix arose before and after the Travers, Jack maintained that not being able to run Alysheba on Lasix medication in New York was a nonissue. "He ran bad in New York last time in the Belmont because he got a pitiful ride. In the G1 Travers Stakes he was no good in the slop because he ran down badly on that off track and burned his heels. It didn't have a damn thing to do with Lasix," steamed Van Berg.

The million-dollar Travers Stakes didn't go well for Jack and Alysheba, but there was one final million-dollar race for three-year-olds. It was a race that was a super stepping stone to the Breeders' Cup Classic—the Super Derby at Louisiana Downs. "It was a one million-dollar race and I liked that," said Van Berg. "And the timing and distance was just right for the Breeders' Cup Classic."

Alysheba showed up in all his splendor and just beamed with class. He bounced all the way to the gate as the 1-2 favorite and bounced right by Temperate Sil when he swept by him at the 3/8 pole. Now all he had to do was get by Candi's Gold, the Eddie Gregson colt who was bulldog tough. Gary Stevens had given him a perfect ride through the first mile of the race and had just a quarter mile more for the win. McCarron had saved ground in the first turn so he could afford to give up ground in the final turn. With a four-wide sweep Alysheba rushed right up to Candi's Gold. Track announcer Dave Rodman shouted, "A million dollars is on the line." And with that Alysheba gradually reeled in Candi's Gold to win by a half length. He then bounced right into the winner's circle, looking no worse for wear, and $600,000 richer. His win in the Super Derby pushed his earnings over $2,000,000 for the year; his wins were the Kentucky Derby, the Preakness, and The Super Derby. The $5 million of the Triple Crown bonus eluded Alysheba's connections, but now they had the winner's share of the $3 million Breeders' Cup Classic in their sights. There wasn't a straw in the path along the way to the Breeders' Cup. Jack summed his training up in one simple sentence: "He couldn't have trained any better."

Okay, now it is time for me, Chris Kotulak, the author of this book, to weigh in. Technically, I guess I already have, given that you've read more than thirty chapters to get to this point. But up to this point, my role has been to explain and describe a chronology of events and races. However, my description of the 1987 Breeders' Cup Classic will be filled with personal reflection, opinion, and impact. As a track announcer I have called more than 25,000 races and I witnessed thousands before that. As a racing analyst for TVG for nearly ten years, I watched and/or commented on close to 150,000 races. Toss in another 2,500 of the races I've seen in my position at Remington Park and about 100 races each year when I fill in for Ed Burgart at Los Alamitos and it's fair to say I've seen close to 200,000 races in my life. Some races are forgettable. I have forgotten some races I shouldn't have, and there are a few races I'd like to forget. However, I will never forget the 1987 Breeders' Cup Classic!

I had seen as many races of Alysheba as I possibly could prior to this race. But keep in mind, the national proliferation of simulcasting didn't occur until after 1987 and Alysheba had never run at a track near Nebraska. The only time I saw him in the flesh was when I was hired by Louisiana Downs to assist the publicity department for the 1987 Super Derby. Because I was the kid from Nebraska, I was assigned to get post-race quotes from Van Berg. Cool! I couldn't wait. But then they went on to explain I would interview Jack only if Alysheba lost. Oh, no! I feared for my life. There wasn't a seasoned turf writer in the press box who wanted to tangle with an unhappy Jack Van Berg. Welcome to Louisiana, kid. Nevertheless, when it came to Alysheba, I had read every word in print, seen every published photo, and watched the Triple Crown races on ABC. I knew Alysheba—I could *feel* him.

You should also know that in 1982 I gave up being a University of Nebraska football fan. Don't get me wrong—I never root against the Cornhuskers, and I have endless pride in being a Nebraskan. I just couldn't handle the weeks of personal heartache and depression each time they were defeated in a bowl game, after a season of winning with a one-dimensional offense. God bless coaches Bob Devaney and Tom Osborne, and the Huskers have won national championships since I turned in my Go-Big-Red card. But I just couldn't handle the tumbler of love, hope, and sorrow. I establish all this with you because as much as I loved the Nebraska Cornhuskers, I loved Alysheba many lengths more. Watching him on the racetrack made me feel like a parent of a young child. As a three-year-old, Alysheba was still young and developing. He was a child, but he was a bright and brilliant athlete. He had personality and character, and he seemed so honest and willing to give. What's not to love about that? There is no doubt that over time he would become very understanding of his role on the racetrack, and to that end, I was smitten with every furlong of his sweet, sincere strides. I was in love with Alysheba.

Once again the Breeders' Cup host track was Hollywood Park, having hosted the inaugural BC card of races in 1984. And once more the sun shone down brightly on that yellow Hollywood Park starting gate as the field for the '87 Breeders' Cup Classic was dispatched. Twelve left the gate in good order and immediately track announcer Tom Durkin's voice seemed to kick right into a high crescendo that he typically saved for the final strides of a race. The fans heard it, felt it, and responded, and the unique reverberation of the loudspeakers suspended from the Hollywood Park infield light poles surely fueled the excitement back into Durkin's call. If ever a case need be made that a race is nothing without a racecaller, Tom Durkin can carry that torch. His songlike delivery, awareness of the aptitude of each horse, and poignant remarks are unmistakable parts of the Breeders' Cup lore. I swiftly shifted to the edge of my seat as soon as a white-faced horse found the lead and Durkin warbled that it was. . . *Judge Angelucci!*

I was watching the NBC television broadcast with my dad, in my hometown of Omaha. We were at the home of my close friends John and Linda Records, who had invited us over for a small Breeders' Cup party. Dad and I were on the couch together. John was trying to watch from the kitchen while he and Linda wrangled their brood of children. The Grambling State University marching band could have been performing in the dining room—it mattered not. I was dialed in. I was in a crouched position and I heard and saw only one thing: Alysheba. I saw that he broke okay and was taken back safely off the pace as Judge Angelucci and Candi's Gold raced to the front. With all the camera cuts, I really didn't see much of him until the field turned up the backstretch; by then he was in ninth, about ten lengths off the lead.

The next time I saw those blue and white Scharbauer silks was only for a few fleeting strides, but I could see that McCarron had taken Alysheba off the rail and was already asking him to run. I was horrified because I was certain McCarron had asked him to run too soon. "Not now!" I screamed. After another camera cut I saw that Shoemaker, in the pink and sky-blue silks of Mrs. H. B. Keck, had also come off the rail, and he too was making what seemed like an early run. All the while, Tom Durkin continued to reel off thrilling descriptions of the race. And then, with extra inflection, Durkin said, "And now, Alysheba begins to roll from the back of the pack." "Shit, yeah! But where the hell is he?" I yelled. Just then, I saw him, and he was rolling—in fact, he looked like he was sprinting. But there was still a half-mile to run.

I don't smoke and I don't chew my fingernails, but through the first half of the race I could have gone through a pack of Marlboros, chewed my fingers to the bone, and peed my pants (I'm not a pants-pisser either). And there was still a half mile to run! By now my dear dad had seen a side of me he'd never seen before. He knew racing and he knew I loved racing, but seeing my passion, I feel like he almost started to cheer for me, rather than Alysheba. God bless loving parents. But that was *my* boy out there streaking by the 3/8 pole. "Come on boy!" I screamed.

Finally, with an uninterrupted pan shot, I saw the tremendously long strides of Alysheba as he was bending through the turn. He was working and so was McCarron. Alysheba was chugging and chugging and he had made up ground, but he had so much more to do. He had to catch Ferdinand, who was completely cruising and waiting to pounce on the leaders. Then I saw Chris reach back and pop Alysheba. Was this confirmation that he might already be running out of gas? Evidently not, because one pop was all he got. He was still chasing, but he was still in sixth, and now he had to go four wide. At the top of the stretch, there was yet another camera cut and for a few strides, Alysheba disappeared off the screen. The shot showed a very still Shoemaker perched atop Ferdinand with hands clenched on his reins. "Shoe" not only hadn't uncocked his whip, he hadn't moved a muscle, and Ferdinand had easily reached the dueling pacesetters, Candi's Gold and Judge Angelucci. He was no longer parked in that pair's hip pocket; he was parallel to them and ready to go right on by. From frantic to panic, I screamed, "Where's Alysheba?"

Just then, he appeared. He had swept through the turn and now he was nearing Ferdinand's hip pocket, but McCarron was asking him furiously and that damn Shoemaker was still coolly coaxing Ferdinand to the front. Oh, it was awful—McCarron whipping, Shoe sitting. But Alysheba was responding. Nearing the 1/8 pole the blue and white diamond blinkers of Alysheba seemed to have come alongside Shoe's tiny leg, but then he stalled, or Ferdinand repelled his challenge. Or both? Suddenly there was daylight between Ferdinand and Alysheba. Time was running out—there were now less than 100 yards to run, Alysheba needed to make up a length and a half, and Shoemaker hadn't turned a hair. Just as it looked hopeless, here he comes again, somehow; Alysheba had more to give and he was surging. But there was no way he could make up that much ground. With 50 yards out he was a half length away; 25 yards out he was within a neck. Ferdinand was now driving, Alysheba was rushing. When they hit the wire, it looked like Alysheba was beaten by a head. But there was a shadow on the track just one stride after the finish line and it caused a deceptive view of the finish. Then came the most wicked and haunting camera shot of them all: the cut to the top two horses, just two strides beyond the finish, showed that Alysheba had passed Ferdinand. What had happened? Of course it would be a photo finish, but did Alysheba win a miraculous head bob? Tom Durkin's racecall hadn't cleared anything up. In one of his most popular Breeders' Cup calls of all time, he exclaimed, "The two Derby winners hit the wire together, in the world's richest horse race!" It was a perfect, yet chilling exaltation. Durkin's work was done; now it was up to the photo-finish results. I looked over at my dad; I looked around the room; I looked at the television. Time stopped, everything hung in the balance. Who won? There were no camera shots of any celebrations, just uncertainty. Then I heard a roar on the broadcast and saw the camera cut to Ferdinand.

To this day, when I watch the replay of the '87 Breeders' Cup Classic—and I have seen it dozens of times since 1987—I still have hope that dear colt gets up to win it. Now, that's either delusion or unending love. And the pain of defeat is still in my heart.

It wasn't until I interviewed Chris McCarron for this book that I learned what also happened. After the finish line, Shoemaker looks over to McCarron as they're galloping out past the wire and says, "Well, what do ya think?" McCarron, uncertain of whether or not his horse won, replies, "Geez, Shoe, I have no idea." To which Shoemaker quickly asks, "Do you want to save?" The term *save* is a rather unmentioned term in horse racing, but it is not unheard of among thoroughbred jockeys. In a tight finish, when neither rider is confident that they have won, but may be fearful they have lost, the two may agree to *save*. That means they will combine whatever they each earn for finishing first and second, then split that total sum. The winning horse earns 60 percent of the purse, and the runner-up earns 20 percent, so clearly there is incentive for jockeys to ride to win. It happens very infrequently, but when the save is on, neither jockey gets stuck with only 20 percent, but neither gets the larger 60 percent, either; they both get 40 percent.

In this instance, just strides after the Classic, rather than combining first and second purse monies, McCarron suggested a nickel ($5,000), to which Shoemaker countered his offer with a dime ($10,000). The numbers seem hefty, but they are light compared to the weight of the Breeders' Cup purses. In the $3 million race, $1.8 million goes to the winner and $600,000 to second place. Jockeys get 10 percent of that split, so we're talking $180,000 due to the winning jockey and $60,000 to the runner-up rider. Evidently a $120,000 net save on the $3,000,000 Breeders' Cup Classic was never up for discussion. They saved for $10,000. Comparatively, the agreed-upon dime *save* felt like loose change. Chris recalls what happened: "A few days after Shoe picked up his check from the horsemen's bookkeeper, he says, 'Okay, McCarron, I owe you $10,000.'" But Chris had other ideas for the money. He asked Shoemaker to donate the $10,000 to the Don MacBeth Memorial Jockey Fund for injured and disabled riders. "He wrote them a check, and that was important seed money for the account in the early days of our fund," said McCarron. Long live Shoe and ever the classy McCarron—each man a sparkling reminder that a noble journeyman athlete can be one of the finest jewels in sport.

To further accentuate the magnitude and blur of Jack's life and lifestyle cast by the shadow of Alysheba's three-year-old campaign, Van Berg reached a monumental milestone midway through the year. On July 15, 1987, in the ninth race at Arlington Park, Jack won a $10,000 claiming race as the favorite with Pat Day up. None of that information is newsworthy, nor was the horse that won: Art's Chandelle. The significance of that win is, with that horse, Jack C. Van Berg, at age fifty-one, became the first trainer in North American racing to record 5,000 wins. After the race, Arlington Park chairman Richard L. Duchossois was waiting for Jack at the winner's circle to congratulate him. He also presented Jack with a new stock saddle to commemorate the event. Jack thanked Duchossois and thanked the Chicago racing fans for their support. Then he gave credit to his father, saying, "My dad was the greatest horseman who ever lived. I had the best teacher in the world." The beautiful saddle is showcased in the Van Berg Racing Collection display at Fonner Park.

It was a year to remember for Jack Van Berg—from what he could remember. As usual, his horses had him traveling all across the nation, but there was one unusual horse that had his absolute attention. Alysheba was that unusually special horse. He won the Kentucky Derby when it looked hopelessly impossible and he lost the Breeders' Cup Classic when it looked hopefully possible. He raced like a champion and was voted one, too: Alysheba, 1987 Champion Three-Year-Old Colt.

35

Alysheba
Evolution of a Champion

Another racing season had come and gone. In North American thoroughbred racing, 1987 progressed into 1988 in a rather routine manner: Hollywood Park concluded, Christmas arrived, Santa Anita opened after Christmas Day, and a cork popped a fresh new year of cheer. But the spirits of Chris McCarron weren't as bright from one season to the next. Reflections on the Breeders' Cup loomed gloomily in his mind:

The worst defeat I suffered with Alysheba was to Ferdinand in the Breeders' Cup Classic. Yes, the defeat in the Belmont was bad, but I feel that Alysheba was not going to win the Belmont. I did not ride fourteen lengths of a bad race, if you will. I cost him the bonus, there is no doubt in my mind. My poor judgment in the turn cost Jack, the Scharbauers, and me that nice bonus. But the 1987 Breeders' Cup at Hollywood Park stings the worst. At that time Alysheba was still maturing mentally. He was very tricky to ride. Sometimes you could hit him to get him to go and he would really respond favorably and other times he would sulk. I could really feel his acceleration and decelerations then, and it was at those times that I really wasn't sure exactly what to do. When he was a three-year-old, he would run to a horse, say within a neck or a head, and then I could feel him gear down. In the Breeders' Cup Classic he ran up to Ferdinand and then there was a lull and then he'd have to run up to him again, and then there was another lull. And he did that through the length of the stretch. And he always made a habit of waiting once he made the lead, which made it difficult for him to impress a lot of people because he seldom won his races by daylight.

Despite the haunting defeat in the Breeders' Cup Classic for the jockey (and the author of this book), the trainer was already looking optimistically down the road. Jack knew that Alysheba was just now hitting his best stride, and he didn't want to disrupt the flow. Alysheba was kept in training in California during the winter, and everything was going according to plan until Mother Nature rained on things. The horse was entered for the 1 1/8-mile G1 San Fernando Stakes in mid-January at Santa Anita, but the rain really fouled the track. Jack had serious thoughts about scratching Alysheba, so he took his concerns to the Santa Anita Park director of racing, Frank E. "Jimmy" Kilroe. "I thought Mr. Kilroe was a genius of racing," said Van Berg. "When I asked him about the track surface, he said, 'Young man, let me tell you something, if he was my horse I *wouldn't* run him.' I always admired him for that remark." Van Berg scratched Alysheba from the San Fernando. He was then pointed for the 1 1/4-mile G1 Strub Stakes at Santa Anita. The Strub is run annually in February; that would mean Alysheba would be returning to the races off a nearly three-month layoff. It's a lot to ask of a horse to win at such a distance off such a layoff, but Jack Van Berg had a special plan for a special horse.

Jack knew that in order for Alysheba to be at his best, he needed to work at least a mile. He decided to work him the actual 1 1/4-mile distance of that race. He told Chris McCarron that as soon as the track dried out at Hollywood Park he should be ready to come and work him a mile and a quarter. A few days later McCarron reported for duty.

As was the norm with Alysheba, when he would come out onto the track we would stand there for nearly a half hour and he would intently watch the other horses train. Alysheba was so intelligent; he'd just stand there and take it all in. So after that, Jack told me to jog him a lap and then come back and he'd tell me what we were going to do. So I jogged around there with him and when I came back to Jack, he says, "Look, I've got this other horse warmed up, I want you to break off at the quarter pole (the top of the stretch) and I want you to go with this horse. He'll be on your outside, but I want you to lay a couple lengths behind him and follow him to the 7/8 pole or about the middle of the first turn. Then another one will hook in with you and work with you until about the half pole (about midway down the backstretch), and then another horse will join you at about the 3/8 pole and go with you all the way to the finish line. You'll work a mile and a quarter." Jack emphasized how important it was for Alysheba to get in a strong work and get him tired in preparation for the 1 1/4-mile Strub Stakes in about three weeks. Alysheba outworked all three of those horses. He worked awesome! I mean, he felt like he was flying around there. So I'm pulling up down the backstretch after the work and Jack lopes up alongside me on his pony and he's yelling at me, "Damn it, Chris—I told you I needed a good, strong work in that colt." I'm thinking, What the hell is he talking about? I said, "Jack, he's a little tired now, but he finished up really strong." But Jack is not happy. So I asked Jack, "What did I go in?" And Jack says, "You went too damn slow. You went in 2:15." I said, "No way, the clock in my head is not that far off, for crying out loud." And then I thought a bit and said, "Holy shit! Wait a second, we worked him a mile and three-eighths."

It was a peculiar way to conduct a peculiarly long work and then it ended with an even more peculiar time. Van Berg and McCarron had forgotten that the year before, the circumference of Hollywood Park had been expanded from the standard 1-mile distance to a 1 1/8-mile oval. When they realized their mistake, the two Hall-of-Famers transitioned from red-faced anger, to blushed embarrassment, to glowing ebullience.

What exhilarated the two men even more was that their colt had taken the happy accident in complete stride.

Alysheba *crushed* in the Strub Stakes. He was a short-priced favorite and he won like it, winning by three lengths over Candi's Gold. "He didn't typically win by a big margin, but I think he won by open lengths because he was an incredibly fresh horse. It was almost like he forgot to pull himself up," said a thrilled Chris McCarron.

In his next start, the G1 $1-million Santa Anita Handicap, Alysheba would face Ferdinand again. It would be a rematch of the '87 Breeders' Cup Classic. In the "Big Cap," the two raced as a team throughout and Alysheba edged Ferdinand by a half length. It was two-pronged sweet revenge—Alysheba turned the tables on Ferdinand and Van Berg turned the tables on Whittingham. Just two years before, Charlie Whittingham's Greinton at 3-1 had nipped Van Berg's 157-1 Herat in the '86 Big Cap.

The entire North American horseracing world was abuzz. Another rivalry had been born, and once again, Alysheba was part of it. Two popular, bald-headed Hall-of-Fame trainers had two top-shelf handicap horses; they were both based in Southern California, and their encounters together—horses and trainers—were electric.

The rivalry that developed was between the two horses, not the two men. Van Berg has unending respect for Whittingham: "Let me tell you, Charlie Whittingham was a great man, a great horseman, and a dear, dear friend of mine." Charlie was in Louisville with Temperate Sil in 1987, trying to win the Derby back-to-back years, having won it in '86 with Ferdinand. Unfortunately Temperate Sil got a respiratory infection at Churchill Downs that last week in April, and it caused him to miss the big race the first Saturday in May. Nevertheless, Whittingham and Temperate Sil remained for Derby Week. Jack at age fifty-one and Charlie at age seventy-seven were apart in age but not in interest; the two spent much time together leading up to the May 2 Kentucky Derby. "Charlie and I were watching Alysheba come off the track and walk back to the barn and Charlie says to me, 'Jack, this horse has a great nervous system. You could throw a handful of flour between his hind legs and not an ounce would stick.' He saw that Alysheba didn't have a drop of nervous sweat on him. I'll never forget that," said Van Berg. "Charlie was a real gentleman, too. I wish he was here today."

The million-dollar Big Cap had been won; now the Scharbauers and Van Berg had designs on the Oaklawn Handicap. But there was evidently still more money left on the Santa Anita stakes table, although it had to be dredged up from their coffers—or at least their marketing budget. The G2 $250,000 San Bernardino was bumped up to $500,000 under the terms that both Alysheba and Ferdinand would run in the race. They did. The plan to pit the two most recent Kentucky Derby winners succeeded; there would be one more Santa Anita superstar showdown. But as the race played out, it became much more than a two-horse race.

On April 17, 1988, 52,487 showed up for the *Super* San Bernardino. Traffic backed up onto Baldwin Avenue and Huntington Drive; the entire majestic facility was a swell of people who had one race on their mind. Alysheba was sent off as the 4/5 favorite and McCarron had him up close early, just off the pace-setting Good Taste. When they turned up the backstretch, Shoemaker pushed on Ferdinand all the way down the backside and the race was unfolding like a replay of the Big Cap. Then, as Alysheba and Ferdinand looped past Good Taste at the 3/8 pole, track announcer Trevor Denman exclaimed, "Here's the match race we've been waiting for—Alysheba at the rail, Ferdinand alongside; 127 pounds each and they're going to go nose and nose to the wire." Trevor nailed it, except what he—and the hundreds of thousands who watched at the track and on television—didn't expect was that Gary Stevens was playing possum with Good Taste, who was in receipt of 14 pounds of the two giants. The steely Stevens had given his mount a breather and suddenly Good Taste rolled up to the outside of Alysheba and Ferdinand. Within an instant, the top pair felt the heat and they instinctively switched into desperation mode. The race was on! It set up for a memorable, three-way thriller to the wire. Ferdinand forged his head in front approaching the furlong pole, but Alysheba stayed on at the rail, as did Good Taste on the outside. In a blanket finish, Trevor Denman assured us, "Alysheba won it by a nose!"

Having won the battle against Ferdinand and Good Taste, the war was still on for Alysheba. He was then deployed into battle in Baltimore, to face his archrival, Bet Twice. One year before, Alysheba had edged Bet Twice in the Preakness; this time, in the Pimlico Special Stakes, Bet Twice was a strong winner in his East Coast backyard and Alysheba ran a weak fourth.

Alysheba then returned to the West Coast for the $500,000 G1 Hollywood Gold Cup and once again faced Ferdinand. Gary Stevens had just missed beating that pair of rivals a few months before in the Big Cap with Good Taste; this time he gave them the slip with the razor-sharp Cutlass Reality. Ferdinand was a distant third. After six races in six months, Alysheba was awarded a summertime vacation.

Chris McCarron knew that Alysheba was maturing both physically and mentally as a racehorse. His ripening was evident by his three big wins at Santa Anita in the winter. In his three-year-old season he had still been developing, and his curiosity had been costing him; he was acting like a young boy. However, as a four-year-old he totally understood what was being asked of him, and he thrived on the challenges. "He was much more businesslike as a four-year-old," Chris McCarron said. It was something instinctual that McCarron could feel beneath him. Horse racing and racehorses are not derived from arithmetic equations. Yes, important numbers are involved, such as race times and purchase prices, but racing is much more art than math. Alysheba was an evolving masterpiece. Suggestions about his performance and potential flowed between Scharbauer, McCarron, and Van Berg, and there was a discussion about his competitive nature. "I was concerned about leaving the blinkers on him even though he had won all of his races wearing blinkers," said McCarron. "I just felt he should have his complete field of vision now that he had matured so well and understood things much better." The suggestion and ultimate decision by Scharbauer sure made a difference, and it sure didn't hurt.

Alysheba's return off his respite brought him right back into the teeth of the dragon—or dragons. In the 1 1/8-mile G1 Iselin Handicap at Monmouth Park, he faced a familiar foe in Bet Twice, but beyond his known enemy, he would also face the multiple-stakes-winning Gulch and the emerging local star Slew City Slew, among others.

Alysheba, the even-money favorite, broke well but didn't race out to chase the leaders. Without blinkers, he settled back six or seven lengths going into the first turn, and by the time the leaders were midway down the backstretch, he had dropped back nearly a dozen lengths from the lead. Alysheba hadn't run in two months and he had a flight of serious racehorses well in front of him. Approaching the far turn, McCarron asked him to run, and he did. In the meantime, Craig Perret had moved Bet Twice out from behind Slew City Slew and just inside of Gulch. Alysheba was now gaining on the front group with each and every stride. But at the top of the stretch, Bet Twice punched away from his nearby rivals and was headed for home. Alysheba whizzed by tired horses, but at the furlong pole he still needed to make up three lengths to get even with a surging Bet Twice. Just then, Dave Johnson, who was calling the race for the live ESPN telecast, said, "The rivalry continues." And then Johnson roared out his trademark expression: "And down the stretch they come!" Fans at Monmouth Park couldn't hear on-track announcer Bob Weems's concurrent racecall, nor could the millions at home hear any racecall once they leaped to their feet after Johnson's signature saying. Alysheba not only reeled in Bet Twice, when he raced by him he hazed close to him in the final strides, as if to ask,

"Remember me?"

The next race on the radar was the 1 1/4-mile G1 $750,000 Wood-ward Handicap, but that would require a return to the track of Alysheba's most costly defeat. It was back up the turnpike to Belmont Park. A salty field of eight handicap horses went to the post, including a few fellow heavyweight handicap horses such as Waquoit and Cryptoclearance and a pair of proven three-year-olds: Forty Niner and Brian's Time. Alysheba settled into third early and prompted the pace throughout. Approaching the far turn Alysheba remained in third but had dropped back nearly four lengths off the pacesetters. But with three-eighths to run, McCarron eased him right back into contention just as other rivals also began to find their best strides. Nearing the furlong pole there were five horses about two lengths apart and not one was tiring. From the rail out it was Waquoit, Forty Niner, Alysheba, Talinum, and Cryptoclearance. Horse, riders, and even the track announcer Marshall Cassidy kicked it into overdrive for the final 1/16. In the final strides the blue and white diamond Scharbauer silks emerged, as did Cassidy's patent racecall, when he said, "It's Alysheba *in front!*" Alysheba had just broken the Belmont Park track record for the 1 1/4 mile, covering the distance in 1:59 2/5 under 126 pounds. He had just edged the mark of 1:59 3/5 set by Silver Buck in 1982, when he had car-ried 15 pounds less than Alysheba's high weight impost in the Woodward. As he was being led into the winner's circle astride Alysheba, Chris Mc-Carron recalled Jack's riding instructions to him before the ill-fated trip in the Belmont Stakes. He looked to Jack and said, "Jack, you're right, he *can* gallop faster than they can run." A not-so-amused Van Berg snapped back, "You're a year late and five million short!"

The penultimate race in Alysheba's career was also the ultimate en-counter between him and Bet Twice. It came in the G1 $500,000 1 1/4-mile Meadowlands Cup. Alysheba was the 127 high weight and Bet Twice carried 123. Under the lights and over a fast track, Alysheba was on edge in the minutes leading up to the race. But when they broke from the gate his professionalism showed. He broke sharply and then allowed McCarron to draw him back off the pace, settling nearly eight lengths off the lead. Slew City Slew set fast, uncontested fractions of 23, 46 1/5, and 1:09 2/5; Bet Twice was a few lengths off the tempo, and Alysheba tracked him. However, by the time the field reached the top of the lane, Alysheba had swept by Bet Twice and was breathing fire on Slew City Slew. With ample gas left in the tank, Slew City Slew had plenty for the drive and he kept the race interesting all the way to the wire. Fans had grown accustomed to Alysheba edging by the leader to get the win, which is exactly what he did. What wasn't as expected was the shattering of the Tunerup and Bounding Basque track record. The previous mark of 2:00 2/5 was whacked down to 1:58 2/5. The highest-weighted horse to win the Meadowlands Cup had just run the fastest of any horse to win at the 1 1/4-mile distance at "The Big M." ESPN horse-racing host Chris Lincoln emphasized in the broadcast that with this win, Alysheba's earnings were now more than $5.2 million. That put him behind only the great John Henry on the all-time earnings list. It was a valued win for John Cherry, too. "The Meadowlands gave the groom of the winning horse a nice mantel clock. They shipped it to me and it had Alysheba's name on it. My mom has it at her place there in Indiana," said Cherry. A mother can proudly display the accomplishments of her dear son, while John is contentedly proud of the memories of his dear "Sheba."

The next start for Sheba would be his last, although his trainer sure didn't believe that, or want that to be the case. Jack was focused on winning the G1 Breeders' Cup Classic with Alysheba, the very race he had lost by a nose the year before. Churchill Downs would host the BC races in 1988 and that suited Jack and his colt just fine. Alysheba had run only once before at Churchill, but the results—despite the near catastrophic stretch run in the Derby—had been satisfying.

In the '88 Breeders' Cup Classic, Alysheba would face a field of horses that he had already beaten at least once in his recent East Coast flurry of G1 wins. While previously defeated, most of the rivals remained a threat; Alysheba hadn't beaten them by much. The new twist was the recent Super Derby winner, Seeking The Gold, and the involvement of Cutlass Reality and Lively One, two West Coast invaders who had just run first and second in the G3 Goodwood Handicap at Santa Anita. Lively One had never faced Alysheba, but Cutlass Reality easily handled both Alysheba and Ferdinand in the Hollywood Gold Cup in the summer. Van Berg wasn't worried:

> Alysheba had gotten so professional by that time. Nothing bothered him physically or mentally. And I told Chris (McCarron) not to worry about the muddy track. The only other time he caught an off track was in the Travers, but he had run bad at Saratoga in the slop because he ran-down and burned his heels. Churchill Downs has one of the best surfaces in the world and I knew he would handle the track just fine.

Mother Nature threw a curveball with the rain, and she followed up with a knuckleball when darkness descended much more quickly than some had expected. Photographers switched to flash mode and opened their lens apertures, video cameramen went to full iris, and television producers simply freaked out. But Jack wasn't afraid of the wet track and Alysheba wasn't afraid of the dark.

Under deepening darkness, the field left the gate. Lively One and Alysheba banged into each other at the start and the two settled back as Waquoit and Slew City Slew went to the front and raced on early. Alysheba was briefly in close behind both Forty Niner and Cutlass Reality until McCarron steered him to the outside and decidedly kept him away from the rail. Alysheba raced into fourth through the first turn as a steady array of flashes popped, freezing the runners in stride with the Churchill

Downs grandstand behind them. Up the backstretch, an honest pace was on. McCarron still had Alysheba in fourth, but his nemesis, Cutlass Reality, was a few lengths clear in third. But approaching the 1/2-mile pole, Julie Krone sent Forty Niner up the rail, to the inside of McCarron and Alysheba. McCarron knew he needed to get going and not lose position. So he set sail. The trip Alysheba was having in this Breeders' Cup Classic was nearly the same as it had unfolded in the BC Classic the year before. Realizing what was happening and sensing the drama, announcer Tom Durkin played his part in stoking up the show. As he saw the blue and white diamond Scharbauer silks stride up to be just three lengths from the lead, he snapped with a pronounced and somewhat growling "Alysheba begins to roll now—he's making his move as they round the far turn." The Churchill Downs crowd roared with enthusiasm and appreciation. Now more than ever they needed Durkin's description and they needed their favorite Alysheba. At the top of the stretch many things happened. Slew City Slew had run out of gas and dropped back, but just as quickly as he did, Cutlass Reality pounced and joined Waquoit, who was still on the lead. This put Alysheba four-wide in his bid, and he now had Seeking The Gold poised to his outside. Meantime, all in contention suddenly had to deal with Personal Flag, who had appeared on the scene via the rail. Five across the track; any horse could win it!

A year before as a three-year-old, Alysheba was uncertain what to do in his attempt to win the Breeders' Cup Classic. He ran up to Ferdinand and then waited and gawked. Now, a year later as a matured four-year-old, he had Seeking The Gold alongside and that was Pat Day astride. Anyone who knew horse racing knew Pat Day always had horse for the final furlong, and Seeking The Gold may have even put a head in front at the furlong pole. Chris McCarron was in the process of putting a perfect ride on Alysheba but he still had some work to do. As Seeking The Gold rolled up to him, he switched his stick to his left hand and signaled Alysheba to fight on. Alysheba got the message, drifted over slightly to the right, and willingly engaged the attackers. While it remained close, McCarron's action on the way to the wire demonstrated he knew he and Alysheba had the measure. Illuminated only by the photo-finish lights and a shower of camera flashes, horse and rider crashed across the finish and into immortality. And to brighten the surreal climax, Durkin, with a now famous racecall, exclaimed, "Alysheba! America's horse! Has done it!"

When he returned to the winner's circle after the BC Classic, "Alysheba for President" signs were raised in support. George H. W. Bush won the U.S. presidential election in 1988, though a few un-haltered fans cast their ballots for Alysheba. Far beyond an elephant or a donkey, a valiant colt had their votes and many others. He was, assuredly, America's Horse!

Jack had finally won his Breeders' Cup Classic. In three of the previous four years his horses took him down the path of ultimate heartache: second by a head twice with Gate Dancer and second by a nose with Alysheba. Jack beamed with pride in his accomplishment, but more so in his horse. "Last year this colt played around in the stretch—this year he still plays, but now he plays with the competition. He is so smart he just toys with them," Van Berg said. "He's like the fastest kid on the playground; he lets himself get chased and only runs as hard as he needs to." Jack enjoyed all the post-race protocol and festivities of a mammoth stakes win, but the next morning both horse and trainer rebounded like it was just another day. That was good news, as Jack now had thoughts of Santa Anita stakes races dancing in his head. Then came the bad news. Through a newspaper story, Jack learned that Alysheba had been retired. "It was just a shame. We barely got to see his best. He had just begun to figure things out and they retired him without a pimple on him. I spoke with Dorothy about it and she didn't want to retire him," Van Berg said. Later, Clarence said Jack was right.

A week after his retirement was announced, Alysheba received a fitting farewell in a final parade in front of the Churchill Downs grandstand, the site of his two most important victories: the 1987 Kentucky Derby and the 1988 Breeders' Cup Classic. No two races in North America are more important. So then, fittingly, America's Horse was led off the track still bucking and kicking, wearing a blanket that read: "Good-bye, I love my fans. Thank you, Alysheba."

Donald Ropp galloped for Jack at Hollywood Park and was Alysheba's primary exercise rider throughout his three-year racing career. Ropp was an important cog in the wheel and world that turned around Alysheba. Jack maintains that Donald was key in the success of Alysheba, while Ropp is more modest: "I galloped him, but there were about a dozen of us that got on him throughout his career. Joe Petalino would get on him when they shipped him east so he got a lot of the attention. But Petalino wasn't the only one," Ropp said. "Alysheba was a real racehorse in the afternoon, but in the morning anyone could have gotten on him. I think Clarence Scharbauer screwed up because there's no telling how much Alysheba could have won as a five-year-old. He was just getting good when they quit on him." When Alysheba was retired, Ropp figured it was a good time to return back to the Midwest. He didn't get to bring Alysheba back with him, but he ultimately got the next best thing. Jack always shipped Red, the Van Berg pony horse, along with Alysheba. Ropp was just as fond of Red as he was the stable star. When the pony's days on the racetrack were over, Donald welcomed ol' reliable Red to his farm in Urbana, Ohio, which became his final resting ground. Ropp, a longtime companion of Alysheba, speaks in a rigid, rough-hewn tone, but as every good horseman should, he has a genuine soft heart for a horse, even if it didn't win millions of dollars.

In the history of North American thoroughbred racing, the pot has been kept thoroughly stirred with some famous rivalries. Those of yesteryear include Seabiscuit vs. War Admiral, and the outstanding filly Gallorette vs. Stymie. Modern-day horse racing has not lacked its rivalries either, the most famous being Affirmed's Triple Crown and two-year hex over Alydar. The brief war that waged between Easy Goer and Sunday Silence was only a four-race battle; however, the '89 Preakness Stakes was one for the ages. But perhaps the most evenly matched rivalry of modern-day racing was that of Alysheba vs. Bet Twice. They faced each other in a total of ten races, with both horses winning four races apiece. On the two nonwinning occasions, each horse finished with one placing in front of the other. Later, though less in incidence, but unquestionable in significance, Alysheba and Ferdinand had their own throw-downs. Alysheba lost that fateful Breeders' Cup Classic in 1987. But in 1988 he repelled Ferdinand, with wins in the Santa Anita Big Cap and San Bernardino; Alysheba finished second in the '88 Hollywood Gold Cup, and Ferdinand ran third.

Alysheba won 11 of 26 career starts and earned $6,679,242. After winning the 1988 Breeders' Cup Classic, he was retired as the richest thoroughbred of all time. The Dubai World Cup debuted in 1996 as the world's richest horse race. Alysheba ranks tenth in all time earnings; those above him include Cigar and Silver Charm, who won the Dubai World Cup when it had a $4 million purse. Captain Steve, Pleasantly Perfect, Invasor, and Curlin all won the World Cup with a $6 million purse. Fantastic Light ran in Dubai and all over the world but didn't run in the Dubai World Cup. Smarty Jones didn't run in the World Cup, but he did earn a $5 million bonus for winning the Rebel Stakes, Arkansas Derby, and Kentucky Derby. Skip Away was kept away from Dubai but was allowed to race as a five-year-old; he won 7 of 9 in 1998 alone. It was a treat to watch him run, and he earned $2.7 million for that extra year of racing. With the Dubai World Cup purse at $10 million, it won't take much for Alysheba to get knocked out of the top ten. In defense of the greats before Alysheba, John Henry only ran in two million-dollar races and earned $88,000 less than Alysheba. The richest race for Secretariat was only a quarter-million dollars. Twenty-five years in the top ten is quite a run, but Alysheba's reign with the elite won't last forever. Black Caviar, anyone?

36

Alysheba
Farewell to a Prince

Alysheba's greatest impact on horse racing is the imprint he left on the racetrack; it was a memorable feat coupled with grit and glory. However, his career in the breeding shed was rather forgettable. His first duty at stud began in 1989 at Lane's End Farm in Versailles, Kentucky. He did sire Alywow, who was voted the 1994 Canadian Horse of the Year. And he sired Desert Waves, a Sam Son Farms homebred who earned more than $1.2 million. He was purchased by His Majesty King Abdullah of Saudi Arabia and stood as a stallion there from 2000 to 2008, but his offspring made little impression.

Kathy Hopkins is the director of Equine Operations and Education at the Kentucky Horse Park in Lexington, Kentucky. One of her duties is to oversee the Hall of Champions, which is a haven for past racing champions and the fans who can reach out and touch them. Kathy describes the touching and surreal moment when Alysheba returned from the desert:

> King Abdullah of Saudi Arabia felt that as a gift to the people of the Commonwealth of Kentucky and America, he would send Alysheba back to spend the rest of his retirement years in Lexington not too far from where he was born at Hamburg Place. It was a long flight—he went from Saudi, to Dubai, to Amsterdam; he was quarantined and then to New York. It was really neat when his flight arrived. It was a beautiful early fall evening. It was warm and you could smell the grass they had just mowed in the farm across the field from Bluegrass Airport. When they opened the cargo door Alysheba stepped up and then stopped. His nostrils

flared and you could see he took a deep breath and let out a big sigh. Then he looked out beyond us and just stood there. He knew he was home. It was just awesome!

Alysheba had a presence about him. You took one look at him and you knew he was a prince. He was such a gentleman and a magnificent horse. His rich being beamed, even through his poor condition. The journey had taken a physical toll on him, so we had to get him back into solid condition before we could bring him to the Horse Park. We actually took him to my farm for a few months so he could rest and recover in private before we could showcase him in the Hall of Champions. We had to slowly reintroduce him to being able to graze on the lush bluegrass. That first morning he was just mouthing in his stall for a chance to get out there and devour that sweet green bluegrass.

When Alysheba was ready to enter the Hall of Champions, the Kentucky Horse Park had a nice ceremony and media opportunity. Jack was there, Chris McCarron was there, Preston Madden was there, and so was Henry Waits, who worked at Hamburg Place where Alysheba was bred. Henry foaled and helped raise Alysheba and was one of his first human friends. "The Prince" was given the same stall that the great John Henry had during his reign at the Hall of Champions. Kathy Hopkins recalls a heartwarming moment the day of the ceremony: "Henry Waits went into the stall and Alysheba started nuzzling on him. He was all over Henry and it was just so sweet. Henry is a quiet and humble man. He didn't say much but you could tell he enjoyed that experience," said Hopkins. "Alysheba didn't do that with everyone. There was obviously a bond between the two." Hopkins also remembers that Alysheba would spend most of his days at the end of his paddock adjacent to the statue of John Henry. "Fittingly, the two thoroughbred champions shared the same paddock," she said. "They were two very special and extremely popular horses at the park. John Henry was more of a character; Alysheba was so incredibly noble."

Tragically, Alysheba's term at the horse park was too short. After less than a half year he was put down due to symptoms resulting from degenerative spinal disorder. Alysheba is buried at the Kentucky Horse Park directly across from the grave of John Henry.

PART IV

37

Family, Finances, and Failures

Jack Van Berg freely admits that he fell far short of being an ideal family man. The remarkably rigorous regime that he maintained did not come without regrets and remorse. Too much time away from his loved ones proved all too much for his family life. "My first wife, Mary Jane, was a hell of a woman," he said. "She'd cook and bake and feed all the help at the barn. Everyone loved her. I loved her, too, but I was a poor husband because I wanted to work all the time. I provided for my children, but I wasn't there for them or Mary Jane as much as I should have been." Jack went on to say,

> I want to apologize to my former wives, Mary Jane and Helen, and to my children, stepchildren, grandchildren, and great-grand-children. I got so involved with training and things that it caused me to neglect my family and my own flesh and blood. I feel awful for that. I guess I treated my family like I did my horses. I provided for them and gave them what they needed to be healthy and strong. I knew they were in good care when I was gone. I made sure of that. But I was gone too much and I put my job before my family. I figured I wasn't being selfish as long as I provided for them. But I found out there is more to being a good husband and a good father than just being a provider. Based on my training accomplishments I shouldn't be in the financial mess I'm in, but bad luck caused plenty of that. I caused some of my problems on my own, but I'd give back thousands of those wins to win back the time I missed and messed up with my family.

Jack's second wife, Helen Murphy Van Berg, from whom he has been divorced since 1993, doesn't see it exactly like that. "Jack is really the kindest human being you will ever meet. I know he says he wasn't a good father. He *was* a good father!" she says, adamantly. Helen first met Jack via her husband at the time, Jack Fiselman, who rode for both Marion and Jack during his riding career. Jack raised Helen's children, Billy and Tonya, along with the five children he had with Mary Jane. He was managing hundreds of horses spread out across the nation, but Helen says Jack also had an awareness of what was going on with his children:

> I've seen Jack with all of his children, and there was never a time that if any child needed help that Jack didn't help them. Whichever child needed Jack, he went there. He solved problems. Jack is convinced that he was a bad father but a good provider, but he was *not* a bad father, because I saw him be a good father. I saw him help every one of those kids out and give, and give, and give, and give. And still today he keeps on giving whatever he can. But I beg to differ with him, and I have always told him that. The children were sort of like me—they all wanted his undivided attention. But nobody gets Jack's undivided attention. He loved them all and he loved me, but you just don't get one-on-one time with Jack.

Helen recalls something Jack said to her before they got married: "Jack told me, 'I'm just like a campfire, Helen—if you leave me unattended I will go out.'" "Hmmm," Helen wondered. Actually, there is no wondering about Jack's remark—it can and should be interpreted in more than one way. And Helen knew that from the start.

"Jack and I had our good times and we had our bad times, and we were each at fault at times, but they were the best times of my life," she said. "Jack provided ways for me to make it convenient for me to live two lives—one on the road with him and the other at home with my children.

But in the end I could not leave my home and my children. I just couldn't do it."

The '80s were the best of times and the worst of times for both Helen and Jack. In that decade alone Jack had won a Kentucky Derby, two Preaknesses, and a Breeders' Cup Classic, but he was riding in the front seat of a jarring emotional roller coaster. Oddly, soothing relief from the manic stress and national attention came from the driver's seat of a purring road grader at his Kentucky training center. "The most at peace I have ever seen Jack Van Berg was when he was out there driving that grader. He was the most content and in the most stress-relieving environment when he was in the cab of that thing," said Helen. "He'd be out there grading that racetrack in the dark. Morning and night. He loved that thing."

Some may say Jack wanted to go too big and have too much. Jack insists that he wasn't frivolous with his money or senseless in his ways:

> I like to look at things and try to devise ways to improve them. I like to develop horses and people, and if I can make more I can do more. I *always* had a plan. The Kentucky farm was beautiful. I developed it the way I designed it and it was making money. Let me tell you, I've bought two farms in Nebraska, two houses in Nebraska, I built a farm in Kentucky, bought a house in Louisiana, and I bought every son-of-a-bitch on my damn handshake and word. And I never had a damn attorney involved in any of that. The first time I hire an attorney to protect myself and I ended up getting the worst screwing of my life. It's very aggravating to hear people saying that I spent my money recklessly and that I was a poor businessman. I'll tell you, the poorest business decision I made was by taking a few people for their word. I trusted them and they took advantage of that.

Failed trust has caused Jack Van Berg to growl a bitter tune: . . . *that damn California ranch!*

38

That Damn California Ranch

Before Jack had visions a of developing a beautiful, functional, and self-providing ranch in Hesperia, California, he had already developed a smart, state-of-the-art horse farm and training center in Goshen, Kentucky.

By the late 1970s Jack had completed an all-inclusive, 500-acre equine training facility. It was an architectural showpiece, complete with a 1/4-mile indoor training track, a 5/8-mile dirt track, and a 2 1/4-mile turf course that wound up and around pastures and horse paddocks. It had a one-hundred-stall barn, a nineteen-horse overhead horse walker, a training observation deck, and a plush horsemen's lounge. It had it all.

But Jack wanted more than a serious facility to train a racehorse—he wanted a facility where a horse could simply be a horse. Jack explains:

> I saw when Montana cattle used to come through our sale barn how dense their bone was. They gained that sturdy density from the good soil and grass up there. I know that Kentucky is the Bluegrass State, but Kentucky didn't have a very strong state-breed breeding program at the time and there were better incentives to raise thoroughbreds elsewhere. And I wasn't getting much business from those Kentucky bluebloods, anyway. So I started looking for a place in Montana. Well, I learned of a place that was in bankruptcy in Hesperia, California, about seventy-five miles northeast of Los Angeles. When I drove up over that ridge and saw that ranch below I fell in love with it immediately. It was beautiful! I guess I forgot about Montana, because I love

the Old West look and this place sure had it. So I got it bought out of bankruptcy in December of 1985. It was 5,000 acres and it had 13,750 acre-feet of water rights on the ranch. Free water! It was like gold. It was such a good setup, I bought 2,500 more acres. I had some partners along with me, and we all came to terms and were happy. Then a land developer outfit by the name of Ameri-Bass came along. They were a group of guys who had three brothers from Texas who were the big money men. I sold them my 7,500 acres on a deal that returned 2,000 acres back to me plus 9 percent of profits derived from the land development. But in the contract, I had to spend $1.3 million to restore and improve the ranch, and they were to spend $2.7 million in development. We would split the water rights, 50/50, and I would own my own 2,000 acres free and clear.

Jack believed he had really struck gold. He had made an acquisition of land for an excellent price and then sold it to the land developers to be developed. Things gradually developed on the land. However, a problem arose when Jack was not getting paid by Ameri-Bass as scheduled. Ever so slowly, after eighteen months, he received what he was owed. Jack bought the property out of bankruptcy with the financial backing of some partners for whom he also trained horses. Now that he got paid, in turn, he could pay off his partners. In the case of his ranch partner John Franks, the two men negotiated an arrangement for reimbursement based off a balance of training fees. Franks had $600,000 involved in Jack's down payment to buy the land. Jack agreed to reduce Franks's monthly training bill by 25 percent until he no longer owed Franks any longer. Jack was to repay Franks the $600,000, plus $125,000 in interest, which he did.

Van Berg then proceeded to develop his prized California ranchland. "I restored a big, beautiful barn built in 1872. It was the largest of its kind in Southern California. I restored six houses on the property. And I built almost twelve miles of pipe fence, a good-looking fence that will last longer than you or I will. I put $1.6 million into that place to develop it," said Van Berg. Jack began investing money according to the terms of the agreement with Ameri-Bass.

But issues about water rights sprang up. Summit Group, the group Van Berg bought the ranch from out of bankruptcy, claimed they still had rights to the water on the land. Jack disagreed because the transcript of the bankruptcy court proceedings reflects that the water rights issue was addressed. Jack knew it would be no small battle to protect his water rights, but he had horses to train and simply could not be burdened with the matter. As the developers, Ameri-Bass, had a major stake in the water on the land, they stepped in and promised to pay for Jack's legal fees if he opposed the lawsuit from Summit Group. Meanwhile, Jack was training several divisions of horses across the nation. Meanwhile, it's Gate Dancer and Alysheba. Meanwhile, it's the Kentucky Derby, the Preakness, the Triple Crown, and the spectacle of the Breeders' Cup.

Back on planet earth—Hesperia, California: a series of lawsuits and countersuits were filed. Serious attorney fees began to mount. There was infighting among the Ameri-Bass partners; a partner left the group and the group was renamed Ameri-Mar. And though Jack was no doubt paying more attention to the actions of his horses than the actions of his attorneys, during the drawn-out process he became suspicious about the land developers and the attorneys involved in the proceedings. He thought there was collusion against him among the attorneys. The more people who got involved, the more cluttered the mess became. Promises were made and promises were broken. Months and years went by but nothing was getting accomplished; nevertheless, attorney fees continued to build.

Jack kept on building, too. He maintained belief that the water rights lawsuit would be won, so he continued to enhance his ranch. With that complete focus, he chose to consolidate his assets by selling his prized training center in Kentucky. Unfortunately, it was a buyer's market at the time of his decision. Jack was advised and persuaded to sell his farm in an absolute auction in order to attract the best possible attention from interested bidders. Under those terms the farm would be sold regardless of price; there was no reserve sale price as there typically is in a horse auction. The complex was appraised at more than $7 million; bidding was weak—it sold for $2.7 million. The tactic was a bust. "If I'd had a gun at the time, I think I may have walked off and shot myself," Van Berg said dejectedly.

The developers, Ameri-Mar, despite their agreement with Van Berg, were not paying the attorney fees. They paid the first $25,000 but then stopped. The fees then mounted to $895,000. That was real money, and payment was demanded. Jack's attorney, John Garrett, needed to assure his firm that they would get paid. He asked Jack the favor of putting up the 9 percent profit clause he had negotiated in his original deal with the land developers as collateral for the outstanding attorney fees. To facilitate the effort, Jack agreed. Then, later, Garret asked Jack for more. "He asked me to put up my 2,000 acres to insure payment of the attorney fees," Van Berg said. "Garret's exact words were, 'It would make me appeal better with my firm if we did this.' Then, right after that, there was a judgment against me for the $895,000." The grip of reality and the vise of the attorneys forced Jack into releasing 1,500 acres. He had been chiseled down to 496 acres. Sadly, what was supposed to be a "California Dreamin'" fortune had become a nightmare and an absolute albatross.

All those years of hard, bone-chilling work in the sale barn as a child; driving horse vans alone through the night as a teenager; the limitless dedication to his father's demands and to his own. The constant travel and monitoring of horses and employees; the hundreds of stakes wins, the thousands of claiming wins; the milestone wins; the Classic wins and Breeders' Cup win. All of the accomplishments and earnings Jack had garnered, exuding blood, sweat, and tears. It was gone; taken from him. Only the intrinsic fortitude of Jack Van Berg kept him going. He was *going*, but he wasn't going on a positive path.

In 1998, one of Jack's daughters, Traci Van Berg Hoops, along with her husband, Rich Hoops, observed the swirling situation Jack was swimming in. With their awareness and wherewithal they chose to throw out a lifeline to rescue Jack from his deepening debt. Traci recalls what occurred:

> After visiting my dad for a few days in the summer of 1998, my husband Rich and I learned about the ranch deal fiasco and began to understand that he had been, and was, accumulating substantial debt. When we returned home we both decided that if we could help my dad turn the situation around and help him focus on training, we would do it. I know this was extremely hard for my dad, but I think at the same time it was a huge relief. He was under an extreme amount of stress. We hired an attorney in L.A. and over the course of several months finalized a loan agreement in 1999. Dad was very worried about us not recovering our money and was insistent that Van Hoops Holdings have the first lien on the ranch in case something should happen to him. Once in place, we began to distribute money as draws against the total loan value. Over the next few years, we paid off service providers (lawyers, hay, vets, builders, etc.) as well as folks who had personal loans to my dad. We also put money into the ranch to get it ready for sale.
>
> But my dad has the biggest heart, and he couldn't make the difficult choices. He kept people on payroll that he couldn't pay. He would give his last five dollars to somebody who was worse off than him. He kept horses that would never run again, boarded horses at the ranch when they had nowhere else to go, auctioned events without asking for payment or reimbursement, and so

much more—all without asking for a dime.

When I attempted to push on with business matters, his response was always, "Damn it, I can't just turn them away; you think it's so easy." I can't imagine how hard it must have been for him—I also know he will never know how hard it was for me to say I couldn't help anymore. We could help financially but we couldn't help change his ways.

Jack had the ranch on the market for years thinking that if he just sold it, everything would be fine. In 2007, a Southern California investment group named Global Investments entered into a contract with Van Berg to buy the remaining 496 acres of the ranch. Global then made an offer to assume the loan. Van Hoops Holdings agreed to the loan assumption so Jack would be free and clear from the ranch. There was a huge relief when they closed on the ranch and Global agreed to the terms of the assumption. Though somewhat skeptical, Van Hoops Holdings and Van Berg were hopeful that the ranch sale was behind them.

Unfortunately, skepticism on their part proved to be justified; there would be slow pay and no pay. The original scheduled payment from Global Investments was extended, and additional extensions were allowed by Van Hoops Holdings. Global claimed escrow delays in Europe, difficulties derived from the 9/11 attack in New York, and anticipation of funds awarded them in a lawsuit.

Global reasoned they could delay their payment again as a lis pendens, or a pending suit, was filed on the property by Franks Farms. Mr. John Franks, a five-time Eclipse Award winning owner and sincere friend of Jack, passed away in 2003. But in 2007 Franks Farms obtained a default judgment against Van Berg. The judgment was based upon Jack's failure to appear and answer a Louisiana complaint against him. Bobby Jelks, a CPA representing Franks Farms in Louisiana, alleged that Jack did not completely clear his debt with the late Mr. Franks. Chuck Quick,

the same man who introduced Global Investments to Van Berg, accepted
$5,000 from Jack to deal with the matter of Jack's summons to Louisiana
court. "Quick said it was taken care of," said Van Berg. It wasn't. Jack
appealed the judgment, claiming he was never properly served with the
summons and complaint.

"Mr. Franks was like a father to me," said Jack. "I spoke with him
in the hospital just before he passed away and he told me that he loved
me. I never charged him one cent for any horse sale commission fees, or
travel fees, or for grading all his foals before all those sales. I didn't charge
him the 10 percent commission when he bought Herat for one million or
charge him 10 percent commission when he sold 50 percent of Herat for
two million dollars." As far as the incomplete debt to Franks Farms, Jack
feels Jelks used extreme methods of suggesting he owed more. "I paid my
debt to Mr. Franks in full and I proved that. But that damn Bobby Jelks
figured out a way to present a bill for hundreds of thousands more. That's
ridiculous!" Van Berg said.

A California title company had given Van Hoops Holdings a clear title
to the ranch, but then the lis pendens filed by Franks Farms threw a wrench
in the proceedings. Jack was red-faced with rage and blue in the face with
demurrers, motions to domesticate, complaints, cross complaints, judgments, foreclosures, lawsuits, and countersuits. The legal chaos was not
only on Jack anymore—Van Hoops Holdings was now named in the lawsuits. Jack felt awful that Traci and Rich were now in the middle of this
muddle.

Global then claimed it couldn't pay, thus starting another salvo of
suits; therefore Van Hoops Holdings couldn't foreclose because of the lis
pendens. Later, Global offered to go to mediation, and Van Hoops agreed.
During the course of the mediation process Jack and Traci realized that if
the lis pendens were removed, Van Hoops Holdings could then demand
Global to pay up. If Global refused, Van Hoops could foreclose on the

investment company. After much consideration and at a massive expense, Van Hoops agreed to pay the Louisiana judgment (removing the lis pendens), enabling them to demand payment from Global Investments. Global refused to pay, so Van Hoops filed for foreclosure and received title to the 496 acres.

Back at the ranch, as claims were made and cases were heard hither, thither, and yon, the California ranch was in the hands of both Jack Van Berg *and* Global. Even though Van Hoops Holdings held the loan, it held no right to the land. Jack had horses, employees, and family living on the ranch while Global Investments had access to the office, equipment, and land. Jack's daughter, Traci Van Berg Hoops, offers further description of what took place:

> Tragically, Global uprooted hundred-year-old trees and discarded them into the creek bed, which was an important water source. They tore up fencing, tilled the large pastures, and generally ruined the beauty of most everything they put their hands on. When they tried to evict the family members living on the ranch, we filed a cease and desist to stop their devaluation of the property before settlement. The motion was granted. Oddly, Van Berg and Global continued to exist on the property until we were able to foreclose. It truly was a nightmare.

As of early 2013, Van Hoops Holdings now holds the title to 497 acres, with 360 acre-feet of water on Los Flores Ranch in Hesperia, California. After a year of clean up, the property has gone on the market. The ranch sits, waiting for a new beginning, and so does Jack. Even though the weight of the ranch should have been lifted, it was just shifted. Now it weighs heavily on him that the ranch has not sold and Van Hoops Holdings has not recovered their money. Dad feels responsible and is desperate to make good on not only his word to Van Hoops Holdings but to others. He truly is a man of his word and will not walk away, even though it would be the best thing for him. Every day I see the tremendous amount of disappointment he lives with—he had such big dreams for the California ranch. It took so much out of him. We want nothing more than to see him move on and to do what he does best—train racehorses.

Don't feel bad if you feel a need to reread this chapter to understand it. It took me seven revisions to write it. I've done my best to tell the story of the "California ranch" as it was told to me. If you are like me and Jack and Traci and Rich, and most everyone else, you are craving the next chapter.

39

Now You Know Jack

Bob Pollock is an even-keeled, friendly, intelligent man who is as wise to the mechanics and logistics of horse racing as anyone you may ever meet. He is utterly unflappable and supremely sensible. What is equally appealing about Bob is that he has the demeanor and uses the spoken expressions of Jed Clampett except he is always clean-shaven, well-dressed, and doesn't wear a tattered hat. He came by it naturally—his father, Alvin Pollock, was a Dust Bowl wheat farmer and horse trainer from Manchester, Oklahoma. Bob grew up there and on the Nebraska horse racing circuit, along with his mother, Ima, and his brother, Dick. He became a respected steward in Nebraska horse racing and he has held both steward and racetrack management positions for decades. As part of the duties of the job, a track steward sees the good, bad, and ugly of horse racing. Bob and Jack are of similar age and the two men have experienced and seen plenty in racing. Typically to the point, Pollock is respectful and on-target with his thoughts: "Jack Van Berg is the most benevolent man in racing that you'll ever know."

The historic G3 Cornhusker Handicap was run for its first thirty years at Ak-Sar-Ben in Omaha. In the mid-1990s, the race moved from the flat-land corn country of Nebraska to the rolling hills corn country of Iowa, and the G3 Cornhusker Handicap now has a home at Prairie Meadows outside of Des Moines. Transporting the trophy of the Cornhusker Handicap is almost as much of an accomplishment as it is to win the race; the iconic award stands nearly four feet tall and consists of a large golden bowl supported by golden columns that are fixed to a heavy wooden base.

Positioned as a centerpiece within this tower of a trophy are three brilliantly gilded ears of corn. It's big, bad, bold, and gold; it's kitschy; and it's conspicuously corny. But you know you've definitely won something big when you've won the G3 Cornhusker Handicap.

Tom Amoss was awestruck when he first laid his eyes on a Cornhusker Handicap trophy. Tom and his childhood buddy Al Stall, Jr., were invited guests with Al's parents at a party held at Van Berg's newly constructed home and training center in Kentucky. The trophy case at the facility was prominent. Seeing all the gold made Amoss feel like he'd just stepped into the tomb of Tutankhamen—Tom was *taken*. "I'll never forget those giant Cornhusker trophies and how they stood out among all the others," said Amoss. It was a remarkable trophy case and a remarkable case of foreshadowing. In time, Tom Amoss would earn a Cornhusker Handicap trophy of his own.

Tom's entry point into thoroughbred racing came at the Van Berg barn at the Fair Grounds in New Orleans, when he spent part of his high school Christmas vacation as a hotwalker for Jack. Vacation was three weeks; Tom lasted nine days. "I was at the barn from sunrise to sunset and I never stopped working the entire time I was there," Amoss said. As a teenager Tom might have been overwhelmed by the demands of working for Jack, but he gained an early and vital understanding of dedication. Amoss was as absorbed and intense then as he is now. Tom would learn more about the Van Berg method of training as he developed his horsemanship under Frankie Brothers, who was one of Jack's early disciples. Amoss, like Brothers, would ultimately leave the nest and hatch into a prominent trainer. In August of 1993, on the backstretch of Ak-Sar-Ben, and just two days before the Cornhusker Handicap, Tom Amoss watched his hard-knocking gelding, Link, step off the horse van lame. Something had gone wrong with the horse during the haul from Louisiana to Nebraska.

Tom's mind began to whir. He rapidly rifled through all the lessons he had learned as a trainer, as well as what he had learned as an assistant trainer to Larry Robideaux and what he had retained from his days of working for Frankie Brothers. And then his desperate search for a solution stopped; he got his answer from Jack. "I recalled a remark Jack Van Berg made when he said, 'Horseshoeing is a lost art.' His statement that shoeing a horse was an art form really stuck with me," said Amoss. "I remembered that Van Berg said Jack Reynolds was the best horseshoer in the nation." Tom was able to locate Reynolds and quickly get him to Omaha to have a look at Link. "Jack Reynolds reshod Link and in one and a half hours Link was walking like new," marveled Amoss. One day later, the red dots on the yellow sleeves of the Stewart Madison silks worn by jockey Ronald Ardoin shone through when Link won a four-horse blanket finish of the G3 Cornhusker Handicap. Bossanova, trained by Jack Van Berg, was in that blanket finish.

At times, it seems like the insight shared by Jack may come back to bite him. In a 1995 Daily Racing Form story, Steve Haskin wrote of Jack's outlook on his willingness to reveal his elements of training. Jack told him, "The main thing I demand is a helluva lot of hard work. If someone wants to learn they'll learn, because I tell them everything we do and why we do it."

Before Donna Barton Brothers became a respected horse racing reporter for NBC television, she became the wife of trainer Frankie Brothers. Before that she was a jockey, and before that she was an exercise rider—for Jack Van Berg. In the mid '80s Donna was at Louisiana Downs and galloping a lot of horses in hopes of getting her license to become a jockey. Donna recalls being on the track on a typical hot and humid morning that became even hotter because Jack was in town to oversee operations. Donna was still a very green rider at the time and was eager and hopeful that she could impress Jack as he looked on to observe the training. Her mount, Friendly Beat, was loping by the trainer's observation stand near the 7/8 pole when trainer Eddie Milligan greeted Donna with a good morning. Just as she raised her head and acknowledged Eddie, Friendly Beat thrashed her head back into Donna's head. The impact smashed Donna's nose and the blood immediately began to gush. Not wanting to show vulnerability, and desperately wanting to satisfy Jack, she galloped an entire round filled with pain and fear, and with a bloodied face. As she completed her gallop, Jack, who had not yet seen her face, was yelling at Donna for not having her stirrups set in the proper manner. When she rode by the stand Jack saw the blood and asked what happened. Donna explained that she had been hammered in the head by the filly. Jack grunted back, "Well, if you'd of had your irons right that never would have happened."

That wasn't the only tough love Jack doled out to Donna. By 1986, she had become an appreciated exercise rider and was frequently galloping horses for Jack. A nice filly named Argentina Lil was shipped to the Fair Grounds from Kentucky and Jack's assistant trainer in Kentucky, Mark Wallerstedt, called and wanted Donna to get on her in the mornings. Mark gave Donna specific instructions to ride with a very long rein and not fight her because the filly liked to gallop with her head very low to the ground. Donna followed the instructions and horse and rider got along very well. At the time, the JVB division at the Fair Grounds had many horses and not many riders. For a period of about two weeks, Donna wasn't able to get on Argentina Lil because her responsibilities put her astride other horses. So here comes Jack, back in town and barking orders again. David Gelpi was Jack's assistant at FG in New Orleans and he knew Donna and Argentina Lil had become a good pair. The problem was that everything Donna had accomplished became undone in the short time she was not on the filly. Argentina Lil had returned to being a witch the very morning Donna returned to gallop her. Unfortunately, all this was unraveling in front of Jack, so naturally, Jack began to howl at Donna. The spectacle was made worse when

Jack told her to make another round with the filly. By the time Donna got back to the barn she was fuming. Donna is an extremely dedicated worker and she was tremendously embarrassed and regrettably wronged in the shadow of what can be a brutal *man's world* at the racetrack. She flung her saddle at Jack's feet and exclaimed, "I quit!" What Donna didn't know is that in the time it took Jack and David to walk back to the barn, David told Jack what a good job Donna actually had done with the filly and that she shouldn't be held responsible for the filly's meltdown. With a crumpled exercise saddle thrashed down at his feet and a trembling exercise rider alongside, Jack put his arm around Donna's shoulders and simply said, "Donna, wipe those tears away and let's go get some ice cream." Nothing more was made of the incident.

In 1995 Donna Barton set a number of female jockey records at Churchill Downs, including most wins, most stakes wins, and most wins in a single day, with four. She rode graded stakes winners for Wayne Lukas, too, including Hennessy and Boston Harbor.

Jack being quiet, or at least in a quiet mind, opinion, and voice, is a rarity. "When he didn't like what he saw, you heard *the voice*," said Jack's former wife Helen Van Berg. When she would reach her limit of hearing Jack's scolding (of her or others), Helen would scold him back and tell him not to yell and be so angry. Jack would then retort, "I'm not angry, it's just the tone of my voice." There are multiple definitions of the word *tone*: 1.) a sound made by vibrating muscular bands in the larynx; 2.) a particular way of modulation or intonation; intended expression of meaning, feeling or spirit: *a tone of command*. The first definition is Jack's alibi, the second is his guilt.

Doc Danner is a longtime jockey agent who worked for M. H. Van Berg prior to becoming an agent. Danner has had the book for such leading riders as Wayne Catalano, E. J. Perrodin, Randy Romero, and Jerry Bailey. But the bulk of his success came from a sixteen-year working relationship with Larry Snyder and nearly eleven years with Pat Day. Doc's riders have ridden the best of the best horses and he has done business with the elite owners of the sport. Danner has seen his share of trainers who got lucky with a few horses for a few years, and he's seen trainers who are genuine horsemen who can make a difference with a horse. "To me it's sad to see Jack out there struggling nowadays when I know he's a tons better horseman than that. But the game has come today where it doesn't matter how good a horseman you are. You've gotta be a salesman! You've got to be able to sell yourself to owners today. Things aren't like they were twenty years ago and beyond. They used to hire you on your horseman-ship. But today it's based more on self-promotion to these owners," said Danner. And that's the rub.

Rick Dutrow, the son of the accomplished Maryland-based trainer Dick Dutrow, recalls a time when he contacted Jack regarding a filly his father was training in Maryland who was tying up badly after training. Tying up is an exercise-induced syndrome characterized by muscle stiff-ness and pain, sweating, sometimes trembling, and reluctance to move. "I met Jack once when I went out to the Los Angeles tracks to have a look around," said Dutrow. "I called Jack and explained that we just couldn't get her to train because she tied up so bad. Jack suggested that we make sure she had urinated before she went out to train. We tried it and it worked. It's still something we use today. Jack is a legend in this game. So many have learned from him and everybody should know about him."

On Monday morning, November 22, 2004, trainer Steve Asmussen received a memorable phone call. The previous day he had just broken Jack Van Berg's record of 496 wins in a single season, a mark that had stood for twenty-eight years. "All I had to do is hear one word from the caller and I knew exactly who it was. It was Jack," recalled Asmussen. "He called to congratulate me on what I had done. He was the first person to call me that day." Steve was appreciative of the phone call and to this day is respectful of the iconic figure Jack is: "John Wayne. That's Jack. He has the walk, he has the talk, and he has the game."

Hugh Miner, Jr., has been the general manager at Fonner Park in Grand Island, Nebraska, since 1983. He assumed control of the racetrack after the passing of general manager Al Swihart. Hugh has always been appreciative of Jack, even after he left Nebraska. "Jack Van Berg never forgot his roots. He's always been there to help Nebraska horse racing and Fonner Park," said Miner. When the demolition of Ak-Sar-Ben began, Miner was informed that all of the Van Berg possessions which had been on display in the AK Hall at Ak-Sar-Ben were piled up in a corner. The priceless trove was in peril of being destroyed and disposed of. "Jack and I spoke on the phone and I offered to house all the trophies and mementos at Fonner Park. I promised to construct a fitting tribute," Hugh said. For decades, Fonner Park's ultra-modest slogan has been "Nebraska's Finest 5/8ths Mile Track." It's always been true. Now, the Van Berg Collection makes it finer.

Birds of a feather flock together, and if ever there were two peas in a pod, it was Jack Van Berg and his good friend Blane Schvaneveldt. First names only, *Jack* and *Blane* are two names that can stand alone in their two respective breeds of horse racing: Thoroughbred and Quarter Horse. "Blane and I had been casual friends until the first year Hollywood Park ran that quarter horse meet back in '86. Then he and I really became close friends," said Jack. "We'd have breakfast in the track kitchen every morning. Then we'd sit together in the afternoons during the races." Just imagine Vince Lombardi on the sidelines alongside Don Shula; Mark Twain jawing with Will Rogers; or Thomas Edison tinkering with Henry Ford. The astonishing accomplishments amassed between the two titans of their industry were simply staggering. Jack remembers Blane and all their fun times together:

I had some of the best times I've ever had in my life with those quarter horse folks. Blane was so funny—everywhere we went he would brag to people about all the races I won and this and that and never say anything about himself. I knew he was the leading trainer at Los Alamitos for years and one hell of a horseman. But I didn't know until he passed away, and I went to his memorial service, about all he had really accomplished. Hell, he won thirty-eight training titles at Los Alamitos and four thousand races there alone. There's no telling how many he won back home in Idaho. And he won that AQHA champion trainer award twelve times. They named the damn award after him. He'd always call me whenever he wanted to come to the thoroughbred races and he'd want me to come down to Los Al and sit with him. He and his wife, Shirley, were great people. Class, class people! And Blane used to be in the cattle business, too, like me. They don't make them like that anymore. He was a genuine good horseman and a good person with it. When he told you something, that was it. You didn't need any paper—when he said something or shook your hand, that was it.

Jack was with Blane Schvaneveldt on the night he won the 2008 Los Alamitos Two Million Dollar Futurity. Jack drove down to Los Alamitos Race Course in Orange County to sit with Blane, Shirley, and their family in the Vessels Club clubhouse at the track. "It was inspiring to see how good friends they were," said Ty Wyant, longtime *Daily Racing Form* quarter horse correspondent and media relations director at Ruidoso Downs Racetrack. "I watched them after Blane won the big race; let's just say Jack was very pleased for Blane. They were two very good friends and are two legendary horsemen."

Spending a day at the races with the two legends would have been a priceless experience. Mark Brown, a longtime Idaho quarter horse owner, trainer, and breeder, was lucky enough to enjoy the show for free. "I never

laughed so hard in my life as I did when Blane and Jack would get to telling stories at the races," said Brown. "It was such a treat to sit with them,
along with Duayne Diderickson (general manager of Les Bois Park racetrack and father of five-time AQHA champion jockey Kip Diderickson)
and Henry Moreno (trainer of the tremendous turf mare Sangue). Those
four cowboys told stories all afternoon long and they never told the same
story twice."

Shirley Schvaneveldt, Blane's widow and a cowgirl herself, chuckles
at one of her favorite stories: "Jack was around so much that my grandson
Braydon once asked me, 'Now how is this Uncle Jack guy my uncle?'
Jack was good with my whole family. He's a great friend and he came to
see Blane when he was in the hospital before he passed away."

Those blessed enough to stop by the Van Berg barn in California
might see a jovial fellow nicknamed "Cuba." He's the guy who resembles
the Wolfman character portrayed by Lon Chaney, Jr. I'm not sure what he
does for Jack, but he makes some tasty microwave *papas y huevos* when
the JVB barn chores are done. Cuba, whose given name is Tony Mansito,
got his first California racing license at Los Alamitos in 1973. When he
arrived at Santa Anita, he found work with Charlie Whittingham and then
went to work for Jack after Charlie passed away. "I used to look at that big
man Jack on that horse and he scared me. I wanted to know about him but
when I heard him yelling in the barn I ran away. When I heard his voice I
was very afraid," Cuba said. To get to the United States, Cuba spent three
days adrift in a tiny boat before he washed ashore in Florida. The shadows of death and deportation didn't discourage him, but the voice of JVB
made him want to swim all the way back home. Viva Cuba!

The employee to work the longest for Jack is his assistant, Sammy
Almarez. He began working for Van Berg with Gate Dancer in 1984. His
father, Adalberto Almarez, Sr., worked for Jack before any of the initial
Van Berg horses had even arrived at Hollywood Park. "Jack hired my dad

and gave him $200 and told him to look after the barn and get it ready for some horses that would be coming soon. A week went by, then ten days, and my dad is wondering if he really had a job because he had no horses to take care of. Then about two weeks after Jack hired him, here come twenty or thirty horses," said Sammy. "My dad sent for me and my brother Jesus and we arrived from Jalisco, Mexico, together; then more brothers came and an uncle, too. My youngest brother, Adalberto Jr., still lives on Jack's ranch in Hesperia. Jack has always been very good and fair to work for." To this day, the constant smile and pleasant demeanor of Sammy Almarez have been incredibly important assets under the shedrow of Jack Van Berg.

If the perpetually sunny Sammy hasn't yet warmed you, then get ready for a showering of Little Miss Sunshine. Payton Hoops is one of Jack's very likable grandchildren. She is what any parent, grandparent, or citizen of planet earth would want to see young people evolving into in our world. She is only seventeen, yet her mind has matured well ahead of her age, as her following report reveals.

I was sitting in class in early November when we were given our "Self-Directed Learning Opportunity" assignment. We were asked to spend the second week in January intensively studying a subject, taking a class, learning a new skill, or shadowing a person who we felt we could learn from. I knew I wanted to do something that wasn't like me and something I had never done before. After conversations with my mom (Traci Van Berg Hoops), I realized this would be an incredible opportunity to learn about horse racing, and most importantly, spend time with my Grandpa Jack. At first I was nervous—I was unsure about how I would feel spending a whole week with someone I have never spent more than a handful of times with. I was nervous it would be awkward and hard and that I wouldn't know how to fill someone in on all the things they didn't know about me and my life. But something kept me so intrigued. So, I went for it. I flew out to Los Angeles to spend six days with my grandfather, learning about the horse racing business, and about his life. I remember how I walked out of the airport into the beautiful California sun and anxiously waited for him. I saw his white truck start to slow down and a man with a cowboy hat and a big smile sitting peacefully in the driver's seat. I immediately felt relaxed and a rush of excitement filled my body as I became determined to learn as much as I could. I knew I had six days to essentially "get to know" my grandfather in as many ways as possible.

The first few moments were silent in the car, as I didn't know where to start with him, and I am sure he didn't know where to start either. As we began to drive away and head towards the barn, the conversations started rolling. One comment sparked another and so on. If there is one thing to say about Jack it's that he is sharp; he has an incredible memory and an amazing ability to tell stories. He is beyond intelligent. The memories that were brought up about his childhood and moments with his father brought laughter and smiles between the both of us. From the outside, Jack intimidated me very much. He came across as "the person you don't want to mess with." He kept talking about how sorry he was to have been such a poor father and grandfather all these years. It hurt to hear him so sad about something, but I felt closer to him when he let that part of him be real. It wasn't until he talked about my mom, her strength, and how proud he was that she was his daughter that he shed some tears and began to let his soft side shine through. My heart warmed, my eyes swelled, and I began to feel a true connection for the first time. From then on, every conversation was fascinating to me. I began to understand the way he sees the world. I was able to see the way he connected with people, his love of teaching, and his desire to help others in their endeavors.

The barn was an incredible place to be every day, the foundation of his life. Everyone around us knew Jack, and everyone worshiped him. He knows everything there is to know about horses and will share that knowledge with anyone. He is happy to help anyone with anything they might need, which shows a true part to his character. I was able to sit and visit with trainers, exercise riders, jockeys, and owners to better understand the way the racing industry worked, the money and people in it, and the future of it all. I came out to California with the intention of creating a photo journal as well, which was so fun for me. I was able to capture perfect moments of Jack interacting with his riders and staff, which I knew would be neat to bring back home and have for years to come. Something I learned about Jack while out there is that he likes routine. Every place we went, he knew people. Every restaurant we ate at, he knew the best dish to get and the best server there was. And every place or person had some hilarious story to go along with it. Every morning we would stop at Larry's doughnuts before heading to the barn, bring two dozen of them to the workers, check in with Sammy to see what horses needed to be worked, and then take a thirty-minute nap in his office. The simplest things like that brought me so much joy—seeing Grandpa Jack in his most comfortable environment made me happy.

So time went by fast and each day I learned more and more about him. Yes, the initial purpose of my trip was school and learning about the key components of the racing business; however, the most valuable learning came from that of Grandpa Jack and his life story. I came away with Jack being one of my largest inspirations. I aspire to one day have as much compassion as he does. He is a man with unconditional love. The hardest part of my trip was seeing Grandpa Jack's health decline, which was very new to me, not having been around him much before. It came up in conversation every day how frustrating it is for him to be 100 percent present mentally, but not there physically. To sit around sometimes because sometimes it is hard for him to breathe, but have so many passions and goals and still want to get out and do great things. Ever since my trip I do not want to leave him. I have connected with him in such a way that has filled my heart with a whole new feeling of love. He means so much to me and has become an important figure in my life. I am so thankful and lucky to have Jack Van Berg, an amazing horseman, a great mentor, and a wonderful teacher as my grandfather. He, a genuine, trustworthy, and caring soul, is an inspiration to many and forever will be.

Now you know Payton. The fruit hasn't fallen that far from the Van Berg family tree.

40

What Happened

Anyone who began attending the races in Southern California within the last ten years might easily think of Jack Van Berg as "that guy who trains all those 20-1 horses." The association is true and the numbers don't lie. But those numbers nowadays are not derived from Jack forgetting how to train winners. In recent years many of the horses Jack has trained are those that he took over from thoroughbred owner and breeder Ben Warren, who for many years operated a prolific breeding operation in California. Warren ultimately downsized and discontinued his assembly line of Cal-breds. The bulk of those downgraded racehorses may have been able to compete elsewhere, but probably shouldn't have been racing on one of the most competitive circuits in the nation. The bulk of horseplayers are not stupid, so a lot of those horses go off at 20-1, as they should. The savvy horseplayer knows Jack Van Berg is not a 20-1 trainer.

Logistics and evolution also had an impact on Jack's destiny. Jack has always stood by his assistants and their accomplishments. Once they left to go out on their own, many stood on their own. But sometimes the owners also left with them when the assistants left the pride to build their own den.

Jack will defend his training assistants and barn help 'til the cows come home, but some owners simply preferred Jack to be home with their horses.

Jack also has his own take on the pros and cons of settling in California. Once settled, he essentially cut off the flow of clients that he had in so many other states outside of California. He went from training hundreds of horses across the nation to training just one division in California. Widespread full-card simulcasting did not kick in strongly until roughly 1990, so in order for owners to see their horses run they needed to go to the track. They had to be able to conveniently get to the races—watching from home or a simulcast outlet wasn't an easy option. Southern California horse racing is almost like an island. It has a relatively finite pool of racehorses and limited, regional racing out of state. Equally, there is a relatively finite number of racehorse owners who participate in SoCal racing. Jack did try to establish himself within the California base of owners, but so were many other talented trainers. That's an ocean out there to the left of California and the pool of active owners is an evaporating pond. For a modern trainer, the competition to win owners is often more fierce than the competition to win races. And that's the rub. Jack can bump elbows with all types, but he's not the type to stab backs. And he's not modern.

"So many owners think when you get old you can't train. They want to go for these young trainers," said Jack. The idea that mature people can't train horses is unreasonable, of course—but that there may be a stigma could be true. But Jack was in his early fifties when he trained Alysheba, and that surely isn't an old age. So his age alibi (at least at that age) has some holes in it. Maybe there is more to it? Van Berg had some further, albeit simplified thoughts:

> When I had Alysheba I spent a lot of my time with him. I think that hurt me somewhat. I'm sure some of my other owners might not have liked that. And then when I came to California and stayed in one place, I didn't get horses from many new people. The people that were already in the game in California already had their own trainers. Good owners don't come easily. And I'm not gonna call owners and try to hustle them away from their current trainers. I'm grateful for the owners and horses I have and I'd like to have more. But I'm just not gonna steal owners like that.

The timing was and is not conducive for JVB. He arrived to California before the flood of simulcasting and the present-day ongoing rush of the information highway. Van Berg has a cell phone and he returns voicemails.
But don't ask him to watch a race or access a chart on his phone. Jack has
what he needs to train a racehorse in his head.

The cache of experience and insight Van Berg has under his bald dome
is appreciated so much that in 2008 he was called to serve and speak under
the dome of our nation's capitol. He has been a longtime advocate for the
strict policing of drug use in the sport of horse racing. The use and abuse
of some permitted drugs has created not only negative consequences in
public perception, but also damaging effects in the physical wherewithal
of the modern-day thoroughbred. Over the years Jack has let his voice
and opinion be heard: while seated on his pony during training hours, in
the horsemen or clubhouse seating at the races, or higher up in the private
boxes with racetrack executives. On June 19, 2008, Jack went all the way
to the top to be heard, when he went to Washington, D.C., to address the
United States House of Representatives. He spoke to the House Committee on Energy and Commerce Subcommittee on Commerce, Trade, and
Consumer Protection. It was at this meeting that Jack spoke candidly on
his beliefs of what he calls chemical warfare on the racetrack. The following is his testimony.

In order to bring integrity back to the great sport of horse racing, the first and most important act should be to implement the
most sophisticated drug testing available. It should be funded by
a small percentage of the simulcast money; approximately 1/8 of
1 percent. Three labs should conduct the testing—one in the West;
one in the East; one in the Midwest. It would be the responsibility of the trainer, or his representative, to monitor the collection
of the sample(s) after the race. Half of the test sample should be
immediately frozen and put in a locker that requires two keys

to open. One key should be held by the trainer and another one held by the lab technician. The other half of the sample should be sent to the designated lab and tested. If this sample is positive, then the trainers and lab technician would unlock the other half of the sample and send it to one of the other designated labs. If the sample is also positive, then very strict penalties should be imposed. As for medication, it would be in the best interest of this grand sport and these grand equine athletes to abolish any and all medications. This would mean no race-day threshold levels of Lasix, bute, steroids, or any other medication. The present rule permitting the use of steroids and other drugs has comprised the integrity of horse racing and has been a major factor in attendance and for interest falling to an all-time low. Steroids do not give these "non-consenting" athletes the time they need to develop and mature. Steroids given to young horses, they cause an unnatural increase in muscle mass and make them heavier than their still-maturing bone structure can often tolerate. Let the horse develop on his own and the trainer should be enough of a horseman to know when he has matured. As for racing surfaces, they should be a good sandy loam and maintained for the soft cushion. I do not think it helps for fans to be concerned about how fast a race is run. The safety of the horse should be the priority and not how fast the track is. On big days, most race tracks see how fast they can get the track. The surface should be maintained at the same depth at all times. I would like to thank everyone for inviting me to testify before the House Committee. The sport of horse racing is one of the greatest sports of all times. I will always be willing to do whatever I can to bring back the greatness and integrity of this great sport.

Decades ago, Lasix—a trade name for furosemide, a diuretic drug used to treat and prevent Exercise Induced Pulmonary Hemorrhage (EIPH)—began to be approved from one state to the next. It is not widely used as race-day medication outside the United States and now its use as race-day medication is being haltered in the U.S. So what about Lasix? When Alysheba was racing, much was made of the colt seemingly needing to race only at tracks where the drug was permitted. It is not uncommon for horses (and even human athletes) to occasionally rupture capillaries within their lungs due to increased capillary pressure brought on by strenuous exercise or racing. The effect of the diuretic is urination and a reduction of excess body fluids and pressure. "I think all Lasix does is relax a horse. If a human athlete has to go out and compete, they can't perform their best when they have a full bladder. It's the same with horses," Jack said. "When they relieve themselves it offers relief."

What about the common cortisone (corticosteroids) injections? Jack weighs in:

> When I go to the barn I feel legs. If I feel heat, or detect some fluid in a knee or ankle, I start working on them and sweating them or do some sort of therapy with the horse. These Johnny-come-lately trainers, hell, they cortisone them every time you turn around. I'm not gonna lie to you, I'll cortisone a horse now and then, but I make the benefit last. And you gotta rub on them, too. That old stuff still works. Some of these new trainers cortisone a horse in their normal training routine. Hell, that's not training! And that's just not right for the horse.

Then Jack raised his voice and took it a stride further, "I think they should stop all race-day medication. If you are not a horseman and can't figure out how to keep a horse healthy and happy, then maybe you should go lay carpet or pump gas. A good horseman doesn't need all that medication. You have to work on and with the horse."

Being a good horseman and knowing what it takes to spot an unsound horse and maintain the soundness of a horse should be as black and white as the required trainer's license test. Some blame soundness issues on the racing surface.

In 1988, Remington Park opened as a state-of-the-art racetrack in Oklahoma City. Prior to installing an all-weather artificial surface called Equitrack, David Vance, the vice president and general manager, selected Jack Van Berg to travel with him to Newmarket, England, and Hong Kong to observe the surface firsthand. Van Berg won the '88 Ponca City Stakes and the '89 Norman Handicap at Remington Park over Equitrack, but the Oklahoma weather was problematic and Equitrack was removed less than two years after it was installed. Presently, some of the most expensive horses in the world train over Equitrack, or Michael Dickinson's Tapeta Footings, or Polytrack, or Cushion Track artificial surfaces.

"I approve of artificial surfaces," said Van Berg, "but those surfaces can be tricky to maintain. The reason it never took ahold at Remington Park is because the people representing Equitrack wouldn't let the track-man Dennis Moore work with the track the way he wanted. Dennis Moore sure as hell knows about maintaining a racetrack."

In 1994, JVB won the Fall RP training title over the native red Oklahoma dirt. It was the final training title of his career. Or was it?

41

A Fight to the Finish

Jack Van Berg remains in training due to some big helping hands. "I am still in the game because there have been many people who helped me when I got into all that financial trouble. I asked them for horses to train and asked some for more than horses. And they came through for me," Van Berg said. "I want to apologize for putting some of them into an awkward position to help me out. I want to thank and honor those people," Jack said sincerely. "I also want to thank the hundreds of people who worked so hard for me over the years." With his longtime and loyal assistant, Sammy Almarez, Jack forges on. "Sammy is my right hand," Jack said. "He does the things for me now that I did for my dad."

Jack shaves every day, he shows up at the races with a pressed shirt, and he takes his hat off for ladies in the elevator. He's old-school. His hands didn't get as big as they are by twiddling his thumbs. That comes from manual labor, and that's old-school, too. If you want some of *that*, Jack's got plenty to give. Fill your boots.

As the author of this book I spent nearly three years visiting, calling, listening to, and learning about Jack. Within that time I learned that I didn't really need to bore down too deep to get *into* Jack because who he is, is basically already out there for you to see. What I saw from Jack decades ago at Ak-Sar-Ben is basically what I still see in Jack today: a genuine, compassionate man, who is big, bad, and bold on the outside and assuredly kinder than most of us on the inside. Truthfully, he has changed a little—he's probably gotten softer both on the inside and outside. And I can also truthfully say that his comprehensive understanding of the inside and outside of a horse hasn't changed at all. I also learned that countless people say they have worked for Jack. Whenever I would mention that I was writing the book on Jack, folks clamored to be associated with him. It's a claim they can be proud of, and that there are so many is not a far-fetched assertion based on the duration and nation of the JVB footprint.

Finally, I learned that Jack is human and does all the things that we humans, who haven't reached sainthood, tend to do. He is aware of his mistakes, and he desperately wants to make things right. He is aware that he is not as physically strong as he used to be, and this frustrates him to no end. But I can guarantee you that JVB is not giving up; he is actively searching for the answers to improve his health and longevity. I have seen men give up, get lazy, cut corners, and quit; if you think that is what Jack Van Berg is doing—well, then you don't know Jack.

Before the internationally famous trainer John Gosden returned to his native England, he was developing Eclipse Award winners in the United States, including both Bates Motel and Royal Heroine. In Europe, he's a master, having won the Epsom Derby, One Thousand Guineas, and Saint Leger. He's won many of the important stakes in France and Italy, as well the Dubai Sheema Classic and the Breeders' Cup Classic with Raven's Pass. Before leaving California in 1989, Gosden voiced a light, yet heavy opinion of Van Berg's ability. He said, "The other trainers are lucky—if Jack stayed put here in California he might win every race." *That* has been discussed.

Jack's mission has always been this:

By the grace of God I have the talent to train horses and the ability to teach people how to train horses. Maybe it wasn't a necessity to train at the vast national scale that I did, but I think it would be a waste and a disgrace not to do as much as I could. My father was a genius horseman and he was God's gift to me, too. I am proud of the young people who I have taught and have helped develop into very successful trainers. One of my favorite things to do is spot and support a horse or a person who may need some help in order to improve. And there is no better feeling in the world than to be able to lend a hand to someone and watch them benefit from it.

Jack is still helping and teaching people. And Jack is still helping and training racehorses. "You watch, I'll train another Derby winner. That is unless I die first," winked Jack.

And that is the gritty truth.

The End

Appendix
Montage Essays

This appendix features artist Gary Simmons's unedited descriptions and explanations of the four montage panels he created for Jack Van Berg. Simmons's illustrations of Jack are realistic and his observations are authentic.

These essays begin on the following page.

LINDELL SQUARE • 101 HICKORY • HOT SPRINGS, ARKANSAS 71901 • (501) 624-6460

JACK VAN BERG PORTRAIT

This is Gary Simmons, October 1984   – I'm addressing these remarks
                                        to Jack Van Berg, concerning
                                        three panel portrait I have
                                        done.

INTRODUCTION

Jack, in my effort to design a portrait of you as a trainer and
as an individual there are two themes which seem to dominate everything. The first one is horses and the second is work. The two are
inseparable in your life, and in this case, inseparable in your portrait. When I came back from Kentucky, after having followed you
around for a week, I jotted down the following impression which summar-
izes the thinking I did while constructing this 3-panel portrait:

> Jack Van Berg is all horses -- it's a total love of
> the animal and the horse business. It is what he
> knows, where he gets his strength, and what provides
> his wealth. As a person he is consistent with his
> business. He looks, sounds, and acts like a mixture
> of cowboy and midwestern farmer. He is similar to
> male athletes and soldiers who abuse one another as
> tokens of affection and who avoid verbal declarations
> of concern for one another. Instead, they state their
> respect and love through teasing, slaps on the back,
> firm handshakes, and friendly nudges.
>
> The personal Van Berg seems very consistent with this.
> His likes, dislikes, politics, and activities all seem
> an obvious extension of his rearing and of his business.
> He is the classic male figure who is fascinated with
> big trucks, fast cars, cattle, farms, making a deal,
> and doing things his own way. He likes male company,
> likes female attention, and doesn't let either one
> prevent him from reaching his goals. Even his family
> falls back when he pushes -- sometimes he doesn't seem
> to notice until he finds they are behind him instead
> of beside him. They seem to respect and love him anyway-
> a testimony to his intentions even when his actions fail
> to meet their expectations.

Jack Van Berg is bigger than life in size, sound,
and behavior. He is the pied-piper of trainers
trailing a wake of owners, employees, media people,
and admirers. He roars through these people like
a large truck coming through a field. He stirs
up clouds of dust, insects and leaves which finally
settle again after he is gone. His personal energy
is contagious and legendary and affects those who
participate in his life.

My intention, Jack, is to convey this sense of power, this
whirlwind of activity flooded with horses and people. The power is
your personality. For this reason I chose to make the central figures
in each panel singular and strong. They represent the three basis attitudes I've seen-- your humor, your intensity, and your authority. The
activity is represented by the surge of elements which swirl around you
in each portrait. You sweep into a place and people are moving everywhere,
either trying to keep up or to get out of the way. The flood of people
and horses is represented literally by the masses of images I have included in the pieces. This is most evident in the personal side of the portrait,
but the other panels have their share of animals and people populating
your life. It may be surprising to think how alone you sometimes seem
amidst all these people, a thought which makes the large singular portraits seem all the more appropriate. It seems to me you are never in
one place long enough to allow the surrounding cast of characters to really
attach themselves to you.

I have handled the Van Berg family as a dream come true-- a statement about your success in the business and a tool for the execution
of ideas and methods you believe in. The farm is an organic entity
growing and improving with time. Its potential as a national equine
showplace is very real. It is also an expression of the real animal
you horse people love--the pastoral environment, mares with foals, acres
of grazing land, and free movement among the horses. It is also a farm
in the true sense of the word. It's a place littered with equipment,
places for fixing, healing and grooming the every-present horse. For
you I think it's an extension of the male who enjoys the tractors, wagons,
trucks and buildings which combine with smells of grain bins, hay lofts,

and fenced in lanes. It's a place of peace, but even here, you just
barely settle down long enough to feel it.

The colors in the three panels are intentional. They carry the
racing colors of the Van Berg name from the father through the current
Van Berg Stables. They are appropriate because of the long days you
put in. They start with sunrise on the left, go through mid-day and
afternoon, and finish with sunset, suggesting the maturation of your
career as a trainer and owner.

Also as an introduction to this project I want to interject my own
feelings which come from my direct participation with you, and which
have led to the images and the total concept I am presenting to you.
I have come from a position of no knowledge of you to a sense of belong-
ing and of friendship. I don't have any illusions about being one of
the inner circle or being someone you are terribly comfortable with.
On the other hand I think I have learned to know you well enough to
recognize my acceptance and respect by you. I have seen you in a lot
of different circumstances and the most comfortable one for me is the
one of working with you. I understand that role and so do you--it makes
conversation and feelings fit because there is no selfconsciousness about
the exchange. Moving gates with you on the farm was one of my favorite
times with you. It helped me understand why your people are loyal to
you and I want that loyalty and respect to be reflected in the images
I have chosen. I want them to be honest, informative, and satisfying
to you. It is important to me that you see that intention in this work.

These impressions are probably simple contrasted with the ones you
really feel and live, but they are the basis from which this portrait
has developed.

-3-

JACK VAN BERG PORTRAIT--PERSONAL LIFE

The general theme is a life crowded with people and influences
which create a strong sense of tradition and progression of events.
The family background almost predicts the present life of Jack Van Berg.
Still an important consideration is the fact that in a family of strong
people and overwhelming achievement before you, Jack, you still dominate
your own life and provide its central force. Another theme I chose for
this side of you is the one which smiles, laughs at life, and is generally the sport who draws so many people to you. More often than not,
you are expressing some kind of humor or jolly demeanor even at the
most intense times of your career. Many of the images in this panel show
that side of you.

The chronology of the panel starts in the upper left corner with
you on your pony. At this stage it is hard to put into sequence which
influences came first. The size of the Van Berg family alone is a considerable force. The nine kids sit on horseback with Marion and Viola
Van Berg. You are the youngest and the smallest at that time. The fact
that the Van bergs chose to represent themselves to the world on horseback,
and that the family was represented as united and a team can surely all be
considered influential on the Jack Van Berg we know today. Added to that
is the almost mythical figure of Marion Van Berg. Your sitting on your
pony is a direct expression of his early influence. Horses start early
in your life and continue to be a main theme. I drew Marion as an almost
smoky figure, not quite real. He is someone so consistently revered that
it is hard to find out anything about him other than glowing praise. His
studious pose and the pensive stare seem consistent with the stories about
the effect this man had on those around him. As the apple of his eye, it's
no wonder you were influenced as you were.

Viola Van Berg is almost part of the same person but still represents
her own kind of strength. In the drawing she flows from him and so it was
in life apparently. They bonded a family tie which is still evident among
the kids and their support of one another. Inspite of their differences and

any distances between them, one gets the sense they are all proud of
being Van Bergs and would circle the wagons at the first suggestion
of attack on anyone of them.

The picture of you and Bud with your dad is from a calendar photo
titled "My Partners" -- you and Bud were already conditioned to the
business and to the idea of running it. Immediately behind is the Columbus Sale Barn as it is today. It's the place still owned by you and
and some of your family, the place you talk about with great nostalgia.
Hearing you talk about the barn makes me aware of how influential it was.
It seemed to be the psychological center as well as physical center of
your universe. The home place sits next door, the Van Berg stables sit
behind, and the people of your young life sat within that barn. Listening to the people in that barn today enables me to understand your own
direct and sometimes tactless answers to others. Here is a whole barn
full of farmers and cattle buyers who speak the same way. There is an
understanding that you don't need to be coddled and you don't need to
coddle others when you're talking to them. One of the more admirable
things I've noticed in you is your consistency in this way. You talk to
the owner of Gate Dancer with the same directness you talk to your help in
the stables. There is no discrimination. When you have something to say,
you say it. Everyone is fair game.

This same period in the portrait finds you with your beloved Olds-
mobile, but more important is your hat and the rakish pose you strike.
That showman still exists in you. When the chips are down the showman
rises to the surface, expressed in a taste for the best -- hand tooled
belts, custom boots, new britches and leather jackets. That same person
shows up in the 50's teenager with the luxuriant flattop. It's a look
challenging all comers. You are the person not to be outdone, the person
who will be the last one caught in 'bump-bump-pull-away' or the first one
in the ranks of his profession. Already at that age, the John Wayne notion
of a man is hidden in your psyche as I have hidden him in the panel next to
you.

The knothole harkens back to the barn and a mischievious Jack who
would entice the older men to stick their fingers in that hole only
to have them bashed by Jack and the kids with him. This is the same
Jack who was a buddy to Boogley Bill, the German-speaking eccentric
who encouraged your sense of adventure and individuality.

Flowing out of this same part of your life is the love of big
trucks such as the Blue Goose, your father's horse van. We never
turned up a picture of that truck, but since your love of trucks
includes "the bigger the better" in your mind, I chose to give you a
giant International of the type you might drive today if you so chose.

Associated with the truck is the cattle auction itself. Your
auctioneering is a source of pride to you, as it should be. Self-taught
and well-practiced at it, it's another one of those associations with
the sale barn -- cattle, coffee, and bantering are the items of the day.
Just as you must have heard in your childhood, I heard you bantering
with the farmers who bid for the best deal. I heard you eliminate a
bidder with the following: "You're out, Charley -- all that's left is
to throw dirt in your face -- you're already dead."

The views of your auctioneering, talking on the phone and sleeping
make up their own kind of typical sequence which represents your lifestyle. It's a breakneck pace. In this case, it's auctioneering, talking
on the phone and then dropping for a five minute nap, sometimes less.
Your morning at the auction was fueled with aspirin, coffee, cough syrup,
and a quick breakfast in the barn cafe. The ever-present phone calls
interrupted all of these events. You remind me of a high-powered engine
fouling out for a second due to heat and overuse, only to sputter twice,
catch, and again roar into motion.

The center view of you on the phone has a lot of things I've seen you
do consistently. Your hands are always busy -- they're a study in themselves. Typically in this picture, they are rubbing your face, pulling

at your hair, or pointing in some explanatory gesture. Even your
phone hand is busy with your index finger riding on your upper lip
in some secret ceremony only you understand. I've wondered if you
talk so loud because you're always knocking down the words with your
hands. Your phone conversations have the same flavor as personal
dialogues. They are direct, edged with teasing and commanding.

The sleeping pose was at the homeplace in Columbus. It was a
momentary doze between a phone conversation and a talk with Bud.
The same pose is likely on a plane, in a van on the way to a track,
and in the farmhouse. You frequently preface the nap with an announce-
ment that you're going to sleep and then follow up with some instruction
or question about whether some detail has been attended to, such as getting paddock passes to someone like me.

This last phrase is more significant than might appear at first. You
manage to remember about people around you, those on the edges of your
circles. That quality is expressed in the way you have taken kids and
people down on their luck, given them a place to work, and given them a
place to belong. As you did with me, you make sure people are included
and feel accepted. That reassurance may be disguised in a rough joke or
a chewing out, but you still communicate your concern. I saw this on the
farm, in the track sheds and in my own experiences with you.

Your profile coming out of the sleeping figure is a favorite of mine.
It shows a gentle and pensive Jack who doesn't show up unless one has an
opportunity to hang around you alot. I chose it as a transition from your
galloping pace to your family of five kids who spring from the same background you did. At the same time there is the ever-present influence of
the horseracing, competition, and the personal standards of manhood and
leadership you find in someone like John Wayne. The desire to win and to
be first is the same whether it's winning on ice skates, being patriotic,
making a deal, or taking a claiming horse and making a winner of it.

The homeplace and the family are positioned together because I see a
tradition again. It's a tradition that sweeps all the way from the left
side of the portrait to the right. It extends from one father and his
two sons to another in a different time and place, but with the same intentions. The old-fashioned family ties survive despite your mobility and
your separation from your kids. Tami and Tommy still live in Columbus
and are growing from those same roots your family sprang from. Tracy and
Tory still show up at racing events which celebrate their father, and he
is disappointed if they don't. Tim more directly than any has stepped into
the horseracing world as a trainer. These ties are not especially neat as
far as I can tell. There are knots and some holes torn in the fabric of
this tradition, but it holds together partly from the long life it has had,
and partly from the force of your own love and personality. You admit your
love of the business has led to shortcomings as a father and as a husband.
Typically, your honesty seems to suggest that you understand the prices you
pay, yet you and the family seem to understand and to prosper. I felt this
when I saw the love between you and the kids at Churchhill Downs and Columbus.
I saw Tracy cry when she almost missed being in the paddock with you. I heard
Tommy say he wanted to be like his dad. I saw Tim help you saddle Gate Dancer
and sit with his hand on your shoulder after your loss. I saw Tory watch you
with pride before the race, and I saw you walk both sons to the barn to check
Gate Dancer after a heartbreaking loss in the Kentucky Derby. The sharing
is there despite any of the other struggles which come from their not seeing
you often enough or from wanting more than you can give. That sharing helped
me understand more about you and who you are under all that terrible mass of
people and business which surround you.

The final image is the scene at Jack Van Berg Day -- Columbus, Nebraska.
The tribute is one home folks made in their own humble way, one you seemed
to appreciate for its very connection with your own past. The farmers with
their wives and kids lean on the rail and talk crops or machinery, some of
them the same ones who listened to you auctioneer that morning. A rather
plain marque announces Jack Van Berg Day, a horse blanket given in your honor
hangs on the rail, and you wait through the afternoon to do your part.

Signing autographs, greeting boyhood friends, and visiting with your
family are activities of the day. The banquet in the evening is a
fitting tribute to you, but this day at the track seems to say more
in the honest fashion you are more comfortable with.

The main figure of this portrait panel is one typical of the more
engaging Jack Van Berg. When you smile and break into a laugh, it is
so engaging that you diffuse any tension you might have set up when
chastising a late employee or snapping at someone who has nagged you
about a place schedule. It's the best side of the Jack Van Berg I've
spent time with. It's the side I think makes hometown folk want to pay
you respect, makes workers try a little harder for you, and which helps
the world step back and give you room.

JACK VAN BERG PORTRAIT -- TRAINER PANEL

The main theme of this panel is the activity and work required to
be the best. The secondary figures of the portrait tumble down around
the main figure in a strategy of preparation, concentration, and finally
performance.

While the white silouette of the 1976 trophy symbolizes a year of
winning the most races and the most purse money, it is only a prelude to
the Preakness trophy looming in the foreground. The '76 trophy is the end
of one era and the beginning of another. From 1976 to 1983 there seemed
to be a regrouping of the Van Berg forces and a re-intensifying of the
effort which led to the 1984 Preakness victory. The Preakness trophy
stands for the pinnacle of your career and a new confidence as a winner
in the triple crown competition, but it also represents the support you
have from Helen and her sense of what is important to you.

Below the trophy is Gate Dancer working out at Oaklawn -- a warmup
to the victory which was waiting at Pimlico. You and Mark work Gate Dancer.
The image epitomizes your direct involvement in the training, your staying
tuned to the horse inspite of your traveling and concern with other horses.

The black-eyed Susans symbolize the coming victory and are scattered
among earlier moments of near victories at Oaklawn and Churchhill, moments
which your attention, concentration, and skill converted into the Preakness
victory. The figures showing you watching, timing, studying, talking all
are evidence of your best asset -- the brain which remembers, analyzes,
experiments, and communicates ideas. These figures remind me of a general
in battle calculating the smallest increments of time and gambling on years
of experience.

The stop watch and the place accentuate the critical schedules and
living by fractions of time. You seem to live more by these increments

-10-

than by any notion of a 24 hour day. Your life and your success is
expressed in times like Gate Dancer's Preakness time --- 1:53 3/8
minutes.

Gate Dancer is featured in this drawing as the premium horse in
your immediate career. It's not just a matter of performance. I
have the feeling you admire this horse for his unorthodox performances
and his ability to back up his eccentricities. With his earmuffs,
blinkers, special bits, and tendencies to run from behind, he represents your own willingness to buck the odds, to experiment, and to run
in the face of established ideas. In this same horse is your confidence
and willingness to risk ridicule and doubt with something as unorthodox
as earmuffs. I've seen you take someone's wisecrack about it, add your
own humor about it, and diffuse the remark while capturing the moment
for yourself.

Behind the running Gate Dancer in the drawing is the training center
in Kentucky. As a trainer you have created a physical plant which expresses and uses the ideas of someone who really understands the elements
of training and the soul of the horse.

The main figure of the portrait gives the look which stops those
who dare to go too far in their challenge of you. It is the competitive
spirit and the personal intensity which aren't about to be run out of
the game or to be distracted from the goal. I've seen this look -- I've
even received it in a glance. Combined with a large body and a booming
voice, this look will get results from anyone within it's range. The
most important thing about the look is that it is always temporary. Within seconds it will revert to a grin or a kindness which reassures the
victim that he hasn't been sentenced to permanent disfavor.

I included your name on this portrait -- the first time I've done
that on a portrait. Your name somehow fits the boldness of your personal
image. It is coupled with the years you won the award as North America's
most winning trainer. Unfortunately, the dates alone seem inadequate to

describe the achievements they symbolize. They don't reflect the
Guiness Book of World Records you are in for the most wins by any
trainer, the houses which run over with trophies and awards, or the
celebrity status you have achieved in the racing world.

The mounted figure of you above the dates is a favorite of mine.
Again, it's one of those images which show the Jack Van Berg I've seen
at work. I like the statement it makes of early morning light, cool
temperatures, hot coffee, gloves, jacket, and fidgeting horses. This
is the image of a man who loves the business. There is a patience about
you in this situation which I fail to see in other parts of the business.
I think you savor the time on that horse, perhaps because you are most
comfortable with yourself at that moment.

The saddles behind you reflect the thoroughness of the Van Berg
image-- the Van Berg name is stamped on the saddles and they are cared
for with a thoroughness which again is not found in every aspect of the
business. I think they may symbolize one of those elements you see as
really important to the welfare of the horse and the rider. You speak
often about concern for the horses and the daily soaping and cleaning
of these saddles may be part of that philosophy.

JACK VAN BERG PORTRAIT -- FARM PANEL

You've told me more than once that the farm is a dream come true.
That makes sense for a man who has his own ideas about how to solve a
problem as complex as training and maintaining thoroughbred horses.
The basis treatment of this portrait is aimed at looking at the farm
as an expression of your ideals about training. It's the reality of
your notions probably once considered by you as pretty grand for a
young man. The elements I think you've dreamed about are the ones you
talk about when you're obviously feeling some fulfillment of your efforts.
For example, the automated hotwalker is typical as a Van Berg innovation
both in its solution and in its scale. In the portrait, the view of you
looking into your thoughts about the hotwalker comes from my first time
with you at the training center. We walked out on the balcony overlooking
the track, and you looked into the evening sunset with the look of a man
more peaceful than any time I had seen you. The schematic of the hotwalker
symbolizes your creative thinking which comes when a man really knows
which problem he is solving and knows the satisfaction of seeing it work.

Below that same view of you is the carriage and the four-horse hitch
which symbolizes the romantic notions you have about the tradition of horsemanship and farms. I remember the satisfaction on your face when you were
perched on the carriage bench behind Ted. Like a small boy who is experienc-
ing the epitomy of his wishes, you looked as though you had to fight not to
burst out in a smug grin. Maybe I appreciate that so much because I have
never outgrown that formative era you and I have in common with the American
cowboy and his trappings. It's fun everytime I experience it.

The farmhouse in the drawing is treated like a rather unreal place too.
Again I recognize something from that midwestern background inspite of the
Kentucky setting -- the white frame farmhouse with its big porch, shadetrees,
fireplaces and rolling lawn. It's the only place I've seen you in that you
really treat like home. It seems to fit you a little better and to feel

-13-

like you own it. In the other places I've seen you, it's obvious you're just passing through.

The portrait's view of the farm's racetrack and the sheds in the background are also a view from the training center. The deep-sand walker is obscured, but the whole view involves the nurturing part of the farm -- the layup barn, the foal barn and the walker. The view of you looking over this part of the farm with radio in hand deals with your active direction and participation in the farm's functions. When you're there, your presence obviously dominates the farm.

The drawing of the running horse is recognition of your philosophy about healthy and happy horses. They should have freedom and should live outdoors in their native environment -- no sissies or hot house tomatoes here. Keep the horses healthy and happy and they'll do their best for you. I see the same application to the many people in your operation and the ways you care for them when they least expect it. It may be free plane tickets for a man to see his family on a holiday, the including of a spouse when someone is your guest, or the concern for a fledgling photographer who needs your interview.

The view of the training center in this portrait is not treated like an architect's rendering. It is treated like an extension of your own dreams. In fact, it projects in the drawing as an element straight from your heart. In the time I spent with you there, I saw you as a man who really loves the place he has created. The comfort and satisfaction you show in your office seemed appropriate. This view of the clubhouse includes no specific riders or viewers. It's an endless troop of people and horses who come through the operation of the training center. The whole place is probably not permanent with you, because you have told me you would like to take the experience you have with this farm and build another, a better one.

The view of you as a rider is a tribute to your willingness to work like your help does, probably more. But is is also intended to recognize the image you perhaps dream of when you think most warmly about yourself. I think it's

a natural projection of a Nebraska boy who grew up in a saddle. It's
also apparent from the posture that this is someone in charge. Your time
on the farm is an outpouring of decisions and instructions. I learned
this quickly enough. Twenty minutes after arriving on the farm, I found
myself moving gates and cattle with you. I enjoyed it, even if I did
accuse you of putting me through the paces for beefing you up in the Derby
Invitation.

The horses across the top of the drawing say what I think the farm
really means to you. It's a place to prepare for racing, but less obvious,
it's a place to make you and the animal you love happy.

The main figure here is one I've chosen to represent your authority.
I've never been around a more forceful personality than yours. Everything
you say, every move you make, suggests control and confidence. I don't think
in my time with you I've seen anyone successfully resist you. This strength
is your virtue and your vice in that it impels people to follow you while
it exasperates those who want to object. I have a suspicion that if you
never won a race, you would still have people following you. In fact, that
may have been borne out in the testimonies of those who knew you as a kid.
Even then you were the Tom Sawyer of the town, the kid who could lead others
inspite of themselves. Your strength is no less today.

The color in the portrait is consistent with your racing colors, gold
and purple. The sun is that old man you see more than most of us since you
get up with him and see him to bed nearly every day of your life.

JACK VAN BERG PORTRAIT-- CLOSING

As a closing note to this project I owe recognition to Helen Van Berg, the unsung hero of the whole job. It was she who established the project and it was she that made it possible. Had I been left on my own to keep up with your itinerary, Jack, I would probably have disappeared in a cloud of dust on the Oaklawn track. Helen provided most of the family materials, the information, the authorizations, the accommodations when I needed them, and gathered materials from the media and the racing community. Once you became involved, you too were most helpful, but it was Helen I relied on to actually get the materials. I feel like the original intent she had of giving a unique gift to you has been amply fulfilled by her role in making the project work. I'm impressed, Helen, by your caring, your stamina, and by the kindness you've shown me and June. I thank you.

Your own kindness, Jack has made this project possible in another way. Without your obvious concern for my welfare and for my participation, I would not have had the confidence to continually assult your privacy in search of the materials I needed. Another contribution you made was your generosity. Every logistical problem has been handled by you in such a way that a minimum of the burden has fallen on me. Again, without that consideration there are times when it would have been impossible for me to participate. For that, June and I both thank you. You not only made it possible, but you made it fun.

THE ARTIST AND THE PORTRAITS

The Van Berg Portrait is comprised of three separate panels, each
dedicated to a particular aspect of his life. The left panel is
composed of images which reflect his personal life, the middle panel
concerns his achievements as a trainer, and the right panel shows him
in conjunction with his farm in Kentucky. The three panels are accompanied by a manuscript and a cassette tape by the artist who speaks
directly to Jack with a description of the images of the rationale
behind the portrait's construction, and with his own personal insights
of and experiences with the subject and the project.

Overall, the three panels try to capture Jack Van Berg in as many activities and postures as necessary to reveal the essential man. The
three main figures of the panels show his three basic attitudes of laughing, of intensity, and of authority. The other activities are as diverse
as his day-dreaming, talking on the radio and on the phone, working, riding,
timing, writing, auctioneering, sleeping, and relating to his children.
The various ages represented include young child, boy, teenager, and present
age. He is accompanied in the portraits by other people who figure significantly in his life, such as his parents, eight other siblings, his own
children, and people from his hometown. The physical locations important
in his development are represented by his homeplace, the sale barn, tracks,
and the farm in Kentucky.

The elements or artifacts which physically represent Jack's achievements,
ideas, and activities include the farm, its training center and tracks,
horses, trophies, stop watch, dates of his years as most winning trainer,
tack, transportation, Gate Dancer, and personal anecdotes such as trucks,
a knothole, and his hero John Wayne.

All of the material was gathered by the artist and the Van Berg family who
worked together through visiting, corresponding, photographing and inter-
viewing. The artist followed Jack and photographed him during occasions
considered important and appropriate for the project.

APPENDIX321

In all, these three panels contain 23 views of Jack Van Berg, 68 figures of people, 6 buildings, and 45 horses. Each panel measures 30" x 40" and is executed in the medium of pen-and-ink with supplemental watercolor as an accent.

Pen-and-ink is an ancient technique which has many types of execution. This particular style is called cross-hatching because the various tonalities in the drawing are achieved by the successive building up of short lines drawn one over the other. As the lines become more numerous in selected areas, the drawing gets darker. By combining these light and dark shapes, the artist achieves a likeness of the subject he is drawing. The medium is notable for its rich textural feeling and for the difficulty it imposes on anyone who masters it. One of those difficulties is the permanence of the ink, which prevents any substantial changes in the drawing once the lines are drawn. The watercolor is applied with brush and is laid in first when the images it surrounds are masked off to prevent the uncontrolled spreading of the color into unwanted areas.

This project was commissioned by the Van Bergs and was executed by artist Dr. Gary Simmons, a partner in the art firm of Stephens & Simmons located in Hot Springs, Arkansas. Simmons is trained in the areas of art, literature, photography, and education and has been a professional artist since 1973.

His work is recognized nationally, but in particular, Simmons has gained a reputation for his unique montages such as the Jack Van Berg portraits. Montages are portraits which comprise several views of a person combined in a complex composition with important elements in that person's life and in his or her development. These portraits are commissioned by companies as well as by individuals. They grew out of Simmons' frustration with trying to capture a personality in one view, and out of an interest in solving complex composition problems. Simmons tries to explore the more personal side of the personality by using very candid poses surrounded by other people and by physical items important to the subject's development through time.

LINDELL SQUARE • 101 HICKORY • HOT SPRINGS, ARKANSAS 71901 • (501) 624-6460

MARION AND VIOLA VAN BERG PORTRAIT   3-18-85
by Gary Simmons

Jack,

I am addressing my remarks about this portrait to you, since you
commissioned it for yourself and for your family. I realize that I
speak to the whole family, particularly those with whom I have spoken
and from whom I have gathered information, pictures off their walls,
and pieces of their memories. I thank you and all who have helped. I
consider myself privileged to have been part of this effort. I want
the portrait to fill a space you might have in the memories of your
parents. They were apparently exceptional people.

The portrait format features both Viola and Marion. A natural impulse,
when confronting Marion's career and personality, is to feature one of
horseracing's major participants. I think that misses the purpose of
this commission, which is a portrait of your parents, not another
special tribute to Marion Van Berg. Because he is a 'grand old man
of racing' the challenge for me was finding him in another context,
finding the Marion who was father and husband. I look at Marion and
Viola as a team, as two midwesterners who faced the challenge of combining their lives and their efforts, raising a large family, earning
a living, and following their personal dreams. Both people have been
hard to find, but for different reasons. Your dad is a mythical
character who is spoken of in such reverent terms that only the family
really knows who he was. Even they may have lost sight of the real man.
Your mother was so obscured by the myth and was so private in her role
that again it's the family who must describe her. My assumptions are

- 2 -

necessarily shallow and intuited, but I offer them as a start in
remembering this impressive couple.

Marion was born January 15, 1896 and died at 75 on May 3, 1971. His
father was a farmer and barber in Aurora, Nebraska. Viola was born
June 28, 1899 as Viola M. Swartzendruber, later changed to Swartz by
her grandfather. She died at 70 on September 14, 1969. They married
February 10, 1917. They reared nine children and shared 52 years of
marriage.

The portrait tries to feature both people at the same times in their
lives. Unlike many of today's couples, they go back to early childhood. They experienced the same values and expectations. Their roots
were planted early. Maybe because they didn't tear them out and attempt
numerous transplantings, they flourished and bore fruit in their family,
their business, and their friendships.

The two central figures show them near the 70 mark, a time of financial
security and success, well past crying babies and hotrodding teenagers.
I like the peacefulness on their faces and the confidence with which
they look at the viewer. Each displays his own evidence of success.
Marion is typically understated in his suit, sweater, and hat. Viola
displays the manifestations of his affection and success, but the
jewelry and fur don't hide her earthiness and warmth. Neither person
looks pretentious. It's no wonder they continued to gather respect
from the people they grew up with.

To each side of the main figures begins a journey back to their childhood. The first figures are the middle years of child-rearing and
fighting for a career. These images show the strength and purpose any
couple needs in that time of their lives. Behind those images are the
beginnings of marriage. Viola at 17 and Marion at 20 were married.
The most striking thing to me in dealing with the images of this period
is the extraordinary beauty of Viola. The drawing here doesn't come
close to the quality I saw in the photo. There is a sensitivity and
vigor I found genuinely appealing. Behind these images are the youngest

- 3 -

available to me. Viola at 12 already looks capable of taking what life
has to offer. Marion as a baby has a surprising cherub in his face
which probably didn't show up again until his grandchildren crawled up
on his knee. I have made a token gesture to his racing career with a
horse who may have been Rose's Gem, but under any circumstances fore-
shadows the preoccupation which was to dominate his life.

The center portrait between the two main figures shows them together at
the track probably not too long before their deaths. Perhaps it best
symbolizes what I want to say in this portrait. It is a couple, a combined force and a success which comes from dedication to others, to
personal goals, and to responsibilities. I find joy in the picture of
them together here. It seems fair that they found reward and happiness
together in their world of kids and horses. Viola's involvement with her
racing form and poised pencil seems like an appropriate symbol of her
wisdom about staying in touch with the driving force in Marion's life.
Her expression looks like genuine pleasure with this involvement, a
perfect tribute to his success. His sitting with her, even though he
watches the track, says to me that he didn't run off from her physically
or spiritually in spite of the dedication and intensity he brought to
his career. Just as he called her every night from the track, this
physical presence is a reminder that one doesn't raise a family and
share 52 years of marriage by wandering off and doing your own thing.
Maybe the real homage to these two is that they managed to live their
lives together as well as individually, each managing to leave a world
of people who speak well of them and remember them for what they were
rather than what they weren't. It strikes me as the best of the midwestern character.

The gold bars connecting the two main images is fitting in two ways.
The gold of their 50th wedding anniversary is coexistent with the gold
in the Van Berg colors. Both forms of gold came from their union, from
their cooperative efforts as a couple. Between them and between the
bars is a subtle, but distinct Spinnette piano, a symbol of the more

- 4 -

intimate relationship these two shared and a symbol of the sensitive
soul of Viola. It is unoccupied, quiet, but nonetheless a reminder of
the peace she found when she sat down and played. Sometimes that was
a moment of private imagination, creative sensitivity, perhaps a rare
chance to look for those things she would have expressed more openly
in another life. Sometimes it was pure escape from anger and a life
which undoubtedly seemed a little too much at times. It is presented
as a presence not quite gone. The piano still sits in the homeplace,
but without the vitality it once offered.

The two roles played by Marion and Viola are beautifully symbolized by
the very structures each spent the most time in. Viola maintained the
homeplace. Marion ran the sale barn, and later he also managed the
stables. The homeplace in Columbus, Nebraska, still houses some of the
family. It still looks over the sale barn lot and toward the golf
course given to the city by Marion and Viola. It is the place where the
nine kids were reared, where Viola tended her flock, where the center of
her universe could be found. On the other side is the sale barn, built
in 1933 by Marion and is still maintained and run by the Van Berg family.
The barn was the basis for Marion's success and still stands as a monument to him. The bison head on the wall, pictures of Marion and the
sons, calendars from the 30's announcing the sales, and the general
feeling of the occupants sitting in the cafe and drinking coffee all
speak of tradition and a sense of farm values.

At the bottom of the portrait are Marion, Viola, and the kids Eleanor,
Helen, Jean, Betty, Alyce, Wilma, Bud, Virginia and Jack, in that
order. After all this time I still can't keep everybody sorted out. I
wonder that Marion and Viola did. Not pictured here are the rest of
the dynasty represented by spouses, grandchildren and great grandchildren.
As I worked with the photo of this family on their horses, I was taken
with how appropriately the picture represents this group. When I
looked closely I saw Marion still directing the show, probably
shouting some order about getting the line straight or looking

- 5 -

into the camera. Viola seems unaffected by the whole thing. I looked
at the photo through a magnifying glass in order to draw the faces. I
thought about one mother rearing seven daughters all wanting different
clothes, hairdoes, and horses. Each face under the magnifying glass
revealed individuals, different attitudes and surely different feelings
about this whole business of sitting on a horse for a calendar photo.
I thought about the person it takes to allow so many individuals to
emerge into adults, to suffer with nine growing lives, heartaches, and
needs. It seems no small feat to have survived physically after bearing,
rearing and nurturing nine kids. The Marion Van Bergs of the world are
rare enough, but I marvel that even one Viola Van Berg lived.

What I know of these two people is sketchy and was gleaned by talking
to family, racetrack people, and by reading the literature provided to
me by the family.

Marion's central image here is based upon a photo taken in 1966 at
Oaklawn in Hot Springs. Sports Illustrated photographer Lynn Pelham
captured this view of Marion and it seems to be the favorite of the
family. It hangs in Jack's office in Kentucky and in the Columbus
homes. Gin said to me that seeing this picture is like knowing the man.
The photo seems to portray the man at peace with himself. He is universally acclaimed as a gentleman, a genius with horses, and a man who
didn't forget his friends. He was strict in his principles and demanding in his standards. He said, "I've just never been one of them
society folks. I've just been an everyday guy, that's all."

When he died, Marion Van Berg was eulogized throughout the racing
community. "Marion was the greatest horseman that thoroughbred racing
has ever seen....This man has done more for thoroughbred racing than
any other individual. He was a horsetrader and he represented the
little guy well. Through his example he has proved that there is a place
for the little guy in racing."

- 6 -

Apparently a lot of his genius was based upon common sense and a lack
of pretentiousness about what he was doing. He is quoted as saying,
"Some horses take different care. You've got to figure 'em out.
They're mean sometimes, but it might be just caused by bad help, or
sometimes they might need somebody who can handle them pretty good and
show 'em who's the boss." He combined this common sense with an intensity which required reward for effort. He said, "When I'm doing
something, I like to make it worth my time. It's no fun unless you're
in deep enough to really get interested and make something out of it."

Marion's achievements are legendary, and they read like a litany of
racing's most desired results. Just on the surface, this man sitting
on ol' Buck and feeding him coughdrops would seem like an unlikely
candidate for the following records:

Leading owner, races won---14 years
All-time record for races won---4,691
Single-year record for races won---396 in 1969
Single-year record for purse monies---$1,453,679 in 1969
All-time record, number of starts---1,872 in 1970
Most years heading both winners and monetary lists---4
Nebraska Sports Hall of Fame
Saratoga Hall of Fame

Viola Van Berg is a little more difficult to identify because it is
almost impossible for me to talk about her without doing so in a
context with Marion. As I drew these portraits I looked more and more
at them as parents. I looked at Viola's pictures and saw a woman who
fulfilled her role as a true earth mother and as a wife as wives were
expected to be in her time. Some of her role was stoic as I understand
it, but no one I've talked to suggested she suffered or lived a life she
didn't choose. There is evidence that she had considerable capabilities
outside of her mother and wife roles, but found little opportunity to

- 7 -

explore them. She had considerable talent and intelligence, but their
expression was confined to a traditional home where her activities
centered around her family. She was dedicated to that role with an
intelligent understanding that stability for families comes from a
strong domestic center. She was apparently dedicated to the family and
to her man. She had the task of seeing to seven daughters, and in
stormy times, two sons who needed her motherly love as much as the girls.

Viola was a gentle, non-violent woman. She was musical and artistic,
and in other times might have found fulfillment in the professional
creation of beauty. She was philosophical and intellectual, but from
the start was denied most opportunities to seriously study. Her father
was traditional in his views and saw no need for a girl to waste her
time with study--marriage and child rearing were the goals he set for
her. He took her out of school and hurried her along to marriage, an
act that probably benefited Marion as much as any other in his life.

Viola loved to play the piano. Her playing was self-taught and by ear.
It was a source of joy when she was happy and a source of consolation
when she was upset. The family learned to recognize the signals. When
she sat down to the piano for her own peace, they knew to leave her
alone--this apparently included Marion. When she played for others, it
was frequently for Marion and he was readily among the listeners with his
own request for his favorite, "When You Wore A Tulip and I Wore A Big Red
Rose." Her artistic abilities seemed to miss the mark in her own children,
but they surfaced again in her grandchildren who exhibit her own flair
for music.

Part of who Viola was can be found in how Marion treated her. He
treated her as someone in his life who deserved his respect and he insisted upon that respect from others. Their relationship was endearing
and he tolerated no rudeness toward her from the kids or from anyone
else. He learned to trust her intuition and her philosophical notions
about others. Gentle as she was, Viola was someone who looked others

- 8 -

squarely in the eyes for it was there she made her judgments. She
insisted the eyes are indeed the windows to the soul and she counseled
Marion about whom he should trust and not trust.

She had few women friends, perhaps due to the arduous task of child
rearing, but probably in part because the world of cattle and the racetrack is a man's world. Devotion to Marion would have insured that
few women would find their ways into the couple's life style. Her
solace was within herself and with Marion. She loved to read, to play
the piano, and to comfort others.

Viola was a protectoress for her kids. Marion loved them, but his love
had to be interpreted and filtered though the extremes of impulsive
tongue-lashings and lavish gifts. One of the kids described him as a
man with a tongue that could strip the skin off a snake. It was Viola
who understood what he was trying to say and understood what the children
needed to hear. She was the link which held the family together and
kept Marion's intensity and single-mindedness from destroying the very
ones he loved. This is not an indictment of him. His intensity and
vision provided well for them, but he didn't know how to express his
love as women and children understand it. He did it financially and
with the gruffness men use to show affection among themselves. Viola
understood him, his gifts, and his intentions. She helped the children
understand and sheltered them when they didn't. They didn't expect
physical affection from him. Not until his mellow years was he assaulted
with kisses and conversation from grandchildren to whom he responded as
any other loving grandfather. With his own children he was sometimes
oblivious if not stoic. He sat in his favorite chair reading the
racing form or the newspaper while the nine kids roared through the
room on all sides. One of them made a hard turn around his chair and
grabbed it for balance. The chair and Marion upended. He got up and
announced with little fanfare that the house was too little. The result
was the front room which now extends across the entire front of the
house.

- 9 -

As Marion and Viola grew older, there was more time to discover their
children. After Viola's death, Marion made even more of those dis-
coveries by himself. When Gin was about 31 she had come to his aid for
some purpose now forgotten. They sat over coffee and he said the kind
of things he probably felt all along the way but discovered late in his
life. He said, "You know, Gin, I never did know you too good...you've
grown up pretty good. You're a good gal."

Marion and Viola, like the rest of us, were expressions of their time and
their rearing. He was raised with the business which made him his money
and reputation. She was reared with the expectation that she would
serve her family at all costs. That rearing in Marion, coupled with an
inherently serious nature, created a man whose stoic standards for himself were extended to those around him. When he was 12 or 14 he was put
on a horse and sent to Grand Island 23 miles away. He had a herd of
20 or 30 horses tied together and his job was to deliver them. His
mother cried as he left, but both of them apparently understood he had a
job to do. He grew up with cattle and horses. That's what he knew and
understood. Horse trading and operating a livestock auction were his
tools and they were the standards by which he measured others. He was
rigid about the things he believed in. No drinking and no smoking were
the rules and he expected performance accordingly. The real tribute to
him, I think, is that his own personal merits were high enough and his
personality charismatic enough that those around him conformed and still
praised him for their own behavior.

It is important, when talking about a man in these terms, to confirm
the rest of his character. Marion was a gentle man. He never hit the
children--but he still managed to adequately impress upon them what he
expected. Jack was perhaps the only one in the group who challenged
that authority and even seemed to thrive in the challenge. Marion was recognized as someone who remembered friends, was fair, and used little or
no violence to enforce his point of view. He had a deep and authorita-
tive voice and a look which shows in the central figure of this portrait.
It does not suggest weakness or indecision. Marion's daughters probably

- 10 -

had little chance for dialogue with him except through the inter-
pretations Viola offered them. She was a quiet listener but a good one.
She kept not only her children's confidence, but apparently that of
Columbus itself.

I would summarize my impressions of Marion and Viola in the following
terms. Marion is universally characterized as a genius with horses,
as a man of principle, someone generally kind to others, and as a man
who spoke softly and carried a big stick. He was, however, someone
who must have used the stick sparingly because he is also considered a
gentle man physically if not always verbally. He is idolized by the
thoroughbred racing world and seems to be remembered more for what he
stood for than for what he did on a daily basis.

Viola is remembered mostly by her kids. Perhaps that is the tribute
she would have chosen. She is characterized as gentle, understanding,
artistic and sensitive. She seems to have been nurturing above all
else. She is the symbol of a devoted wife. There is not much physically
which reflects who she was. The piano perhaps is the only tribute
to her artistic sensibility. Her children are her monument.

Bibliography

Cattau, Dan. "'Nebraska Cowboy' Making Self Known in East. *Omaha World-Herald*, August 11, 1985.

Equineline.com.

Gordon, Mark. "Van Berg Tribute Paid." *The Lincoln Star*, May 7, 1971.

Haskin, Steve. "Van Berg Passes on Demanding Work Ethic." *Daily Racing Form*, December, 1995.

Kotulak, Chris. Transcription of 1987 Kentucky Derby broadcast. Author's collection.

Mann, Jack. "Tradin' Platers Is Mr. Van's Game." *Sports Illustrated*, March 21, 1966.

McCracken, Sam. "Rose's Gem Romps at R.I." *Daily Boston Globe*, October 3, 1959.

McEvoy, John. "See Trainer Jack Van Berg as Merlin of the Midlands." *Daily Racing Form*, July 1, 1975.

Mearns, Dan. "Working with His Head." *The Blood Horse*, May 26, 1984

Rees, Jennie. "Alysheba Kicks Up His Heels." *The Courier-Journal*, November 20, 1988.

Scholz, Harold. *Van Berg Thoroughbred Racing Record.* 1937–1963.

The American Racing Manual. 1994 Edition. New York: Published by *Daily Racing Form*, May 1994.

Marion H. Von Berg on his horse Tony in 1936, the day of the Columbus Sales Pavilion grand opening.

First Sale at New Yards 1936

*Grand Opening of the
Columbus Sales Pavilion,
March 6, 1936.*

*Nebraska governor
Robert Cochran
in attendance at the
momentous event.*

Jack grew up with the Columbus
Sales Pavilion in his backyard.
He frequently worked at the sale
yards with his brother, Bud, and
all of his sisters.

He is shown here (above) astride
his pony, Tiny, along with Bud
and their father, Marion.

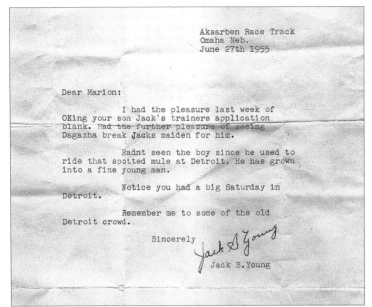

Letter from Jack Young (an Ak-Sar-Ben steward) after Jack Van Berg
won his first stakes race with Dagazha, in the 1955 Brandies Stakes.

...ckie Van Berg wins at Hazel Park. A nice way for sixteen-year-old "Jackie" Van Berg
...conclude his summer high school working vacation in Detroit. A very hot day; it was a
...are occasion that M. H. Van Berg appeared in the winner's circle without a suit coat.

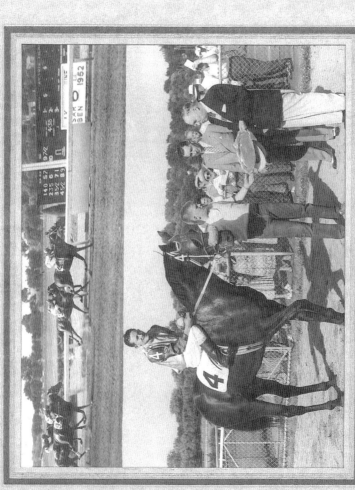

Jack at age sixteen accepting the trophy for his father's assistant trainer, Charlie Tanner. French Admiral was one of Jack's favorite horses as a child because the horse was very unruly until the two became friends. Even at a young age Jack was transforming horses for the better.

*Cal's Choice on Ak-Sar-Ben backstretch with Marion and Viola Van Berg.
The gelding was claimed for $6,500 and won stakes races at Ak-Sar-Ben,
Waterford Park, and Hazel Park.*

*Morning training at Detroit Race Course (DRC): Richard Rettele, Jack Van Berg,
Jesse Dehoyos, and "Mr. Van" (Marion Van Berg).*

Van Berg purple and gold horse van; Marion Van Berg out front, December 1947.

Ray Irwin leads Henny Penny (the goat-killer); Jack oversees, circa 1951.

Top left to right: unknown, Chuck Karlin, Sonny Pensick. Bottom left to right: Dick Karlin, Will Richardson, Bud Markey, Royce Fairchilds, Don Cheloha, unknown, Jack. July 6, 1958.

Spring Broker wins the $15,000 Arkansas Derby. The race was always important; now it has a $1 million purse. Marion then ran Spring Broker in the Kentucky Derby, where he finished eighth at 40-1. He was the only horse M. H. Van Berg ran in the Kentucky Derby.

Winner's circle: Harold and Betty (Van Berg) Scholz, Marion with trophy plate, Jack on hip of Spring Broker.

	Horses	Starts	Firsts		Seconds	Thirds	Winnings		Trainer
Fair Grounds	31	96	13	(1T)	13	13	$ 28,915	(4)	Kepler (3T)
Oaklawn	27	81	13	(1T)	11	12	48,733	(1)	M H V (2)
Sportsman's	38	100	19	(1)	26	17	66,700	(1)	M H V (1)
Ak-Sar-Ben	34	115	27	(1)	21	17	95,150	(1)	J.Van Berg (1)
Ascot	2	4	2		1	0	2,600		Fitzgerald
Churchill	2	3	0		0	0			M H V
Detroit	46	170	32	(1)	22	34	77,880	(1)	Irwin (1)
Balmoral	5	10	1		2	1	4,575		Kepler
Arlington	13	37	0		5	4	5,525		Kepler
Cahokia	3	3	0		0	0			
Wheeling	1	1	1		0	0	1,070		M.C.Johnson
Randall	1	1	0		0	0			
Hazel Park	57	254	61	(1)	51	31	157,890	(1)	Irwin (1)
Hawthorne	9	24	6		2	1	14,180		Kepler
Maumee	3	6	2		1	1	1,650		Nutter
Thistledown	10	21	6	(5)	5	2	8,080	(5)	Irwin
Sportsman's	37	103	22	(1)	25	15	83,597	(1)	M H V (1)
Churchill	6	11	0		3	1	3,052		Irwin
Fair Grounds	27	82	16		12	10	42,900		Kepler
Totals 19	116	1,122	221		200	159	$ 642,497		

LEADING HORSES

Rose's Gem	20	6	10	2	$ 52,267	
Spring Broker	15	6	1	2	33,128	
Safe Message	26	6	3	7	31,095	
Redbird Wish	23	3	1	6	26,125	
Severn	21	5	6	3	22,749	
Dashing Dquaw	28	7	6	4	21,106	

LEADING PURSES

O P	Spring Broker	1st	$11,498	Arkansas Derby	$15,000	1 1/8	1:54-2
Spt	Spring Broker	1st	4,225	Sprinters	6,500	6 fur	1:15-3
Spt	Redbird Wish	1st	6,500	Chicagoan	10,000	1 mi	1:41-3
Aks	Severn	1st	7,994	Ak-Sar-Ben Governor	12,500	1-70	1:48-2
Aks	Spring Broker	1st	4,500	Ak-Sar-Ben Ambassador	7,500	6 fur	1:10-4
Aks	Spring Broker	1st	6,000	Ak-Sar-Ben Council	10,000	1-70	1:41-4
Aks	Captain Dick	1st	5,355	Ak Breeders Spc	7,500	1-70	1:46-1
Det	Safe Message	1st	4,875	Bully Boy	7,500	6 fur	1:12
Aks	Mr. M. H.	1st	4,566	Ak Futurity	6,000	5 fur	1:00
H P	Safe Message	1st	4,600	Inaugural	7,500	6½ fur	1:21-3
H P	Rose's Gem	1st	6,200	Maple Leaf	10,000	1 mi	1:39-2
H P	Safe Message	1st	4,600	Michigan Sprint Championship	7,500	6 fur	1:11-4
H P	Cable King	1st	5,75				
H P	Rose's Gem	1st	4,12				
Spt	Rose's Gem	1st	7,71				

Example of the records Harold Scholz kept for the M. H. Van Berg racing stable; photo of Harold and Jack taken by Betty Scholz (one of Jack's seven sisters), 1966.

Marion H. Van Berg sitting proudly on his Appaloosa mule. As a child, young Jack Van Berg often escorted racehorses to the post on this giant, spotted bunny. What a sight!

"The Michigan Derby" Purse $25,000 Added

SONNY FLEET Hazel Park September 7 1963 Track Fast
Jerry Noble Up   M. H. Van Berg Owner   R. L. Irwin Trainer
Dr. Giddings 2nd   One Mile and 1/16   1:43   Moral Suasion 3rd

HAZEL PARK 1963

Michigan Derby, Hazel Park, 1963.

Marion Van Berg and his wife, Viola, with their speedy colt Sonny Fleet.

Van Berg also won the Michigan Derby in 1957 with Redbird Wish.

"SONNY FLEET"
JACK VAN BERG, T.R. BILLIE WHITT, UP
M. H. VAN BERG, OWNER
1 1/16TH MILES 1:43   30 MAY 64
2ND, LONESOME DREAM 3RD, RODEO HAND
THE AK-SAR-BEN KING'S PLATE HANDICAP
PURSE $12,500 ADDED

Sonny Fleet edges Lonesome Dream; the popular Rodeo Hand finishes third.

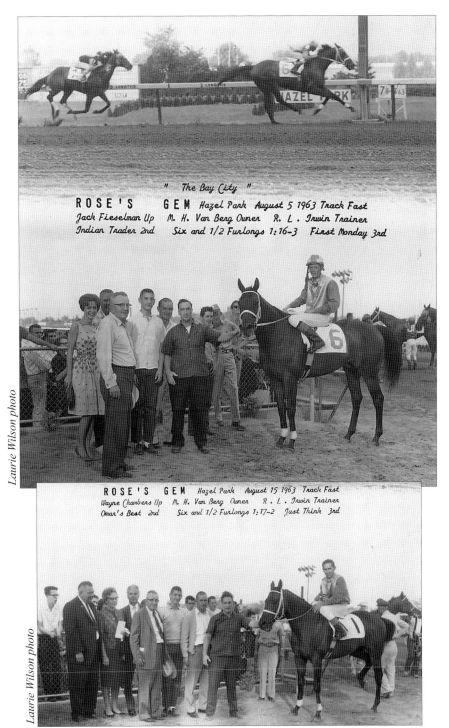

" The Bay City "

R O S E ' S   G E M Hazel Park August 5 1963 Track Fast
Jack Fieselman Up   M. H. Van Berg Owner   R. L. Irwin Trainer
Indian Trader 2nd   Six and 1/2 Furlongs 1:16-3   First Monday 3rd

R O S E ' S   G E M Hazel Park August 15 1963 Track Fast
Wayne Chambers Up   M. H. Van Berg Owner   R. L. Irwin Trainer
Oman's Best 2nd   Six and 1/2 Furlongs 1:17-2   Just Think 3rd

Rose's Gem retired as the leading Nebraska-bred of all time, but he won well beyond the boundaries of the Cornhusker State. He earned $230,964 with a race record of 125-41-34-12.

Jack C. Van Berg, at age twenty-five, received his third-straight Ak-Sar-Ben train-
ing title award. From 1959–1977, he won nineteen-straight titles at the popular
Omaha, Nebraska, racetrack. Jack won the "Aks" title for a final time in 1984.

" The   Hamtramck "
R A M B L I N   R O A D *Hazel Park   July 17, 1965 Track fast*
Charles Baltazar Up   M. H. Van Berg Owner   R. L. Irwin Trainer
Little Lu 2nd   One Mile 1:40-3   Touch Bar 3rd
                  5.80   3.20   3.00

Ramblin Road wins another stakes race in 1965. Marion Van Berg's trainer and longtime assistant R. L. "Bob" Irwin is in the photo.

In 1965, Ramblin Road won stakes races at Sportsman's Park, Ak-Sar-Ben, Hazel Park, Hawthorne, and Fair Grounds. At some tracks he won more than one stakes race, and he led the Van Berg stable in 1965 with a record of 15-7-5-1 $85,685.

Hamtramck, the stakes name, is a Detroit neighborhood once inhabited by Polish and Slovak emigrants.

Marion Van Berg (left) and Jack Van Berg.

*Gate Dancer with Mark
Wallerstadt astride; training for
the 1984 Arkansas Derby.*

*Eddie Delahoussaye up
in the Arkansas Derby
at Oaklawn Park; Hot
Springs, Arkansas. Notice
the eye of Gate Dancer.*

*Debut of the shadow roll and the
hood in the 1984 San Felipe at Santa
Anita. Led by groom Sammy Almarez.
Notice the eye of Gate Dancer.*

Jack at play
in the auction
stand at the
Columbus
Sales Pavilion.

Howard Cosell and
Jack exchanging
barbs on the Pimlico
backstretch before the
1984 Preakness.

Jack with
AQHA trainir
legend Blane
Schvaneveldt
and trainer
Henry Moren

The Marion H. Van Berg family. Standing: Betty; Eleanor, Bud, Alyce, Jack.

Seated: Helen, Jean, Virginia, Wilma, Marion, Viola.

Living room of the home in Columbus, Nebraska; located adjacent to the Columbus Sales Pavilion. Virginia and her huband, Dwayne (Smith), currently reside in the home.

Circa 1965.

Circa 1965.

Jack, Virginia, Bud, Wilma, Alyce, Betty,   Jean,   Helen,   Eleanor,   Viola,   Marion

The Van Berg ladies . . . .
Jack's aunts (his father's sisters):
Aunt Alberta
Aunt Visa
Jack's sister Helen
Betty and her daughter Ann
Aunt Mary
Aunt Edna
Aunt Helen

British Fleet 1972 Omaha Gold Cup. Looks like British pants, too.

1975 Omaha Gold Cup – Gray Bar defeats My Juliet and Master Derby. Jack and Laurie Bale in center.

Jock alongside Laurie Bale, the namesake of Miss Laurie Bale; Sam Maple up.

Jack at his full-service training center in Goshen, Ky.

500-acre facility with training track and turf gallops.

Nineteen-horse overhead walker.

Training center office adorned with priceless mementos. Large photo of his father, and idol, M. H. Van Berg.

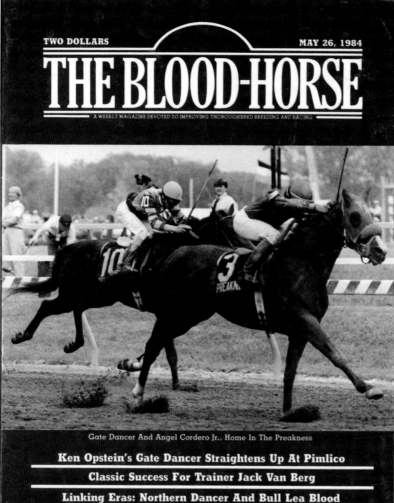

TWO DOLLARS · MAY 26, 1984

THE BLOOD-HORSE

A WEEKLY MAGAZINE DEVOTED TO IMPROVING THOROUGHBRED BREEDING AND RACING

Gate Dancer And Angel Cordero Jr., Home In The Preakness

Ken Opstein's Gate Dancer Straightens Up At Pimlico

Classic Success For Trainer Jack Van Berg

Linking Eras: Northern Dancer And Bull Lea Blood

Gate Dancer
wins the 198
Preakness
Stakes.

© Blood-Horse Publications

Milton C. Toby/Blood-Horse Publications

From left:
Jack Van Berg,
Angel Cordero Jr.
Sammy Almarez,
Ken Opstein.

Gate Dancer in paddock before 1985 Cornhusker Handicap at Ak-Sar-Ben.

Gate Dancer training at Santa Anita; Chris McCarron up.

Illustration created after Kentucky Derby disqualification and Preakness win.

Artist: Gary Simmons

1984 Breeders' Cup Classic; Gate Dancer disqualified from second and placed third. Official order of finish . . . First: Wild Again (pink); second: Slew O' Gold; third: Gate Dancer.

T. Abbahazy

1984 Eclipse Award Outstanding Trainer

Helen and Jack Van Berg; National Museum of Racing Hall of Fame Induction, 1985.

Benoit photo

1987 Kentucky Derby – Alysheba defeats Bet Twice after nearly falling in the stretch.

1988 Breeders' Cup Classic – Alysheba "America's Horse!"

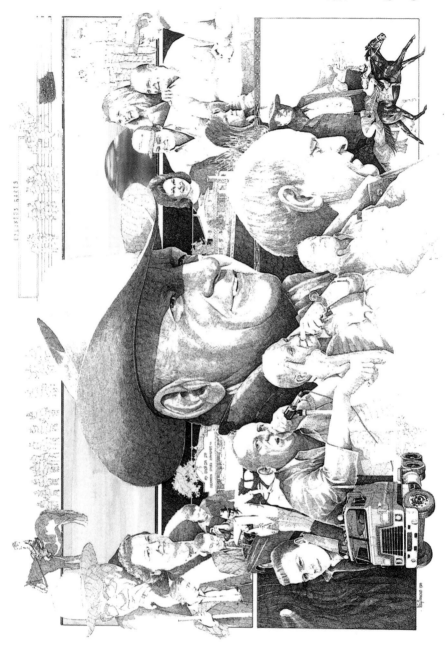

Montage no. 1, Personal Life.

Gary Simmons 1984

Gary Simmons 1984

Montage no. 2. The Trainer.

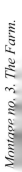

Gary Simmons 1984

Montage no. 3. The Farm.